For Dick & Mary Dunn

In hopes that this book
will contribute to their
enduring interest in the role of
the sacred in American life.

With affectionate regards,
from
Bruce

• TO EVERY THING A SEASON •

Shibe Park and Urban Philadelphia

1909–1976

by Bruce Kuklick

PRINCETON UNIVERSITY PRESS · PRINCETON, NEW JERSEY

Copyright © 1991 by Princeton University Press
Published by Princeton University Press, 41 William Street,
Princeton, New Jersey 08540
In the United Kingdom: Princeton University Press, Oxford

Library of Congress Cataloging-in-Publication Data
Kuklick, Bruce, 1941–
To every thing a season : Shibe Park and
urban Philadelphia, 1909–1976 / Bruce Kuklick.
p.   cm.
Includes bibliographical references and index.
ISBN 0-691-04788-X
1. Shibe Park (Philadelphia, Pa.)—History.
2. Philadelphia Athletics (Baseball team)—History.
3. Philadelphia (Pa.)—Social conditions.   I. Title.
GV416.P477K85   1991
796.357'64'0974811—dc20

This book has been composed in Berkeley Laser typeface

Princeton University Press books are printed on acid-free paper,
and meet the guidelines for permanence and durability of the
Committee on Production Guidelines for Book Longevity
of the Council on Library Resources

Printed in the United States of America by
Princeton University Press, Princeton, New Jersey

3   5   7   9   10   8   6   4   2

To see a World in a Grain of Sand,

. . . . .

And eternity in an hour.

• **WILLIAM BLAKE** •

•CONTENTS•

Part III. 1953–1976

•LIST OF ILLUSTRATIONS•

PHOTOS

MAPS

•ACKNOWLEDGMENTS•

My thanks go first of all to many, many individuals—members of the Society for American Baseball Research and a considerable number of other fans—who showed an interest in this project and offered assistance in numerous ways. Those I actually quoted are listed in the section on sources at the end of the book, but I am grateful to all of them.

The following people were kind enough to read various drafts of the manuscript and comment on it: Joe Barrett, Bob Bluthardt, Wayne Bodle, Jim Brown, Jerrold Casway, Harry Cerino, Thomas Childers, Richard Dunn, Walter Licht, Walter McDougall, Clifford Pearlman, Charles Rosenberg, and Jonathan Steinberg.

Sarah Brown, my research assistant for two years, was a great help.

Larry Shenk of the Philadelphia Phillies gave me access to some of the franchise's material. The staff of the Eleutherian-Mills, Hagley Foundation was cordial and efficient in locating business records of the Phillies for me, as were various librarians at the Free Library of Philadelphia in obtaining a wider variety of material. William Yancey of Temple University graciously made available statistical material that he has generated for more comprehensive studies of Philadelphia. Peter Levine, editor of *Baseball History*, granted permission to reprint as Chapter 7 of this book my essay "The Demise of the Philadelphia Athletics," which appeared in his 1990 issue. George Brightbill and his staff at the Urban Archives at Temple were unfailing in their assistance for over five years; without them this book could not have been written.

The staff at Princeton University Press has performed in the exceptional manner that people have told me is customary. Their abilities are extraordinary. The two helpful but critical readers for the press allowed their names to be revealed: Sean Wilentz and Peter Levine. My special thanks go to the press's director, Walter Lippincott, whose enthusiastic support has made it a pleasure to work with him.

Some years ago Marya Kuklick and I conspired to create her interest in baseball and to revive my own. This book, which I hope she likes, is one of the results. Elizabeth Block initially inspired my fascination with the affectional importance of public places by taking me to the minor league Reading Phillies during the major league strike of 1981.

• TO EVERY THING A SEASON •

•INTRODUCTION•

In April 1909 the American League Philadelphia Athletics—the A's—opened Shibe Park, the first of the many concrete-and-steel parks in which major league baseball teams would play for the next fifty years. The Phillies, the National League franchise, came to Shibe Park as tenants in 1938. They stayed in the stadium, renamed after the Athletics' longtime manager Connie Mack, after the A's left the city in 1954. Even in the mid-fifties, the Phillies regarded the park as outmoded. When the team departed at the end of the 1970 season and closed the building, it was decrepit. The franchise eagerly moved to its new quarters, Veterans Stadium.

Nonetheless, the Phillies wanted to trade on the feelings fans had for the old place. The organization hired newsman Al Cartwright to step up publicity for the transitional seasons of 1970 and 1971. Cartwright made the last game at Connie Mack Stadium "one of my babies." He coordinated festivities on that evening, October 1, 1970, and arranged for guests of honor to attend. Connie Mack, Jr., would come and so would Claude Passeau, first winning pitcher for the Phillies at the park in 1938.

Throwing out the first ball is a ceremonial activity sometimes reserved for the president of the United States. Cartwright wondered who could do it at the finale. He dug into various record books to see if any old-time ballplayers associated with the beginnings of Shibe Park were still alive. After some research Cartwright located Amos Aaron Strunk, who played in the majors from 1908 to 1924, mainly with the old A's. A native Philadelphian who broke into the big leagues when he was a teenager, Strunk played odd games for the A's in 1908 and 1909 before becoming a regular at the end of 1910. He was, however, in the starting lineup in the 1909 opener at Shibe Park and indeed was the last man alive who had performed on the field that early spring afternoon.

Cartwright wrote Strunk at his home in nearby Llanerch, Pennsylvania. Stressing that "the program would be most inadequate without your presence," Cartwright told Strunk that he would be introduced "as the man who played in the very first game," and asked him to throw out the first ball.

The reply was immediate: he would not come.

July 8-1970

Mr. Cartwright

I wish to tell you in Answer to your letter, pertaining to closing the Connie Mack stadium Oct 1st That I will <u>not except your</u> invitation to be present.

I hold no sentimental value about the closing of this property and it means nothing to me at all.

<u>This is final.</u>

Yours very truly

Amos A. Strunk

Strunk's letter is hardly indirect, but two points should be made about it. First, although Shibe Park may have had no "sentimental value" to the old ballplayer, the "property" surely did not "mean nothing" to him. When he wrote the letter, Strunk was almost eighty-one and had retired from baseball forty-five years earlier. Yet when I first read it—seventeen years after he wrote it and some eight years after Strunk's death—the author's anger was palpable; it still smoldered on the page. And I suspect that my readers will have no trouble in grasping Strunk's emotion. Second, the emotion is startling. Strunk was not caught up in the binge of nostalgia on which the Phillies capitalized, nostalgia that was not limited to fans and baseball writers. His bitterness contrasted with the feelings of most others.

Although Robert Carpenter, president of the Phillies, acted slowly and not always decisively, no one was more responsible for the new stadium and the desertion of Shibe Park than he. When the A's left in 1954, circumstances had forced Carpenter to buy Connie Mack Stadium, which, he said, he needed "like a hole in the head." Several years later he sold the park and became a tenant once more. Thereafter he used his power as owner of the Phillies to push metropolitan officials into finding a new home for his club. He expressed a lack of interest in what he regularly called the "real estate," and for close to fifteen years worked to vacate the park. Carpenter dickered with officials in other cities about moving his franchise; he suggested that the team might use facilities across the river in New Jersey; and he cajoled Philadelphia politicians into seeking various forms of public funding for another stadium.

Yet on the evening of October 1, when Carpenter was introduced with the other guests of honor, he was near tears. "Progress, I guess that's what you have to call it. . . . But damn it," he said, clearly upset, "I hate to leave this place."

The feelings of Strunk and Carpenter differed dramatically. Nonetheless, the "grounds," as Connie Mack had called the park when he occupied it, had a grip on the emotions of each.

This book is a history of the parcel of land on which Shibe Park sat, of the neighborhood around the park, and of the baseball played in it. But the focus is not the baseball, the locale, or the physical aspects of the site. I am interested, rather, in conveying the feelings that people had about the park. Some of these feelings, like Strunk's, were negative. Many more, like Carpenter's, were positive—even paradoxically so. People's emotions varied, depending on expediency and situation, but the "grounds" always stirred individuals and groups.

In one sense a physical object like the site of Shibe Park over one hundred years does not have a biography: a study of physical changes over time may not be considered history. The connection to the interests and goals of human beings gives the site a history. People do not just "have feelings"; they have them *about* things that are significant to them. As I was able to learn, Amos Strunk was angry at Connie Mack, but it was Mack's association with the park that became the target of Strunk's wrath. Men and women infuse things with meaning. Without the attachments of human beings, objects are meaningless.

The book tells the story of people insofar as their stories intersected with the park. Owners, neighbors, ballplayers, employees, fans, real estate speculators, and local politicians figure most prominently. Shibe Park, however, additionally touched the lives of others—novelists, baseball businessmen in other cities, architects and engineers, presidents of the United States. Readers should understand that though this is a story about Philadelphia, it is also a story of urban America.

The first part of the book focuses on several such urban histories. I discuss the career of Benjamin Shibe, the baseball entrepreneur who built the park that bore his name, the local community, and other important groups—Connie Mack and his teams from 1909 to 1932 and the fans who celebrated their triumphs.

The middle four chapters cover roughly the time from the Depression to the era of prosperity after World War II. They lay out the tensions among the owners, politicians, fans, employees, and community over changes at the park in these two decades. I also look at those besides the Philadelphia Athletics who used the park. Most important were the Philadelphia Phillies. The emphasis finally shifts to the Mack family—Connie Mack, his wife, and his three sons—during the time in which the park became the central issue in the Athletics' move from Philadelphia in 1954.

The last part of the book covers the thirty-year period from the 1950s to the 1980s, when the neighborhood around the park went into decline and the stadium itself was abandoned and demolished. This part explores the story of politicians, developers, urban planners, and the new owner, the Phillies' Bob Carpenter, who were committed to moving the team from the area. I also investigate the black and white communities that contested the neighborhood and the connection of the new dominant black community to the baseball played in the park during the 1960s. I concentrate on Dick Allen, a controversial black player of great talent.

The Epilogue reflects on changing civic tastes and the vicissitudes and transience of achievement as these themes are tied up with the history of the ball field. Shibe Park no longer exists, and neither do the Philadelphia Athletics, the team preeminently connected with the stadium. The parcel itself is occupied by development unrelated to its past. It is then, it seems to me, proper to ask: Who cares? Who will remember? I want to answer these questions by suggesting that seeking larger issues in history or threads of continuity with the present is not necessarily all important. There is something to be said for memorial and remembrance of a world we have lost.

• Part I •

1909–1932

• 1 •

Ben Shibe and Shibe Park

At 7:00 A.M. on the morning of April 12, 1909, George McFadden arrived at the corner of Twenty-first Street and Lehigh Avenue, the first person in line for the opening game at Shibe Park. By 8:00 A.M. two hundred people were behind McFadden. An hour later the line circled the block—down Lehigh Avenue to Twentieth, up Twentieth to Somerset Street, down Somerset to Twenty-first, and back down Twenty-first to Lehigh. Well before the building opened shortly after noon, the "line" was a friendly mob of ten thousand, although McFadden and others managed to keep their spots. Trolleys and nearby trains deposited more and more people in the vicinity of the park, until all the neighborhood streets were thronged. The vendors hawking peanuts, lemonade, popcorn, and A's pennants soon exhausted their supplies and vanished from the scene. Afraid that they might not get in, some fans made frenzied attempts to buy a position in line. McFadden turned down an offer of twenty-five dollars for his place, saying that no one had enough money to buy him out.

At 12:15, three hours before the game started, a whoop went up from the assembled masses as tickets went on sale. In the next two hours some thirty thousand got in, McFadden first. Twenty-three thousand had seats. Another seven thousand bought admission to stand, mainly in the outfield behind ropes. The ticket windows were shut shortly after two. Before that time other fans, knowing that the game would be sold out, began ringing the doorbells of the residences surrounding the field. They offered money to homeowners to view the game. Soon the houses and the roofs of Twentieth Street and along Somerset were thick with people. Still others packed the streets. Shortly before three a crush of fans broke open one of the big exit gates at Twentieth and Somerset. Before police could lock it, five thousand more people streamed into the outfield behind the ropes. Reporters said it was the largest crowd ever to watch a game.

Many fans remained in the streets around the park to be near the excitement. Some, however, left for the business hub of the city. There, downtown, thousands congregated to watch the game on a scoreboard that the *Philadelphia Inquirer* had erected.

Eighty years later George McFadden's son—then an old man—proudly displayed the ticket stub his father had kept from that ancient game. But the son had little articulate sense of the tradition of which he was a part. From the 1860s George McFadden's father had been a fan. Yet even in 1909 it is unlikely George himself had much of an idea of the history that had brought him and so many others to the door of Shibe Park.

Baseball had been popular in the United States from the middle of the nineteenth century, played in cities and in more rural districts. Prosperous folk enjoyed it in private clubs. After the Civil War working-class people increasingly took pleasure in the sport. By the 1870s the game flourished as entrepreneurs made money sponsoring teams of professionals, men who played for a salary. Great numbers of people paid to see unusually skilled athletes compete. Professional clubs did especially well in large cities such as Boston, New York, Philadelphia, Baltimore, and Washington in the Northeast; and Pittsburgh, Buffalo, Cincinnati, Detroit, Chicago, Milwaukee, and St. Louis in the Midwest.

In the 1870s businessmen formed the National League, the first "major" league. Centered in the East Coast, it fielded the most illustrious players and commanded the allegiance of fans. Many factors made the league profitable. Railroads increased rivalry among cities, whose large populations were a reservoir for baseball enthusiasts, the "kranks" or "bugs," as they were called. Among immigrants and first-generation citizens, commitment to the sport signaled that one was an American; commitment to a team showed that one was devoted to one's locality. Club owners appealed to the ethnic composition of their cities in selecting players and consequently in attracting patrons. The telegraph and telephone instantaneously transmitted events and, so, gave drama even to faraway games. Developments in photography added to the attractiveness of baseball coverage, already a major element of newspapers. Fast travel within cities and advances in building construction allowed the safe aggregation of large crowds to witness athletic contests.

Historians have offered various explanations for the popularity of baseball. It provided, among other things, escape from the drudgery of industrial life and was a cohesive force in expanding towns while at the same time reminding Americans of a vanished and mythically simple rural past. Many adults played the game as children and knew its intricacies. Familiarity and nostalgia made kranks out of adults. Many took their sons to the park as an indoctrination into manhood. In addition the owners pandered to youth, grasping that the boy of today was the bug of tomorrow.

For whatever reasons, baseball absorbed all sorts of Americans, who were willing to pay to watch it. The bulk of weekday afternoon attendance appears to have come from the middle class, both men and women, from professionals, and from craftsmen who in some measure controlled their time. On the weekends workers swelled these ranks.

Yet the period from the 1870s to the turn of the century was unstable for baseball. Players were frequently not loyal to a team and might "jump" from club to club in search of more money, or not show up to play at all. Owners occasionally did not maintain schedules or distribute receipts as agreed on if these obligations threatened their finances. The search for profits meant that franchises erratically took up and abandoned cities as their homes. Leagues rose and fell. In the 1880s the American Association challenged the National League in a ruinous competition. In the 1890s the Players League tried to obtain for the ballplayer-workers the prerogatives of their owner-capitalists. The same irregularities characterized baseball that characterized all U.S. business at the end of the nineteenth century.

The dubious status of the game complicated matters. Ballplayers seemed a rough group, and women, liquor, and rowdyism were friends of the athletes. Alcohol and gambling made baseball gatherings often seem unsavory if not downright dangerous to public order. Calculating entrepreneurs, however, knew that the sport could enrich them. They needed and wanted mass patronage but tried to make the game respectable; they stressed its "American" qualities, wooed a "better class" of customer, and promoted an image of manliness and decency. The baseball "magnates" were often nouveaux riches, men who had got their money in trade or worked their way up. They desired the notoriety baseball management gave them but also wished for the prestige attached in the United States to solidly run commercial operations. In constantly espousing business values, the owners struggled to imbue the sport with a high-toned quality, to place it in a social niche between the womanish and the unmannerly.

Critics, then and later, have condemned the avarice that was from the start part of the baseball business. Yet while the greed and fakery of owners and players were frequently obvious, the profit taking went along with the development of extraordinary ability and of a form of excellence. The sport might lack the morality some people demanded, but the "leisure industry" produced aesthetic benefits: the achievement of the exceptional. Spectators participated imaginatively in what was beyond their power and received a few moments of enjoyment that lifted their lives above the ordinary.

In the mid-1890s Ban Johnson, an Ohio sportswriter, gained the presidency of the Western League, a successful "minor" league that had eight franchises and moved among sixteen midwestern cities from 1894 to 1899. Despite his interest in the money and power that could be had in baseball, Johnson was a gifted and imperious administrator, anxious to secure the reputation of the game. He strove for a predictable enterprise, encouraged well-behaved clubs, and upgraded the status of umpires. Emphasizing standard rules, equipment, prices, and schedules, Johnson also believed that two major leagues could coexist and that the National League had not fully exploited the eastern cities. At the turn of the century he created an "American League." It contained the most lucrative of the Western League franchises and also competed with some of the teams of the National League, which had recently cut back from twelve cities to eight.

Johnson's financial angel was Cleveland industrialist Charles W. Somers, who had made several million dollars running his father's coal firm. Somers initially supported franchises in several cities in the new league. Commentators sometimes stigmatized such arrangements as "syndicate" baseball. If each team was not independent, a connected group of investors who represented no city could buy and sell players simply to maximize profits. On the other hand, Johnson and some baseball officials hoped that evenly distributed talent would assure close, exciting races and, of course, fat gate receipts. In any event Johnson believed that once he built up the American League, local interests would buy out Somers to avoid the stigma of syndicate ball.

In its first year, 1900, the American League was very much the old Western League, battling the National for the kranks only in Chicago. In 1901 Johnson expanded his assault on the older league. One of the critical eastern cities was Philadelphia. An important baseball town since before the Civil War, it had had a representative of the National League—the Philadelphia Nationals or Phillies—for almost twenty years. Johnson placed an American League franchise there. To manage the new team he chose Connie Mack, a thirty-eight-year-old Irishman who had begun his working life in a shoe factory in Brookfield, Massachusetts. Tall, handsome, and soft-spoken, Mack was "lace curtain" Irish. He had used his skills as a catcher to escape from the factory to baseball and by the nineties was making his way as a manager. In 1900 he led Milwaukee in the American League. This franchise would vacate Milwaukee for St. Louis in 1901. Johnson figured that Mack, who had also managed in Pittsburgh, was better known in Philadelphia and might attract fans there. For his experience and an estimated five to ten thousand dollars Mack received one-quarter of the stock in the new club. Johnson expected Somers, who got a three-quarter interest, to ante up more than thirty thousand dollars

At the end of 1900 Johnson dispatched Mack to Philadelphia to organize a team and find a place to play. He put the new manager in contact with two local sportswriters—Sam "Butch" Jones, baseball writer for the Associated Press, and Frank Hough, sports editor of the *Philadelphia Inquirer*. Jones and Hough helped Mack lease a site for a park. The franchise quickly threw up stands around a lot at Twenty-ninth Street and Columbia Avenue in Philadelphia and called it Columbia Park. It seated ninety-five hundred, mostly on uncovered wooden "bleacher" benches. With Somers's money Mack also stole some of the players of the Philadelphia Nationals—including the great star Nap Lajoie—and was set to begin his maiden season in the city.

In addition to recommending a playing field, Jones and Hough introduced Mack to the "dour and crusty" sports manufacturer Benjamin Franklin Shibe. Shibe had been born in the working-class Kensington section of east Philadelphia, known as Fishtown, in 1833. As a young man he drove a streetcar, but his zeal and interest in sports led him to manufacture and sell baseball and cricket bats. He also fabricated baseballs, employing women working at home to sew on the four-part cover by hand. An expert in leather, Shibe was an adept mechanic and the most prolific technical innovator in the sport. He popularized a novel two-piece cover for the ball and invented a machine for winding balls. Determined to improve baseball equipment, he later introduced the cork-centered ball to the majors.

After the Civil War Shibe became partners with his brother in John D. Shibe & Co., originally a hardware firm that as a sideline produced baseballs for the trade. By the 1870s, however, the principal business of the partnership was selling baseball equipment and other sporting goods. In the late 1870s and early 1880s Benjamin Shibe allied himself with Al Reach, a prominent Philadelphia baseball player, who also sold baseball equipment. As a partner in Shibe and Reach in 1881 and then in A. J. Reach & Co., Shibe supplied the manufacturing knowledge, Reach the sales skills. By the late nineteenth century Shibe's Kensington workshop had become a factory. "Uncle Ben," as people called him, was rich.

In addition to his fascination with sports equipment, Shibe followed baseball. He had gotten to know Al Reach when Reach played for a team known as the Philadelphia Athletics, or A's. This professional baseball powerhouse had existed from before the Civil War until 1891. For a time Shibe was a small shareholder in the franchise.

In December of 1900 Mack met Shibe in Philadelphia and offered to designate the baseballs of A. J. Reach & Co. as the official baseballs of the American League. He also asked Shibe to invest in the new franchise, which Mack was calling the Philadelphia Athletics, after the old team.

Shibe liked the idea of two "big leagues," and the revival of "his" old club intrigued him. It also intrigued his sons, Tom and John, now active in their father's business. Near the age of Mack, with whom they became friendly, the young men wanted to try the management side of professional sports. On the other hand, the new league was bound to be risky. In Philadelphia the Athletics would compete with the entrenched Philadelphia Nationals.

To make matters more complicated, Shibe's partner, Al Reach, co-owned the Phillies. But for a long time the sporting goods business had absorbed Reach more than his franchise. He could see the benefits for his company of a second league, even if the Athletics fought with the Nationals for fans. In addition Reach was feuding with John Rogers, his co-owner in the Phillies. Rogers controlled 51 percent of the stock and had in fact alienated the Phillies players who jumped to the A's in the winter of 1900–1901. These disputes motivated Reach to recommend Shibe as a possible owner of the new A's. Shibe conferred several times with the principals but remained unconvinced. Not until after he witnessed a capacity crowd and a multitude of onlookers on opening day of 1901 did he agree to buy into the Athletics. At around the same time Reach sold his stock in the Nationals.

It is unclear how much cash Shibe put out. He purchased 50 percent of the club from Somers and set the total stock value of the A's at fifty thousand dollars. Mack retained his one-quarter interest. Somers sold his remaining one-quarter to the sportswriters Jones and Hough, which they split between them. Shibe might have furnished all the cash and might have given the two sportswriters their interest for nothing in exchange for favorable publicity. Writers and baseball have always been dependent—the sport giving writers employment, the writers giving the sport publicity. In Philadelphia the Athletics' stock agreement formalized this arrangement between baseball and journalism, perhaps contributing to the tradition of banal and uncritical sports reporting. Mack himself remembered that Hough's column, "Don't Knock—But Boost," greatly helped the franchise. Later, in 1913, Mack bought out Jones and Hough and became co-owner, but Shibe and his family continued to manage the finances.

The Shibe-Mack partnership satisfied both men and exemplified the style of baseball business in the first part of the century. Shibe's main source of income was his factory, not baseball. As someone who had started out poor, however, he wished for social standing. He liked the fame that surrounded an owner and wanted to foster the sport's good name. The quiet and clean-living Mack was made for him.

On the other side, Mack earned his living from baseball and accurately determined that the game would earn him money. Shibe provided owner-manager Mack with the capital he needed to build a team without risking his own cash. Like many others, this franchise brought together new money concerned with prestige and an entrepreneur familiar with the sport itself.

The Shibes worked quietly but powerfully on the A's. Ben was president, but, as vice-president, Tom performed many of the ceremonial duties while his father ran the factory. But business also involved Tom more than the baseball team did. Younger brother Jack, however, typified the twentieth-century American "sportsman": he was a wealthy entrepreneur who associated with athletes and who promoted the political and social aspects of professional competition. Jack liked horse racing, football, boxing, and speedboat racing as well as baseball. He looked after the family's money in the franchise. For a time he owned the publication *Sporting Life* and also had interests in contracting and in amusement parks. Jack became the Athletics' business manager or "secretary" in 1902. He oversaw the finances and the club's physical plant— its maintenance and the nuts-and-bolts of running a business out of a ball park. Perhaps more important, as a prominent Democrat Jack dealt with the city and state governments. An associate of Philadelphia politicians, he made it comparatively easy for the franchise to get a start and understood real estate, taxes, city services, and municipal regulations.

The Shibes cooperated in a division of labor with Mack. They handled the cash but allowed him freedom with the club, a big money-maker in the first decade of the century. Mack won the American League pennant in 1902—there was no World Series until the following year—and again in 1905. Although defeated in the 1905 series, the A's were almost as famous as their opponents, the National League New York Giants of John McGraw and Christy Mathewson. Mack was becoming what the *Sporting News* described as "wealthy." In a detailed analysis in 1907 the magazine revealed his 1906 salary as $15,000. His share of the profits from 1902 to 1913 ran from $6,000 to $37,000. In the same period the Shibes made almost $350,000.

The money flowing into the Athletics' treasury resulted partly from the end of the baseball war in 1903. The National and American leagues, with eight teams in each league and homes in ten of the industrial cities of the East and Midwest, would dominate baseball for the next fifty years. The early years of the century, moreover, were prosperous for the sport, whose attendance doubled between 1901 and 1914.

Overflow crowds flocked to Columbia Park. Rube Waddell, an eccentric but gifted pitcher whom Mack had let go, visited Philadelphia to pitch for the St. Louis Browns in May 1908. Twenty-eight thousand bugs stormed the wooden stands at Twenty-ninth and Columbia. By that time, with the lease up in two years, Ben Shibe had decided to build a new park.

The A's were not the only team doing well. Many owners enlarged their grounds and added more comforts. Spectator sport vied with vaudeville, theaters, and amusement parks for money spent on "leisure." Luxurious fields commanded better prices for seats and enabled baseball magnates to isolate lower-class customers in distinct parts of the stadiums.

A flurry of ball park fires and disasters occurring between 1894 and 1911 also fueled the push for new and bigger facilities. In 1887, when the Philadelphia Nationals built Baker Bowl, as it was later known, the park was technologically up-to-date but hazardous. In 1894 its wooden stands caught fire. In 1903 a railing collapsed killing twenty and injuring two hundred.

By 1900 it was no longer profitable or safe in the long run to construct a field cheaply from wood. Columbia Park was one of the last of its kind. But fireproof stadiums that would hold large numbers required a substantial investment and initially discouraged owners. Motivated by the crowds, Shibe was bold and slightly ahead of his time in erecting an all concrete-and-steel stadium. Christened Shibe Park in 1909, the building was the first such structure. But seven more were soon built, and others were remodeled. These new sports coliseums—among them Wrigley Field and Comiskey Park in Chicago, Fenway Park in Boston, Forbes Field in Pittsburgh, Ebbets Field and the Polo Grounds in New York, and Briggs Field in Detroit—would house major league baseball for the next half century. The opening of Yankee Stadium in 1923 ended this period of privately financed construction.

In the nineteenth century professional baseball teams in Philadelphia played in what was later called Lower North Philadelphia. Then it was simply North City, some twenty to thirty blocks north of Philadelphia's City Hall, located in the center of downtown at Broad and Market streets. Especially after the consolidation of the city boundaries in 1854, North City opened up to development along the spine of Broad Street and between the two railroad lines that flanked the district on the east and west. The area consisted of small farms and meandering roads. These lanes ran diagonally across North City, but their function does not appear merely to have been to carry people out of the city. The roads took Philadelphians, initially, to cemeteries and, later, to various distant places of diversion—recreation grounds, racetracks, amusement parks, and fairgrounds. Baseball businessmen followed the roads and at their North City intersections built parks after the Civil War. Residential real estate contractors followed the undertakers and the entrepreneurs of commercial leisure.

Proximity to streetcar lines partially fixed the location of the ball parks. Powered by horses and mules in the 1850s, then by cable, and later by electricity, the streetcar was a major innovation, allowing workers for the first time to proceed to and from jobs comparatively long distances from their homes. Even more "rapid transit" came later with the elevated train and subway, separated from street traffic and operated with a string of connected vehicles. The "el" came to Philadelphia in

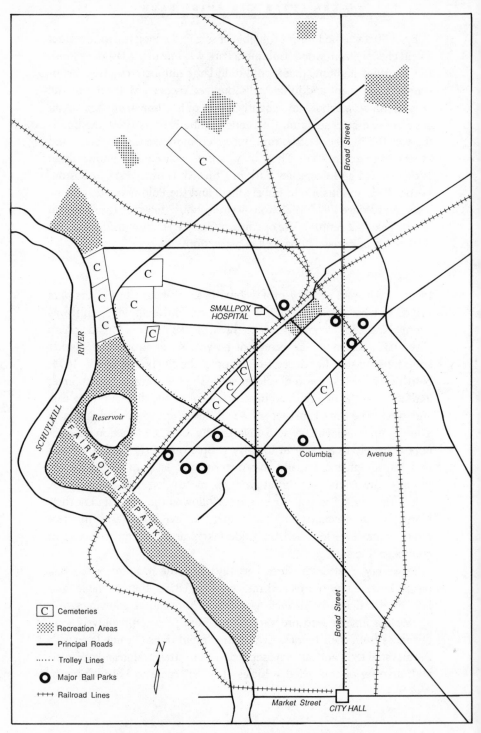

Map 1. Ball parks and North City, 1860–1910

1905, the subway in 1909. Although the Broad Street subway was not running until the 1920s, by the late nineteenth century North City was rich in connected lines of fast and inexpensive transport.

The disorderly aspects of this development vanished as officials realized in North City their plan for the familiar grid pattern of streets. The city's "number" streets ran north-south, starting with Second Street near the Delaware River on the east; going west to Thirteenth, where Broad substituted for Fourteenth; and continuing until Philadelphia's Fairmount Park and the Schuylkill River halted the street network at about Thirtieth Street in the west. The plan for North City called for the northerly continuation of these streets. Running east-west were major intersecting streets. Politicians gave them the names of the counties of the state of Pennsylvania—Jefferson (fifteen blocks north of Broad at 1500 North), Columbia, Montgomery, Berks, Dauphin, York, Huntingdon, Lehigh, Somerset, Cambria, Allegheny, Erie (3700 North), and so on.

Before Shibe's Athletics played in Columbia Park, the old A's hosted teams in three places: near what became Seventeenth and Columbia, Twenty-fifth and Jefferson, and Twenty-seventh and Jefferson. The Philadelphia Nationals played, first, at the intersection of Twenty-fourth and Columbia Avenue and Ridge Road, an old highway that curled through the city; and from 1887 on at Broad and Huntingdon. Three other professional fields were used for brief times near Eleventh and Huntingdon, Broad and Dauphin, and Eighteenth and Master. Although the newer parks tended to be farther north and to the east, all nine fell within a ten-block radius. All were between the railroad lines and close to North City residential areas, yet outside the most built-up zones, near the older diagonal highways.

For his new park Shibe selected a spot slightly farther out than the other ball park sites but in the same general vicinity, between Lehigh Avenue and Somerset Street, Twentieth and Twenty-first streets. Shibe was worried that he might have gone too far north. Yet even when Mack had first looked around in 1900, he had favored land near the Lehigh Avenue parcel, and during the later search two sites rejected for financial reasons lay farther north than Lehigh.

The park would be accessible in many ways. From the center of town, whence baseball drew the clerks and businessmen who came to afternoon games, the field would be a brief trip up to Lehigh by the Broad Street trolley, then a seven-block walk or an even breezier trolley ride. The new field would also be a short distance from the confluence of three railroad lines. The Pennsylvania Railroad had its Germantown Junction, or North Philadelphia Station, at Broad and Sedgley streets, some nine blocks away. For many years these trains brought visiting teams to Philadelphia or carried the A's on road trips or to spring training. Local trains on two other lines also had stops near the site: they carried commuters from what were then near suburbs to and from the city, but could also transport people directly to the park. Finally, many of the working-class districts that still lay hard by the center of town were a trolley ride or walk away.

At the turn of the century the district where Shibe wanted to build was barely a neighborhood at all. Above Lehigh (2700 North) much of the street network existed merely as a plan. Although not isolated, residential housing formed only a series of tiny communities. The Pennsylvania Railroad dominated the geography; its Philadelphia–New York route cut through North Philadelphia on a diagonal, running from Thirtieth and Columbia in the southwest to Sixteenth and Cambria in the northeast. There the Pennsy intersected with a complex of other lines, some proceeding northeast, some turning in various northwesterly directions.

Near the railroad lines, at Seventeenth and Clearfield, was a cluster of houses known as Smokey Hollow; near Nineteenth and Indiana, Stifftown; at Twentieth and Somerset, Goosetown; around Twenty-second and Cambria, Irishtown; at Twenty-ninth and Allegheny, Paradise; around Twenty-sixth and Huntingdon, North Penn. On the north side of the tracks west of Twenty-second below Lehigh was Swampoodle; across the tracks, over the railroad bridge, near Broad Street, was Gillietown.

In the vicinity of Twentieth Street—Twenty-first was only projected—both sides of Lehigh had ungraded vacant lots with diverse scenery. There were high clay bluffs, rain-washed gullies, quagmires, open fields, and even ponds where children could go rafting. The Gillies and the Swampies were sworn enemies. They guarded the playing terrain in their respective territories on either side of the railroad and fought over the high ground, a knoll at Twenty-second and Lehigh, fifteen feet or so above the land around it. The older residents of the district kept chickens and even pigs in yards festooned with honeysuckle and trumpet vine. The area had truck gardens. Door-to-door

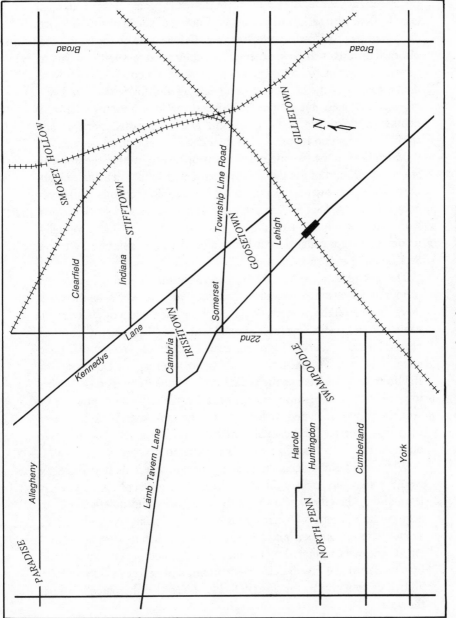

Map 2. Residential communities, 1890s

hucksters lived here, their wagons advertising "Fruit and Produce, Swampoodle, Pa." Other salesmen, not residents, moved through the uncongested thoroughfares in horse-drawn wagons or pushcarts, or even walked with sacks on their backs. They sold goods of all sorts—ice, clothes props, coal, milk, and hardwares. Others were on the lookout for old rags or knives to be sharpened. Customers were often Irish, many recent immigrants or refugees from Pennsylvania coalfields. The residents, too, used the streets for congregating and for parades and religious ceremonies. But picturesque scenes were disturbed by what residents freely acknowledged as "horseshit" and the pigeons, sparrows, and starlings feeding on it and adding their own excrement to the area.

Much later in the twentieth century people who lived in the immediate neighborhood of the ball park remembered fondly that their neighborhood was known as Swampoodle, but people used this name only occasionally after Shibe built the park. More often the district was just North City or later North Philly or "near the ball park." More formally, it sometimes got called North Penn, after the large community below Swampoodle at Huntingdon.

The square block at Lehigh, Somerset, Twentieth, and the still-only-proposed Twenty-first was almost vacant. Only the SPCA had kennels there. In general the property in the neighborhood north of the Pennsylvania railroad tracks was undeveloped and cheap because the land had been informally reserved for undesirable enterprises. At Twenty-second and Lehigh was Philadelphia's Hospital for Contagious Diseases, "the smallpox hospital." Passersby would bring handkerchiefs to their faces to protect themselves from the miasma. People unlucky enough to be sent there often escaped, believing that the cure was, literally, worse than the disease. The hospital's main building was dilapidated. Two ominous shacks contained particularly dangerous cases.

Why would Shibe decide to erect a stadium, where he hoped people would congregate, across the street from such a place? He apparently learned that the city was to vacate the old facility and quietly began to acquire the adjacent 5.75 acres in early 1907. Officials had laid out two smaller streets, Lambert and Woodstock, immediately west of Twentieth. Three owners, including the municipality, held seven plots of land that made up the city block. In a complicated series of transactions, Shibe's general contractor, Joseph Steele, assembled the parcel through the year.

Steele and his brother Edward of William Steele and Sons were pioneer constructors of steel-and-concrete buildings in the United States and put up many of the city's manufacturing enterprises in the early part of the century. They also designed Shibe Park, the first major construction north of the tracks. In February 1908 the city struck Lambert and Woodstock from the city plan, gave Shibe their title, and later laid out Twenty-first Street. In April Shibe held formal ceremonies and turned over the first spadeful of earth. For the first two months thereafter his crews graded the land, much above the level of the surrounding streets, before they started to build. The city closed the hospital in June 1909 because of "the needs of the neighborhood" and tore down the cluster of medical structures in 1911. The land had cost $67,500. By 1913 its value had appreciated by one-third.

At the end of the nineteenth century engineers made the technological advance necessary for the park's construction. Before that time the impermanence of steel offset its strength: it rusts and is not fireproof. But the low resistance to tension of stone weighed against its beauty and permanence: it could easily crack. Steel and stone, too, cost a lot. Builders avoided them in preference to wood when someone wanted cheap construction. Luxury building involved masses of steel (for strength) covered with a jacket of expensive stonework. If builders used stone alone, they faced strict limits on its form that the problem of tension imposed.

The invention of ferro-concrete or reinforced concrete—steel rods embedded in concrete—solved many problems of cost, strength, and durability. Reinforced concrete overcame the high price of stone-cutting by substituting carpentry for masonry. Woodworking for concrete forms replaced the preparation of cut pieces in stone. The rods and concrete in the wooden frames combined to give enormous strength and drastically reduced the amount of steel required. The concrete also fireproofed the steel, and the resulting material required dynamite to get it apart.

Shibe not only wanted a product strong enough to withstand the yearly weight of hundreds of thousands of fans. He was also of the optimistic, "progressive" American frame of mind of the early twentieth century. Shibe Park was to have an abiding element; it was "a lasting monument," built to endure, with a grandiose beauty that should express continuing prosperity and assured advance.

The nature of the game and protracted use of the park over the summer dictated additionally that its layout differ from that of ancient coliseums and of the permanent football grounds erected at many colleges. At one corner at least where owners located the infield diamond, they also desired an arrangement—the grandstand—to maximize the number of good seats. Daily contests made a roof over the seats attractive to shield patrons from the sun or inclement weather.

The original stadium consisted of a doubledecker main grandstand from first base to third, each wing 251 feet long and 77 feet deep. The lower stands held fifty-five hundred steel folding chairs, the upper forty-five hundred. In right and left field astride the foul lines two bleacher sections had rows of wooden benches embedded in the reinforced concrete. The twenty-five-cent bleachers held thirteen thousand. The preponderance of cheap seats meant, as one writer said, that baseball was a game "for all classes." Shibe believed that those "who live by the sweat of their brow should have as good a chance of seeing the game as the man who never had to roll up his sleeves to earn a dollar." Shibe built the park "for the masses as well as for the classes." In addition to making room for seven thousand standees in wide aisles in the back of the bleachers, and fashioning a terraced lobby in the upper grandstand, Shibe "banked" the outfield to permit overflow crowds of up to ten thousand more to watch contests. Thus, the initial theoretical capacity was an extraordinary forty thousand. In 1913 Shibe covered the bleachers and added a new unroofed stand running from left to center field as the new bleachers.

The geographic layout synthesized the imperatives of the urban landscape with the demands of the game as both sport and business. Shibe designed his park like other major league fields so that the high-priced grandstand seats were shadowed during the midafternoon and later, when his team played. In addition, he placed the infield so that the sun favored the batter and was most troublesome to the right fielder and first baseman, who received the fewest batted balls. In North Philadelphia this meant that home plate would be near Twenty-first and Lehigh. The sun would thus shade the grandstands behind first and third in the afternoon. The batter would be out of the sun, and the pitcher would throw to the west. This plate location was at the southwest corner of the parcel, putting the main entrance at the northeast corner of the intersection of Twenty-first and Lehigh.

The square block on which Shibe sited the park was, however, not square but rectangular, its north-south distance some 40 feet longer than its east-west distance. Once Shibe positioned home plate, the urban

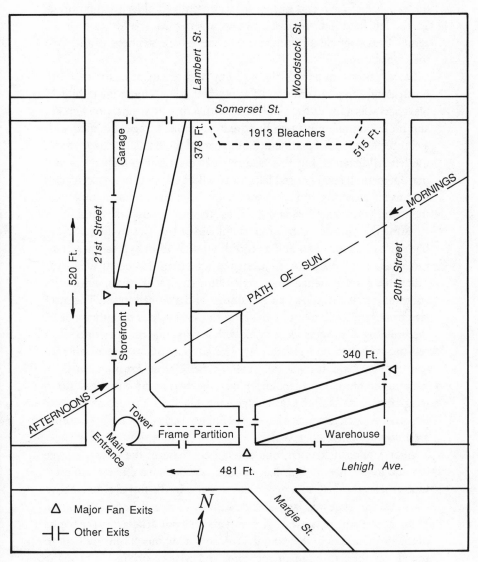

Map 3. Shibe Park, 1909

street pattern prescribed a cramped right field. Fewer balls were hit there anyway, and to the right field foul line was a modest 340 feet, the Twentieth Street boundary determining its size. In left and center, however, the expanse of lawn and distant fences resembled older rural grounds. To the left field line the distance was a generous 378 feet and to the center field flagpole an immense 515 feet—here standees would take their positions.

Storefronts were part of the building and extended to the east and north along Lehigh Avenue and Twenty-first Street. Under the right field bleachers was a furniture warehouse, with a display window on Lehigh, and more prominently a two-hundred-car public garage equipped with a complete service department. Shibe placed an auxiliary garage under the left field stands, but this facility catered largely to ballplayers and management. It soon housed Jack Shibe's fleet of racing boats along with a plant for repairing and servicing them. A group of Shibe's employees then worked in what insiders knew as "the Shibe Park boatyards."

Along the outside of the grandstand and at the Twenty-first and Lehigh main entrance Ben Shibe outdid himself. As an expression of culture, taste, and manners, he designed an ornate facade in what was called the French Renaissance style, with rusticated bases, composite columns, arched windows and vaultings, and a domed tower. The massive front had Ionic pilasters flanking recessed arches on either side of the building. The walls were brick with ornamentation of terra-cotta, a red-brown baked and glazed clay. The copper-trimmed mansard roof was of green slate. It made, all in all, as the *Souvenir Program* stated, "a fetching combination of color." Over the two main entrances stood terra-cotta casts of Shibe (at Lehigh) and Mack (at Twenty-first). Over the other entrances was the letter *A* in English script, and over the corner arch was inscribed SHIBE PARK.

After buying tickets patrons entered the base of the tower, a large circular lobby, twenty-four feet in diameter, the most elegant entrance, writers later recalled, to a major league park. In the tower offices above the entrance level was Jack Shibe's suite with five cathedral windows. Using a mezzanine walkway, Shibe's assistants put tickets into the hands of the ticket sellers in their booths below. Shibe himself directly kept in touch with them through an intercom. Above Jack Shibe (actually on the fifth floor) Connie Mack had his ultimately more famous quarters, done in an equally opulent manner and later known as the oval office.

Two fourteen-foot-wide concourses to the north and east took some fans past the players' dressing area and various other workrooms to the bleachers. The more affluent patron of the grandstand went through turnstiles to a handsome pavilion, walking up a twenty-one-foot-wide stairway to the main grandstand promenade. The journey gradually revealed the expanse of green field, the sod transplanted from Columbia Park. Management claimed that the cantilevered stands provided unobstructed viewing from every seat, though enthusiasts soon noted that steel supports and various other impediments made it difficult to see the entire field from many vantage points. No advertising, however, marred the twelve-foot green concrete wall around the outfield, and an electrified scoreboard recorded who was playing and at bat.

The building cost Shibe $301,000 and the 1913 improvements another $76,000. After his successors demolished the park and others like it fifty or sixty years later, old-timers mourned the loss of the human scale of these stadiums in contrast to the new "multipurpose" facilities of the late twentieth century. But in the early 1900s contemporaries recognized that men like Shibe hankered after an imperial and impersonal look. Many commentators noted a loss of intimacy and the inconvenience fans accepted in walking great distances. The new parks "depersonalized" the game, separated players from fans, and destroyed much of the previous era's informality when customers and athletes were cheek-by-jowl. Cartoonists had a field day depicting kranks crushed in great crowds, collapsing with exhaustion after a climb to their seats, or looking at the game from distant stands. Cartoons also showed the passing of the knothole gang—a concrete wall did not invite peeking boys.

For magnates like Shibe, baseball was a revenue-based enterprise. The construction of a huge building to house the business reflected its complexity. Shibe also wanted a grand showplace as a symbol of his worthiness as an American entrepreneur. He proudly and repeatedly stressed the financial appropriateness of building Shibe Park, "a shrewd business move." It was as if the owner had to *prove* his interest was not merely sporting but one responsibly monetary, in keeping with the values of the well-to-do.

Shibe had to hurry to ready the park for opening day, but after he closed the gates in the early afternoon, everything went off smoothly before the enormous crowd. The entertainment began with the fans rising to sing "America" ("My Country! 'tis of thee"). Thereafter, officials, bands, and players marched to the center field flagpole, where Shibe and Ban Johnson raised Old Glory alongside the Athletics' pennant. Then the bands played "The Star-Spangled Banner" while the crowd, again, stood up "reverently . . . with uncovered heads." Back at the grandstand box seats, Philadelphia mayor John Reyburn threw out the first ball. Umpire Tim Hurst cried, "Play ball!" Shortly after 3:00 P.M. Eddie Plank delivered the initial pitch to Boston Red Sox second baseman Amby McConnell. The A's won 8–1.

When the game ended, as thousands swarmed over the field, the mayor declared that Philadelphia would long remember the day. Shibe Park, said Reyburn, was not just "any business." Baseball had a public dimension, and the stadium was a "pride to the city."

• 2 •

The Athletics and North City, 1909–1923

One man—Ty Cobb, right fielder of the Detroit Tigers—immediately contributed more than any other to the growth of a tradition at the new stadium. Cobb's Tigers won the American League pennant in 1907 and 1908, but the A's challenged them for the 1909 title. In August the Athletics dropped to second place in a bitterly fought series in Detroit, with the ferocious and talented Cobb leading the Tiger offense. He spiked A's third baseman Frank Baker in an attempted steal and, in another play, knocked over second baseman Eddie Collins.

When Detroit came to Shibe Park in mid-September for a four-game series, Philadelphia bugs were raging. Articles in the *Philadelphia Bulletin* stoked their anger. The series drew 120,000 patrons, the best-attended group of games in the city's history. Fans sat all along the outfield wall and on the tops of row houses on Somerset and Twentieth streets. Indeed, a dozen notes had threatened that someone would shoot Cobb from the Twentieth Street roofs if he dared to play. The games in Detroit had disturbed the usually placid manager Connie Mack, who now called the police out in force. A motorcycle squad escorted Cobb to and from the grounds. Officials scattered several dozen plainclothesmen in the stands and stationed a solid line of Philadelphia bluecoats in right field, between Cobb and the kranks standing behind ropes on the outfield grass. At one point in the tense proceedings Cobb jumped at the backfire of a car in the street. But no incidents marked the first ugly crowd in Shibe Park, although such crowds would become the rule.

In the second game, the tension broke. When Cobb stole third, Baker shook his hand to end the feud. The fans cheered when Cobb dove into the roped-off area in the right field corner to catch a foul ball. The bugs cheered again when Cobb returned the next inning with five dollars for the man whose straw hat he had crushed when he made the catch.

Cobb continued, however, to draw the fire of Philadelphia rooters. After a game a few seasons later, a hostile gang mobbed him outside Shibe Park. He tried to escape in a passing trolley, but someone climbed on the trolley's roof and disabled its electric connection. Cobb was safe only after the conductor reconnected it and the vehicle took off. In 1912, after a nasty incident in New York in which Cobb beat up a heckler, Ban Johnson suspended him from play. With the suspension in effect the next day at Shibe Park, Cobb's teammates went on strike and refused to perform. Before resolving the issue, the franchise assembled a "Detroit" team from customers in the stands, largely ballplayers from the local St. Joseph's College. Outfitted in the uniforms of the striking professionals, the amateurs took the field for fifty dollars apiece. Fifteen thousand Philadelphians now delighted that the despised Cobb caused a great Athletics victory, 24–2. By the end of the decade the meanspiritedness of the city's rooters was such a part of the baseball scene that the *Sporting News* went out of its way to note that one should not blame unruly baseball behavior on foreigners, since it was common in Philadelphia, a "bastion of 100% Americanism."

During this period, nonetheless, the fans had much to cheer about. Although the A's finished second in 1909, from 1910 to 1914 they won four pennants, dominating the Tigers in the American League and going on to win three world championships as one of the preeminent baseball dynasties.

The A's boasted a solid group of outfielders, including Bris Lord, Danny Murphy, Eddie Murphy, Rube Oldring, and Amos Strunk; but they were strongest in the infield and in their pitching. Jack Barry played a classy game at shortstop. Three players each regarded as the best at his position in the decade from 1910 to 1920 joined him: Stuffy McInnis at first, Eddie Collins at second, and Frank Baker at third. McInnis consistently hit .300. Collins was one of the stellar players of all time—a powerful hitter, sterling base runner, and brilliant defensive player and strategist. Baker was the number-one slugger of the "dead ball" era, leading the American League four times in home runs. A powerful left-handed batter, he hit the first Shibe Park home run, some 350 feet over the right field fence in 1909—a stupendous feat given the lack of "jump" in the ball in that period. Writers dubbed the four men the "$100,000 infield," and later called them "the million dollar infield," reflecting inflation, short memories, and the legendary aura surrounding the four.

Finally, the team had superb pitching. Chief Bender, Eddie Plank, and Jack Coombs were three of the best pitchers in the majors, each capable of winning over twenty games a season. Aiding them were Cy Morgan, Boardwalk Brown, Bullet Joe Bush, and Harry Krause, each capable of winning fifteen to twenty games.

Louis VanZelst, the Athletics' mascot from 1910 to 1915, was also famous. A tiny hunchback, he became a sentimental favorite at Shibe Park. Eddie Collins discovered him, and the superstitious ballplayers rubbed his back for luck. The fans credited VanZelst with bringing the champions their good fortune and favorably compared him to similar mascots that other teams employed.

In 1910 the A's defeated the Chicago Cubs in the World Series. The next year they faced the New York Giants managed by John McGraw. McGraw gave Shibe Park kranks a rival the equal of Cobb. A brawling Irishman, McGraw and his team regularly played in the city against the mediocre Philadelphia National League club and reminded rooters of the most rough-and-tumble aspects of the game. More important, when Mack established the American League franchise in 1901, McGraw quipped that the new league had a "white elephant" on its hands. The remark prompted the Athletics to make an elephant their symbol. In 1905 McGraw's Giants beat the A's in Philadelphia's first World Series. After the victory, the "little Napoleon," as writers called McGraw, felt he had demonstrated the superiority of the National League and of New York over the better of the Philadelphia clubs.

The 1911 series was a return match. The first series to receive national and international coverage, it was filled with excitement as well as ticket scandals, rowdyism, and miscellaneous charges of foul play. New York won the opener at the Polo Grounds 2–1, with Christy Mathewson besting Bender. In the second game at Shibe Park, Baker won the game 3–1, with a two-run homer over the right field wall. Rounding second base that afternoon to the mad ovation of the bugs, Baker remembered, was the greatest moment in his life. The next day, in New York, he hit another homer off Mathewson in the ninth inning to tie a game that the A's went on to win. These two home runs gave the third baseman his nickname—"Homerun" Baker—a tag that echoed "Home Run Alley," the sometime description of North Twentieth Street, where Baker's right field Shibe Park homers landed.

With the A's up by one in the series, it rained for five days. In his tower office Connie Mack looked out at the gray surroundings every morning and hoped for the weather to break. In the Shibe Park lunch-room a vendor's nightmare occurred. Employees removed the sandwich meat from between the two pieces of bread and put it on ice. They gave the bread to orphanages. After two days, they discarded the meat itself, and the franchise worried about its profits. On the sixth day the rain stopped, but grounds keepers spent the day drying out the waterlogged field with cans of burning gasoline. The A's and Giants then split the next two contests, so the Athletics led three games to two. The sixth game at Shibe Park was the finale, a 13–2 rout of New York. After the fourth inning, McGraw disappeared from the coaching lines, unwilling to subject himself to the taunts of thousands of Philadelphians.

In 1913 the A's again defeated the Giants, four games to one, but the 1911 victory had been sweeter. It even entrenched the A's in fiction. Ring Lardner wrote of Baker's Philadelphia home run "over that little old wall" in his short story "Horseshoes." Over seventy years later Eric Greenberg's *The Celebrant* treated the whole series in a book widely re-garded as the best baseball novel.

Central to the Athletics' success in the eyes of Philadelphia was their manager, Connie Mack. He not only took charge of day-to-day tactics but also assembled and developed talent. Mack's ties to the A's lasted for more than half a century. After his early triumphs at Shibe Park, the public regarded him as the most significant figure in Philadelphia base-ball. In 1913 the owner of the New York Highlanders—soon the Yan-kees—conceived the brilliant idea of luring Mack to New York to offset the attraction of McGraw. Ben Shibe hoped to retain the team leader who had capped a string of victorious seasons with a third World Series. Mack wanted to stay in Philadelphia, but the offer flattered him. To keep him Shibe undertook some complicated maneuvers that promoted Mack to full partnership in the franchise. First, Shibe sold Shibe Park, the Athletic Grounds Company of which he was the principal owner, to the franchise, the American Base Ball Club of Philadelphia. The price, $46,000 plus assumption of a $150,000 mortgage, was a steal. The cost of land and structure, mainly incurred five years before, was near $445,000. Thus Shibe enlarged the value of the franchise, of which he was majority shareholder. Then he loaned Mack money to buy out Frank Hough and Butch Jones and increase his quarter interest in the club to one-half. The loan, for $113,300, meant that Shibe valued the franchise at $450,000, the primary asset being the real estate. Mack stayed in the city, and now had a 50 percent holding in the club and the new park.

In the late nineteenth century young Irish Catholics had four paths to advancement—politics, police work, the priesthood, and professional sports. In baseball, however, Mack did not represent the tough Irish style that people all over the United States identified with McGraw. An important segment of the middle class wanted in this Progressive period to shun effeminacy but also to demonstrate a well-mannered virility. Teddy Roosevelt, president in the first decade of the century, expressed this love of the strenuous life and contempt for "mollycoddle." Yet Roosevelt was a gentleman. Mack embraced this most acceptable conception of manliness. He fit in well with those baseball men who were upgrading the image of the sport.

Even on the hottest days Mack wore immaculate three-piece suits and starched collars that fifty years later, when he still wore them, sportwriters would describe as old fashioned. One of his ballplayers said he looked like a deacon who had mistakenly wandered into Shibe Park. He enforced a curfew, could not abide hard liquor, and eschewed profane language. When Stuffy McInnis once screamed out "Jesus Christ" on a quiet afternoon, Mack remonstrated with him by saying, "Don't do it again." He was so quiet and unobtrusive that in the first two decades of the century people did not know what he looked like. After he entered the Shibe Park dugout for a game, he rarely left it. Coaching from there, Mack instructed his players by a complex wagging of his scorecard. Although these directions later became his signature, in the early years they were the only way Philadelphians knew him. When the game was over, he never went into the clubhouse or made a public appearance.

After his first World Series victory in 1910, over fifty thousand fans packed the streets around the Broad Street Station in the center of town to greet the team on its return from Chicago. Mayor Reyburn gave Mack a key to the city. Nonetheless, he could still ride the downtown subway unrecognized, while other passengers discussed "Connie's" managerial brilliance.

In succeeding years, Mack emerged as more than a first-class manager. Indeed, had he not had one-half interest in the A's, his failures after 1914 would have led to his dismissal. Instead, he became a baseball businessman. He took on the character of a statesman of the national game for which people all over the United States knew him.

Mack's model for baseball enterprise was his first period in the American League before Shibe built the park. From 1901 to 1909 the A's won two pennants and no championships. Mack had a good team but never achieved dominance. He learned two lessons from this decade. First, he believed that the team would prosper when it contended but not necessarily when it was champion. Fans came to see doubtful contests. Enthusiasm and profits might flag if the A's won too consistently. During this decade, too, Mack easily adjusted and refined the abilities of the team and quickly brought together an able group of players. For the rest of his career he wanted an aggressive franchise but not a perfectly built "machine." "When your club is fighting to the top," he said, "the fans . . . come out to the park . . . ; but pennant winners get to be an old story."

Mack learned, second, to respond to socioeconomic conditions. He reacted cautiously to the world outside of baseball but knew to expand when good times were certain. And he cut back severely at the hint of bad times. In effect Mack tried to produce good teams if that was the most profitable way of running the business. He endured wretched clubs if he calculated that a winning team was risky or that champions would not make money. "When you win, you have a general rise in all expenses," Mack opined. "When the club is behind, salaries are low, so are expenses." Another time, expecting a bad season, he warned fans that they should not spend money "expecting too much," and one spring he promised Philadelphians only competent baseball and "nothing more." His evaluation of one year showed exactly how he thought. "With a tail-end club," he said, "we're doing real good."

Mack appears to have learned a final lesson from Shibe's financial moves of 1913 that gave the manager 50 percent of the Athletics stock. Mack's focal point was the yearly bottom line that set the income from gate receipts against the expense of players' salaries, but he grasped that the economics of the business was more complex. The sport also involved real estate, investment in future player talent, and the worth of the contracts of players. For tax purposes he could complexly appraise property, in both players and in the park. The value of the franchise's stock could climb dramatically if the A's had a popular team or be artificially adjusted in a variety of ways. After the stadium became an integral part of the franchise in 1913, manipulations of the value of the business were not uncommon. Manager-owner Mack did what he could to save money on taxes; or to sell stock cheaply to his children; or to convince outsiders that he had no assets.

Mack's troubles arose from frugality and misjudgment about what it took to bring together a good team. Some called him a cheapskate or skinflint, but his thrift was explicable. He did not have other income to offset baseball losses. Although ultimately a wealthy man, he weighed matters closely and conservatively and was always sparing, at least in dealing with his players. Suspicious of the devotion of fans, he used any decline in attendance that went with winning teams as immediate grounds for retrenchment. He was not afraid to spend big, to cash in on boom times, but only when a boom was sure. Prudence was his style. Yet like some individuals who do not usually take risks, Mack could be daring when convinced that he could make a killing. During much of the half century he held stock in the franchise, his efforts produced clubs that were only inexpensive to administer. But from 1910 to 1914 (and later, from 1927 to 1932) his tinkering assembled at Shibe Park two of the outstanding teams in the history of the game.

By the second decade of the century Mack was the dean of American League managers. His style and success with the "Mackmen," in contrast to McGraw's with his Giants, gave baseball fans endless opportunities to discuss which man had the greater genius. "There has been only one manager," said Mack, "and his name is McGraw." Visiting Napoleon's tomb, McGraw said, "I, too, met the Duke of Wellington, only his name was Connie Mack."

A close and informal network of friends, located mainly in and around Pennsylvania, kept Mack in touch with promising players. He shrewdly brought college prospects into the majors, thinking they would make the game more toney. By scouting eastern schools, he also mined a new field for talent and helped his Athletics. Mack worried that college athletes would push up salaries but persevered early on in recruiting them, even when observers laughed at him. Jack Barry played at Holy Cross; Jack Coombs at Colby; Eddie Plank at Gettysburg. Other players could claim more than the rudiments of education. Chief Bender went to the Carlisle Indian School, Harry Davis to Girard College (a Philadelphia preparatory school for orphans), and Stuffy McInnis to the Gloucester Massachusetts High School. When the Tigers traded catcher Ira Thomas from Detroit to Philadelphia at the end of 1908, he feared "going to Connie Mack's team of college boys." Mack got rid of the talented but illiterate Joe Jackson in mid-1910 because he did not fit in with his cerebral teammates. The 1910 A's were the most highly educated club in history. When they won the World Series, Mack's mentor

Ban Johnson said that "dignified men in the best tradition of middle-class American values" achieved the victory. Although the press exaggerated his pious virtues, Mack had a public persona that embodied them. His shy, gentlemanly character was making him the focus of sentimental, even maudlin, admiration.

"The tall tactician" or "the lean sage of Shibeshire," as the sportwriters called him, brought men up and down, juggled his lineups, and shifted players around. He was always searching for the right combination of strength that would make his team a contender. The basic plan was to pick up a cheap buy here, a castoff there, a local star or college man here, a friend's tip there.

The careers of two of Mack's players hinted at different tendencies in the sport. The most famous collegian was Collins—"Columbia Eddie," as he was first known. To maintain his eligibility at Columbia University in New York City, Collins started professional ball under an assumed name. When he joined the A's in 1906, he began a twenty-five-year career in the majors in which he would accumulate more than three thousand hits and compile a lifetime batting average of .333. A smart team captain, Collins commanded the admiration of owners for his prowess, general savvy, and understanding of the larger issues involved in baseball, its business nature and place in the public eye. Many less gifted and educated players resented him, calling him "Cocky" Collins. He left the A's in 1914 for an equally successful and more lucrative stint as second baseman and then player-manager of the Chicago White Sox before he ended his career back with the A's from 1927 to 1930. A cosmopolitan and sophisticated man, Collins then moved to an executive position with the Boston Red Sox. In 1939 he was one of the early inductees into the Hall of Fame.

If Collins represented one direction baseball lives might take, Amos Strunk represented another. Born in Philadelphia, Strunk went to the James G. Blaine Grammar School at Thirtieth and Norris streets, a few blocks from the old Columbia Park and Mack's home. Mack claimed to have recruited Strunk from Blaine Grammar, although he also played for the Park Sparrows in nearby Strawberry Mansion Park and attended Central Manual Training School with Connie's son Roy at Seventeenth and Wood streets, also within hailing distance of the Macks.

Strunk appeared in a few games for the A's in 1908 at Columbia Park and in 1909 at their new home, but did not play regularly till the end of 1910. He was a tall, fleet outfielder, popular with local fans. He batted

.283 over seventeen seasons, although during his peak years he averaged over .300.

Strunk's home was the Shibe Park neighborhood. In his first years with the A's, he lived some half dozen blocks from the new stadium with his sister and close to his brother. He courted a childhood sweetheart who lived around the corner from their school. The local Lutheran minister married them. Strunk moved to nearby Llanerch, Pennsylvania, to what was then the country. During the off-season he sold insurance in Philadelphia, a job he kept long after he retired from baseball.

Strunk played with the Athletics until 1917, when Mack cut his salary after some unpleasant negotiations. As Mack put it, there was "a financial question," which fans could not "care anything about." He wanted to reduce expenses and, after the season ended, sold Strunk and two other starters to the Red Sox for sixty thousand dollars and three unknowns who played the same positions as the men he had traded.

In addition to the comparatively small salary he received from Mack, one reason Strunk gave for dickering in 1917 was that he could earn more selling insurance than playing for the A's. He argued equally strenuously with the Sox about his pay before going to Boston. Playing there, he said, would hurt his Philadelphia business connections. In 1918, his first season with Boston, he hit .257, his lowest average since breaking into the majors, and thus was in a poor position to bargain.

In 1919 Strunk adapted to his new team and was hitting .272 in the first three months of the season. Then Mack brought him back in a trade. Strunk's bat once more collapsed. In sixty games he hit only .211. Nonetheless, he was happy to be playing in Philadelphia again. Naming him team captain for 1920, Mack stated that he would not sell Strunk, and Strunk responded by hitting .297 for the first half of the 1920 season. Then he injured his knee in late July and was to be out for six weeks. Mack sent him to Chicago.

Part of the consideration in the sale may have been Mack's desire to fortify the White Sox. For the rumors about the fix of the World Series the year before were becoming public. In early September, eight players left the club, whose morale and play went to pieces. In any event, Strunk's knee injury did not prevent him from playing in Chicago, but his game suffered. He batted only .230 in fifty-one games for the "Black Sox."

Once again Strunk adjusted to a new club. During the next three years, for a poor and disorganized team, he averaged well over .300 in

267 games. By 1923, however, he no longer started. After one game in 1924 the Sox released him. As a newspaper reported, Mack put him "back at Shibe Park" for a last time when he gave Strunk a contract in May. He played thirty games for the A's before calling it quits.

Eddie Collins was an intelligent star performer who got treatment reserved for an elite group of players. Strunk was not unintelligent but was no more than a regular. Mack bought and sold him according to his own agenda. Repeated trades obviously disrupted Strunk's life, in Philadelphia and in baseball. In later years Eddie Collins could speak no ill of "Mister Mack." Strunk, who said that Mack preferred to sell ballplayers for money than to field a winning team, bottled up his resentment.

Late in his career, Mack was "wistful," Red Smith recalled, about the "old days" and lamented the growth of farm clubs in the 1930s. Even later, Mack deprecated the bonus system, in which major league franchises owned minor league teams stocked with high-priced players. Mack felt most comfortable when talent was on the open market. Then good scouting, managerial initiative, and skill, along with the "reserve" clause that tied a man to one franchise for as long as it wished, might produce a winning club. Yet the balance was so fragile that there would always be a horse race for the pennant and, thus, the possibility of profits for all. Downplaying the advantages of money, this vision of Mack's was somewhere between the syndicate baseball of the early years and the farms, bonuses, and free agency of the future. The vision was not unalluring, despite the problems it made for men like Strunk.

Strunk was not the only major leaguer to live near the park. When Shibe opened the stadium in 1909, rookies boarded on Twentieth Street, behind right field. Monte Cross, who played shortstop for the A's till his retirement in 1907, lived nearby, and Jack Coombs roomed with him. Eddie Collins stayed with Harry Davis, another Philadelphia ballplayer ending a long career with the A's. Catcher Wally Schang joined the neighborhood when he married his girl friend, who resided on the 2700 block of North Nineteenth Street. Chief Bender bought a new house seven blocks north of the park. No one, however, was more of a presence than manager Mack himself. In the first decade of the century he lived across the street from Columbia Park. When the franchise moved, Mack moved too, to 2119 Ontario Street, some seven blocks from Twenty-first and Lehigh. In 1910 his players used their anticipated

World Series shares to present him with an automobile at Shibe Park. A few weeks later, after his series victory, he was given a two-ton live elephant, which walked through the streets to Mack's house, where it was left eating the backyard grass. Even after he moved to nearby Germantown, Mack regularly took the trolley to his workplace.

Around that workplace, where the players continued to live, the familiar Philadelphia row house sheltered a dense population south of Lehigh. The large east-west streets and the numbered streets were themselves crossed by smaller streets running both north and south and east and west. Often alleys further separated, for example, the back of the east side of one small street from the back of the west side of another.

Streets above Lehigh replicated the same pattern. In the northwest, however, from Somerset to Clearfield, Twenty-second to Twenty-eighth, many square blocks were still vacant, although Mayor Reyburn noted that builders were following Shibe's lead in developing the community. Baseball led the way in the real estate move north of the Pennsylvania tracks after the hospital (and other noxious industries) disappeared. To the east, where the railroad turned, were commercial and industrial enterprises or open railroad yards. Here, lumber and brickworks, furniture and pipe factories, and warehouses towered above the landscape.

In addition to Shibe Park, a number of landmarks stood out. More than a business, Freihofer's Bakery at Nineteenth and Clearfield gave food to many down-and-outers, and everyone went there for "day olders." After the city demolished its old Hospital for Contagious Diseases across the street from the stadium, a park replaced it. Originally called Donegal Square because of the prevalence of the Irish brogue of County Donegal, Ireland, Donegal Square soon gave way to "the Square," a name that persisted long after the city officially named it Reyburn Park after Mayor Reyburn.

At Twenty-fourth and Lehigh the Roman Catholic church built Saint Colomba's parish, its parochial school and church completed shortly before Shibe erected his park. At Twentieth and Indiana Siegmund Lubin constructed a large glass studio for the production of motion pictures. "Lubinville," a clutch of buildings covering a full city block on the scale of Shibe Park, housed one of the first movie moguls, whose work added much spice to the locale. A fire in 1914 caused Lubin to move, and a ball bearing company moved in. Although much smaller, a more lasting community institution went up nearer the park. Matt Kilroy, a famous nineteenth-century professional ballplayer and a friend of

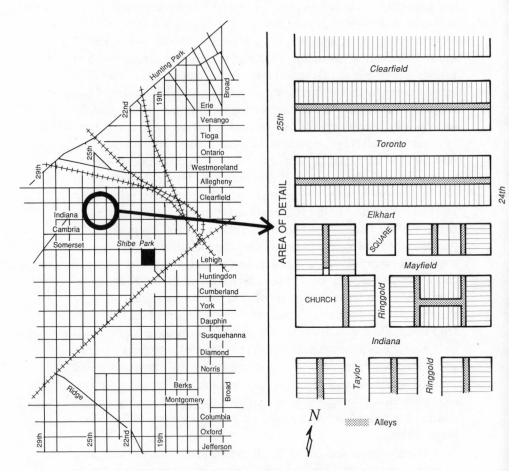

Map 4. North Philadelphia street patterns, 1920s

Mack, opened a bar at the corner of Twentieth and Lehigh. Kilroy's soon became a hangout for fans and players. It remained under his ownership till 1935 and continued to be run afterward for the baseball trade.

Like many parts of the city, North Philadelphia was getting less varied than it had been before 1900. Because of the slowness of transportation in preindustrial Philadelphia, the more well-to-do had lived closest to the business center, with poorer people relegated to the outskirts. The smaller scale of the city, in any event, had meant that all the city's districts displayed varied housing and a mix of social classes. Then, in the middle of the nineteenth century, quicker transportation turned previously undeveloped North Philadelphia into a residential suburb. Later in the century, however, continued urban growth made the area heterogeneous. Its primary axis was north Broad Street. North Philly comprised a mix of ethnic groups and people of various social and economic stations living in close proximity. The territory included mansions—mainly inhabited by upper-class Jews—middle-class row homes, immigrant bandbox houses, and industry. A nucleus of blacks lived at Tenth and Columbia. Yet industrialization and even faster public transportation were again bringing class homogeneity. Overall, the well-to-do moved to the newest parts of town. The less affluent, who could not afford the best housing and who were forced to live near their employment, took over the older areas. Those with larger incomes got away from their economic inferiors and the noise and dirt of manufacturing by retreating to the most recently built and most distant residences accessible by trains and the trolley system. When this housing, in turn, aged, its owners would sell out to lower-income groups on the rise.

The result in "the industrial city" at the end of the century were uniform social and economic districts. Scholars have found, however, that socioeconomic consistency did not mean rootedness in a neighborhood. Evidence suggests that families, certainly renters, moved frequently from one district to another, or from one home to another in the same district, perhaps moving up the housing scale in eras of prosperity, down in times of hardship.

Inhabited by the workers in the industries located in the older part of the city, North Philadephia was achieving a blue-collar look. East of Broad at Columbia the working-class community was black. But on the other side of the tracks, from Twenty-ninth and Diamond northeast to Seventeenth and Allegheny, North Philadelphia attracted members of the white working class, many of them immigrants. Irish and Irish-

Americans were most noticeable. English and Germans, usually a leg up on the Irish, were also in evidence, as well as Italians—usually a leg down. Around Lubinville the houses of a substantial group of Italians were backdrops in comic chase films, in which local Italian children often joined.

The building trades employed many of the Irish-Americans, who also occupied niches in local government and the police force. These connections insured that the Irish constructed and then manned the city's transport system. They also worked their way up in some of Philadelphia's skilled trades—textiles, machine shops, hardware manufacturing, and printing. Finally, the Irish-Americans often "managed" newcomers, the Irish and Italians who did unskilled construction work or had menial employment with the city or with the railroads.

In the vicinity of the ball park the more successful Irish-Americans owned their homes, sometimes three stories high, although a much smaller German- and English-American middle-class elite usually occupied the very best dwellings. Ethnic building and loan associations financed much of the housing. Trees lined the larger streets—the county and number streets—and their houses had substantial porches, frequently graced with awnings. On the smaller streets were renters with laborers' jobs, their pinched and cramped two-story buildings requiring austerity for large families.

The Irish and their culture stamped the area. Even the tiny row houses were luxurious to the immigrants. "Better than thatched roofs," said one resident. Neighbors kept their houses clean, scrubbing steps and windows weekly. The concrete sidewalks were a novelty but also an amenity to be treasured in contrast to mud or unsteady planks. Wives swept and reswept along the curb, even banishing dirt from the cracks in the pavement.

Central to the lives of the Irish was Saint Columba's. It "saw them through from the cradle to the grave," said one observer. The parish priests were respected figures, the most important men in the neighborhood. For children the nuns at school loomed largest. But school and church were one, with good performance in school and regular appearance at mass the sign of respectability. The Irish were proud that the kids who could not behave got thrown out and were sent to the Thomas May Pierce public school just to the north. On the one hand, the Irish would assert that this made Saint Columba's educationally superior to the school of their socially more upscale Protestant neighbors. On the other, the Irish occasionally called the public school "Saint Pierce," and the Protestant parents of children there despaired that Pierce had to open its doors to "harp trash."

The saloon was a focus of solidarity in the community and also its great affliction. Second only in significance to the church, the corner bar was a center of gossip, conviviality, and information about the neighborhood. Saloonkeepers helped patrons in dealing with city officials and welfare services and in looking for jobs. Even the Irish who did not imbibe saw the positive side of the saloon culture and its humor. Residents would relate how regular lines formed outside the confessionals at Saint Columba's from seven to nine on Saturday nights. Male parishioners admitted their failings of the previous week. Then many of the forgiven sinners would promptly go off on another binge, having prepared their stomachs by coating them with milk. Some would manage to show up at mass the next morning. Others, "coming off a load," would be too sick to attend. They would stay at home nursing themselves through a hangover. Buy a pound cake, went the lore, and a quart of ice cream; take a spoonful of cake and slide it down with a spoonful of ice cream; repeat as necessary.

After laughing at the weakness of friends, "more responsible" Irish would still lament the bane of alcohol in the community. They would shake their heads even more because the "pig shit" Irish made them all look bad in the eyes of "the goddamn [Protestant] Republicans, looking down their noses at us." The German- and English-Americans agreed: the Irish were "all drunks."

Despite the pressures creating lower-income enclaves, other pressures made these enclaves accept certain middle-class values. As the city's grid plan was realized in North City, older meandering highways disappeared. Asphalt and concrete covered the new straight streets, intersecting one another at right angles. Cleaner and better for heavy transport, these substances yielded quicker access to and from outlying areas. They replaced gravel, macadam, and cobblestones. The older materials restricted fast and heavy traffic and abetted what one expert has called "the social function" of the street—the socializing, play, and huckstering characteristic of the area around Twenty-first and Lehigh before Shibe built his park. Reformers transformed the old streets so that the middle class could work in a more sanitary inner city and rapidly get to more distant residential areas. The change forced a new kind of life on the burgeoning working-class neighborhoods. Sitting on the stoop of one's house or chatting on the porch with neighbors remained important leisure activities, but the streets themselves were more and more off limits. What authorities called "the Parks movement" was also a middle-class attempt to give workers a less dirty and morally ambiguous place to congregate. Reformers placed the Square across the street from the stadium. This recreational area would expand over the years, as would the various playing fields in Fairmount Park and around Twenty-eighth and Clearfield, at the edges of the neighborhood.

The reforming impulse was part of the constellation of factors that produced Shibe Park itself. After the Civil War, amateur and semipro baseball was sometimes an activity of the privileged. But neighborhood and factory teams offered exercise and sociability for the hoi polloi. Much before the turn of the century, entrepreneurs showed that the sport could attract large audiences and earn money. Shibe and Mack joined an established business that was remaking baseball as a spectator sport. "Old Shibe," said one articulate working-class resident in the early years, "moved baseball off our streets into his park." But then, he reflected, "it wasn't all bad. . . . The boys learned how to act in that swanky park and stopped fighting one another in the saloons. They could sort of fight New York instead and show some of the Philadelphia high-hats [at the stadium] that we were O.K. Maybe they saw that we were human beings too and even learned something from us—how to relax a bit or tease the girls."

This was surely an exaggeration. Baseball did not vanish from the streets as it moved into Shibe Park with paying customers. But nonprofessional athletics lost their public function for both aristocrats and the working classes when baseball showed it could attract a multitude of paying customers.

In promoting the benefits of professional baseball, its owners argued that the game relieved the monotony and tedium of employment in an industrial society and made for worthwhile use of nonworking time, away from bars or street corners. In embracing baseball, the working classes, as the old resident sensed, may have become less threatening and more committed to forms of entertainment that were acceptable parts of the business order. Shibe Park was part of an emerging commercial culture. The sport was as much the invention of industrial America as it was an antidote. "Fun" produced by businessmen was supposed to alleviate the troubles endemic to a business society.

At the same time, capitalists did not victimize ordinary citizens, who also affected the cultural significance of the sport. Great numbers of people who were not working class followed baseball. The game may have assisted in creating a mass democracy, eventually bringing social groups together. The sport may have popularized some working-class characteristics—informality, physical intimacy, and the mixing of sexes—among the nonworking classes. Finally, baseball may have strengthened the working class, ameliorating its ethnic and religious divisions.

The Irish in the neighborhood were staunch baseball fans. Many players were Irish and had a local following. Around the stadium (and in Philadelphia) the ethnic group was devoted to Mack. As one writer noted, the intense commitment of "hyphenated" communities like the one near Shibe Park made baseball, ironically, "America's game." But ethnic groups differed. One woman complained that the nearby Italians were "not even neighbors . . . they didn't even like baseball." An Italian resident downplayed the importance of baseball for his neighborhood.

It is still peculiarly difficult to sort out what made citizens into fans. Professional baseball attracted customers from all over the city, Irish and non-Irish. At times they divided their fealty between the A's and the National League Phillies, whose park was some nine blocks from Twenty-first and Lehigh. The proximity of the two franchises meant that the geographical determinants of allegiance that existed, for example, in Chicago or New York, did not exist in Philadelphia. More important, until after World War II, the Phillies, a persistently poor club, were a distinctly secondary consideration for Philadelphia rooters. The A's were the city's team. Fans of the Phillies were few, and people might follow them without feeling disloyal to the A's. Theories abounded to explain commitments. Those who liked the underdog favored the Phillies. Republicans, in general, were A's fans. Protestants supported the National League.

Cheered by their rooters from the district and around the town, the A's in 1914 not unexpectedly won the American League pennant again. Widely thought of as the premier team of modern times, they faced in the series a weak and upstart Boston club that had been in last place in the National League as late as July 18. Streaking through high summer, however, the Braves finished first, ten and a half games ahead of McGraw's Giants.

Led by former mayor John F. Fitzgerald, enthusiastic Boston fans came to Philadelphia by train for the first two series games. "Honey Fitz," grandfather of John F. Kennedy, led the Boston "Royal Rooters" in a parade on Broad Street and later in a special section of the Shibe Park stands. Baseball insiders, however, heavily favored Philadelphia. Even the Boston manager was diffident in proclaiming his team's virtues. Then, however, the Athletics' pitching and batting both inexplicably collapsed. "The miracle Braves" swept the A's—two games in Philadelphia and two in Boston—the first time this had happened in postseason play. In 1950 the Associated Press polled sportswriters and found that the Braves' victory was the biggest upset in the first half of twentieth-century American sport. Baseball historian David Voigt wrote that if no one had discovered the "Black Sox" scandal of 1919, the upset Cincinnati victory over Chicago in that year would have ranked "somewhat behind" the triumph of the Braves.

One question must inevitably come to mind: Did the A's throw the 1914 World Series? Baseball gambling was common, and many players were not above trying to fix games. In 1920 the revelation that the players on the Chicago team had thrown the 1919 series shook baseball and American culture. A consequent reorganization of the sport gave formidable powers to a commissioner of baseball, Kenesaw Mountain Landis. In the mean business of 1919 the players had revolted against the tightfisted policies of Chicago owner Charles Comiskey, only slightly more stingy than Mack. Later, in the 1920s, Mack acted in concert with Commissioner Landis to vindicate Ty Cobb and Tris Speaker. He hired the two aging stars in an effort to restore their reputations after they had been charged (probably correctly) with shady practices and gambling.

In 1914 it was hinted that the A's had "laid down" in the series. In his dotage Connie Mack mentioned these allegations only to reaffirm that other reasons explained the Athletics failure. The team was factionalized and at odds with itself, said Mack. The factions originated because the Federal League, a short-lived competitor to the two established major leagues, attracted A's stars with the lure of high salaries. The frictions between the "loyalists" and their opponents produced an arrogant club that had gotten off its stride. Pitchers Plank and Bender, who had Federal League offers, merely coasted through much of 1914.

Much that happened corroborated this story. At the end of the season Bender and Plank went over to the Feds. Mack waived Jack Coombs, another dissident, out of the league. The disaffection between Mack and Frank Baker was so great that the star third baseman sat out the 1915 season. Then Mack sold Baker to the Yankees. In the biggest move, Eddie Collins, whom the Feds tempted, went to the White Sox and got a large salary increase.

Faced with these demands and the related instability in the business, Mack continued to dismantle the team. A dramatic decline in 1914 attendance and worries about the war in Europe contributed to his decision. In the next few years he got rid of Barry, Oldring, Strunk, and McInnis, among others. Nonetheless, Mack did what he could to strengthen "organized" baseball, and particularly the American League. If other league teams would pay higher salaries to his stars and money to the A's to obtain them, Mack could at least keep the players from the Federals.

Still, the evidence raises many puzzles. Mack did not try to sell Bender and Plank but simply let them go to the new franchises. Why did the pennypinching manager not try to make a profit and keep them in the American League? The most interesting events concern Mack's friend from his hometown of Brookfield, Massachusetts, George M. Cohan. A famous entertainer and gambling sportsman, Cohan broke with his New York croneys and personally insulted John McGraw in 1911 by betting on the A's. Cohan said he could not root against a man from Brookfield and cleaned up as the underdog A's defeated the Giants. Later, however, he turned on Mack. In 1914 Sport Sullivan, a leading Boston gambler, placed bets against Philadelphia for Cohan, who won a small fortune. Sullivan also handled the betting when Cohan wagered and won in the first two tainted games of the 1919 series, and Sullivan was later implicated in the fix. Whatever one makes of Cohan's infidelity to the A's in 1914, Mack himself was out of character in publicly venting his disgust with his team after the loss.

Mack may have suspected the club—particularly Bender, who had been decisively defeated in the first game—of "lying down." What this meant is hard to say. The team might have been demoralized or taking it easy. Or some of them, for spite, might have deliberately not played as well as they could; or some might have deliberately played poorly *and* bet against the A's. As Mack saw it, he punished some players and protected organized baseball from scandal by dismissing them. He would not heed the players' demands for more money but did what he could to keep others in the majors.

There was, however, more going on than a whitewash of the sport's seamier aspects. Mack undoubtedly thought he could rebuild rapidly and overestimated the ease with which his canny abilities could mold a winner. But from 1914 to 1918 he also sold off good players in what seemed like desperation and would not make even modest investments for the future. For example, he refused to buy Babe Ruth from his friend Jack Dunn of the minor league Orioles.

The Federal League threat, the world war, and a slump in patronage troubled baseball in these years. But Mack's cries of poverty are suspect, too. In 1913, in an adulatory article on Mack, *Harpers* reported that of all the American League teams the A's took in the most money with the smallest payroll. At the same time Mack did have a $113,000 loan to pay off to Ben Shibe. With one-half interest in the club, he could use short-term profits from the sale of players to liquidate his debt.

Whatever the background, the A's precipitously declined. Having lost 63 games in 1914, the team lost 109 in 1915 and finished last. In 1916 Mack fielded perhaps the worst team in history; it lost 117 games. But since the A's finished last seven years running and lost 100 or more games five of those years, the distinction of the 1916 A's, 40 games out of seventh, was obscured. In 1918 Mack began the season with twenty players, only three of whom had been with the A's the year before. Only seven had been in the majors. The next year five of his twenty-seven-man roster were drawn from the Shibe Park neighborhood and an additional pitcher from nearby Germantown.

Grantland Rice said it best when he wrote a tribute to Stuffy McInnis, "the last of the Mohicans," whom Mack kept on in Philadelphia longer than most of his other stars:

> Piking along with the trailers
> Here as the summer flits
> Sometimes isn't it lonesome
> Wasting your two-base hits?
> Batting above Three-Hundred
> While Hanging on to a dream,
> Swept from the years behind you,
> Last of the Old Regime

As one writer put it, "The game offers no parallels for those dark ages of the Mackmen." After making rooters proud of being Philadelphians, Mack had now, another writer said, injured civic pride and done a "monstrous injustice" to baseball devotees. From time to time the fans returned the favor. When Ty Cobb stole his ninetieth base at Shibe Park to break the old stolen base record for a season, three hundred customers were there.

In the late teens and early twenties Mack gave hundreds of kids a chance to play in the big leagues. They merely had to show up at Twenty-first and Lehigh. Mack often put them into a game the day they arrived. One wag said three teams were there—one coming, one playing, and one going. During World War I more practiced professionals came and went, too, depending on their fear of being drafted and the availability of defense jobs. Other ne'er-do-wells whom Mack hired at bargain prices were always available to perform. Jack Keefe, the fictional hero made famous by Ring Lardner in *You Know Me Al*, ended his career with the lowly A's. In hope of having his talent spotted, the central character in one of James T. Farrell's series of novels of growing up in Chicago wrote to "Mr. Connie Mack, Shibe Park, The Philadelphia Athletics, Philadelphia, Pennsylvania." Danny O'Neill knew that Mack, above all others, picked promising players off the sandlots to develop them into stars.

One young man did develop. Wisecracking Jimmie Dykes, a Philadelphia boy, took three trolleys to Shibe Park in the late teens for a tryout. This was the start of a twenty-two-year major league career for Dykes—much of it with the A's—and he vividly remembered the chaos and mediocrity of Shibe Park baseball. Each day, he recalled, he would go through a mock ceremony of introducing himself to other members of the infield because it was never the same two days in a row. "Life was short at Shibe Park," he said. When Commissioner Landis banned the eight Black Sox from baseball, Dykes quipped that Landis "ought to investigate what's keeping us in this League." It was a bleak time for Philadelphia fans.

• 3 •
Days of Glory, 1924–1932

Mack fruitlessly tinkered with his team into the 1920s. By then good times and increased baseball popularity aided his efforts. More customers came to the park despite the woeful teams that played there. Demonstrating that he was not merely a skinflint, Mack started to buy players, shrewdly sensing that spending might pay off.

The tide turned in 1924. Mack brought three rookies to spring training—Paul Strand, Max Bishop, and Al Simmons. Strand was a costly flop. Bishop became a solid infielder with a twelve-year career. Simmons, who had a queer batting stance, keeping one foot "in the water bucket," became one of the strongest right-handed hitters of the next fifteen years. He had a lifetime batting average of .334, and during his prime with the A's regularly hit over .350, his high being .392.

Later in 1924 Mack acquired two other future stars. He got catcher Mickey Cochrane by purchasing an interest in the Portland, Oregon, club of the Pacific Coast League. Pitcher Robert Moses "Lefty" Grove from Baltimore in the International League came for installments totaling $100,600. Grove and Cochrane were the most formidable battery in the sport. Cochrane was a skilled catcher, fierce team leader, and dangerous batsman. His career average was .320. Grove was perhaps the most effective left-handed fast ball hurler ever. He won 300 games. In an era in which hitters prevailed, he stood out as an exceptional pitcher. From 1927 to 1933 he won 172 games and lost only 53, an average of 24 wins and 7 losses each year for seven years. In his worst season during this string (1927) he was 20–12; in his best (1931), 31–4.

Finally, in 1924, Frank Baker visited his old manager in the tower office and ended his feud. He told Mack of a teenager in the Eastern Shore, Maryland, League. Thus, Mack got Jimmie Foxx for nothing and saw "Double X" or "the Beast" grow into a prodigious slugger. Foxx hit on the order of Simmons and Cochrane, but was best known for his 534 career home runs. At his peak, in 1932, he smacked 58 of them.

Cochrane, Simmons, Foxx, and Grove all were elected to the Hall of Fame. While they matured in the mid-to-late twenties, Mack supplemented his lineup with aging stars who could impart wisdom to his younger players as well as draw fans. Future Hall of Famers Ty Cobb, Tris Speaker, Zack Wheat, Waite Hoyt, and Eddie Collins (for a second time) played for the A's in this period. With five or six men destined for the Hall of Fame performing for the Athletics on any given day, Philadelphians saw an aggregate of talent that was perhaps unmatched before or after.

To his stars Mack added a strong supporting cast. Rube Walberg, George Earnshaw, Jack Quinn, Eddie Rommel, and Roy Mahaffey gave the pitching staff depth and could each win between fifteen and twenty games. After Wheat, Cobb, and Speaker retired, Mack put Bing Miller and Mule Haas in his outfield with Simmons. Both players were underrated. Miller had a .312 batting average over sixteen years and Haas a .292 average for twelve. The infield was comparatively weak. Max Bishop and Jimmie Dykes settled down at second and third base, respectively, with Foxx at first; Joe Boley's five years in the majors were spent at shortstop.

In addition to buying minor leaguers, the Athletics renovated the stadium under Jack Shibe's auspices. The remodeling of 1925 resulted in what the management called "Greater Shibe Park." Shibe added more seats and constructed an upper deck on top of the old converted bleachers from third base to left field and from first base to right field. The Somerset Street left field bleachers received another deck. Finally, Shibe rebuilt the original grandstand, increasing expensive seating and relocating home plate. The distances down the right and left field lines eventually became 331 and 334 feet (not 340 and 378). While center field remained a formidable 468 feet, it was not the gargantuan 515 feet it had originally been.

The area around Greater Shibe Park prospered and grew. By the twenties the immediate vicinity was a definite community, its most important boundaries on the south and west. To the west, from the parks at Twenty-ninth and Lehigh south to the railroad tracks and then west to Fairmount Park, lay Strawberry Mansion, a well-known, distinctive, and stable Jewish area. To the south, in "old" North Philadelphia, one of the city's black enclaves had expanded from a nucleus at Tenth and Columbia. But the Pennsylvania Railroad, running on its east-west diagonal through this part of the city, formed an impenetrable barrier to the northern movement of blacks. Only a small triangle, described by Twenty-ninth Street, the railroad, and York Street, was racially mixed. People from York and Cumberland northward—"white and decent," said one of them—identified with the neighborhood that included Shibe Park.

Other railroad lines turned at the eastern edge of Shibe Park, and the tracks and industries that used railroad landings defined the area's further boundaries.

Neighbors called their environs "North Penn," from York to Clearfield and from Seventeenth to Twenty-ninth. The 1928 publication of the *Chat of North Penn*, later the *North Penn Chat*, formalized the existence of the neighborhood. The *Chat* was almost exclusively a vehicle for the thriving small business community—an advertising medium and exponent of genteel business values.

The center of the commercial area was Twenty-second Street. Here neighbors shopped and socialized in cafés like Elraes, the Hop Inn, Jewels, and Wolfmans, which were close to groceries, hardware and clothing stores, druggists, barbers, cleaners, shoemakers, and the like. Lehigh was the main east-west artery, where larger homes were mixed with the neighborhood's public buildings. The more prominent doctors, dentists, and lawyers had offices on Lehigh. The Athletics operated a Building and Loan at Twenty-third and Somerset, but the banks also clustered on Lehigh. Neighborhood men ran the local Lehigh National Bank at Twenty-third and Lehigh. At Twenty-fifth was a branch of the more prestigious Bankers Trust, headed by Albert M. Greenfield, a prominent financier. Lehigh also deserved its name as the "Avenue of Churches," boasting not only Saint Columba's complex of buildings, but farther west on Lehigh the smaller and more elite Saint Bartolomew's Episcopal, as well as many houses of worship of middling status. If Twenty-second was the street of commerce and Lehigh Avenue the cultural thoroughfare, Twenty-second and Lehigh was the hub of North Penn. Neighbors would stroll Lehigh in the evening, stopping at Schillings or Doc Hoffmans for ice cream, or taking in a film at the Lehigh Theater at Twenty-fifth and Lehigh, or attending a community event at one of the churches, or just sitting in the Square across the street from the ball field.

This vigorous neighborhood life gave North Penn its identity. But industries, many on the northern border above Allegheny Avenue, stabilized the community. These enterprises were not a physical presence but provided jobs for the blue-collar workers.

Ballplayers still came out of the neighborhood to perform in Shibe Park. Lefty Grove boarded on Lehigh. Max Bishop lived on Somerset with a dentist and his family. On a summer evening Connie Mack would cruise Lehigh checking on his players, and he could usually find his rookies, who lived in a three-story house across the street from Saint Colomba's, in Doc Hoffman's drinking a cherry coke. Jimmie Dykes and Joe Boley attended dances at Twenty-second and Clearfield. Al Simmons had a second-floor room with the Conwells on 20th Street behind the right field stands. Mrs. Conwell, an older woman, was reluctant to get Simmons up in the morning. She would signal one of the kids on the block, who would scoot in to wake the star: "Hey Al . . . you got to get your batting practice if you're gonna win the batting title." A short time later, after he ate breakfast, Simmons would saunter down the street to his job.

In 1924 the A's finished a surprising fifth, the closest they had been to the first division for a decade. In 1925, with much of the team in place, they finished second. The mid-twenties were the years of a great Yankee dynasty led by Babe Ruth and Lou Gehrig. The A's contended but were far behind New York. In 1927, however, a rivalry began that would last through 1932 and that would pit two of the finest professional teams against each other. The city's enthusiasm for the Athletics was at a fever pitch through the late twenties.

When the team was home, hordes of fans walked up Lehigh, the street alive with the hum of baseball talk. Other rooters pushed out of packed streetcars at the corner of Twenty-first and Lehigh. Frequently coming to work by public transport, ballplayers who did not live in North Penn might rub elbows with the Athletics' socialite devotee Henry Savage, a familiar spectacle on the trolleys in dingy clothes and battered straw hat. At the entrance to the stadium the clanging bells of the streetcars blended with the ooo-gahs of automobile horns, the blasts of police whistles, and the cries of vendors. The ballplayers would thread their way through the crowds to the clubhouse while the fans poured through the turnstiles of the main entrance.

The sounds inside as hawkers made their pitch for peanuts, ice cream, and scorecards were loud but friendly. Once the game started, however, the noise of food sellers would compete with louder and less amicable cries. Fans screamed at umpires, and boos echoed from all over the park. Partisans razzed opposing players, of course, but reserved some of the nastiest assaults for the home team—someone in a slump, a pinch hitter who struck out, a pitcher having a bad day. Even from outside the stadium people could hear the famous "Huckster." He never seemed to shout, but his deep powerful voice coming from the lower grandstand was relentless against the visiting pitcher. The Huckster was so adept at rattling Jimmie Dykes on third base that Connie Mack unsuccessfully tried various ways to have him silenced.

The Huckster was around for years. Who was he? Did he actually sell vegetables from a truck? Did he have a megaphone? Long after his day Shibe Park regulars wondered about him. Was he different people at various times? Was he the peddler Charlie Dougherty? Or the same heckler as "Bull" Kessler and his brother Eddie, who were famous for conducting a stentorian conversation from opposite sides of the field?

At the beginning of an A's rally, the Huckster might briefly stop. Fans would ignore the cries of "Hot dog here" as everyone concentrated on the action. Then other sounds would take over—the steady beat of thousands of hands clapping, and a similar rhythm of stamping feet. The Huckster would return, adding his lungs to the Athletics' efforts.

The excitement carried outside the park. On Twentieth Street opposite right field and right-center, spectators frequently crowded onto the roofs of the houses. Toward the Somerset end of the block, fans on the roof often called the play-by-play for folks hanging around the right field wall. Those outside with a practiced ear—Quill the cop, Charley Score Cards, Peanut Mike, or any habitué—did not need help. Their voice was the noise of the crowd inside.

When a batter is waiting out a walk, there is a feeling of suspense or restlessness. It is followed by the sound of relief as thousands of people suddenly let out their breath and by a smattering of applause. A sharp roar means a single. As it eases off, an afficionado on Lehigh Avenue could imagine the runner rounding first, holding up, then walking back to the bag. A longer roar, broken off, indicates a long hit. When the break is followed by a tremendous cry, it tells the outsider that the baseball has fallen safely and that the batter is scampering around the bases. A gasp of exhilaration from the crowd inside says that the runner has made it safely to second or third. A solid smack and relative quiet mean that thousands of pairs of eyes are watching a baseball sailing through the air. Next a crescendo of shouting, foot stamping, and clapping of hands can mean only one thing. Just the sound of bat meeting ball tells experienced listeners that it is a home run.

This was indeed the era of heavy hitting. At the end of World War I the majors were using a livelier ball and outlawed trick pitches like the spitter. In places like Shibe Park remodeling shortened distances to the fences. More and more colossal home runs resulted, and fans delighted in the exploits of powerful batsmen. In 1932 Foxx, Simmons, and Cochrane hit 116 homers among them. In the vicinity of Shibe Park, too, every home run had a history, a personality. The ball hit someone's roof, broke a front window, or disturbed an afternoon snooze.

Left-handed home run hitters targeted the short right field wall along Twentieth Street. Kids and neighbors patroled the street at batting practice and during games to capture a ball that would admit them to the park. On summer afternoons wives would wait apprehensively in fear of broken glass and further disruption to a household that the antics of enthusiastic fans in the streets had already taxed. In waiting at the park or nearby was a handyman or a glazier, hired by the A's and ready to do his bit to minimize neighborhood distress.

The two most important left-handers, Babe Ruth and Lou Gehrig, made it seem impossible that the A's would ever vanquish the Yankees. Ruth was credited with hitting a home run over two rows of houses, those on North Twentieth and those on the west side of Opal beyond, breaking a window in a house on the far side of Opal, some five hundred feet from home plate. In June 1932, in a game won by the Yankees 20–13 and featuring nine home runs, Gehrig hit four, two over the right field wall and two into the center field stands. In his last at bat in the ninth inning, with the fans cheering, he hit another near the flagpole in deep center, where Al Simmons made a theatrical one-handed catch.

The Athletics' Jimmie Foxx was right-handed. He was called "the Prince of Wales of distance hitters," but old Philadelphia fans swore that he had more power than Ruth. They could tell you how only the changes in the American League ball parks in the 1930s—Ruth swatted his sixty home runs in 1927—prevented Foxx from getting the three more in 1932 that would have put him ahead of Ruth. With his bat cocked menacingly over an enormous pair of shoulders, "the Beast" would hit to left or to center field. No one except Foxx, the oldsters said, hit a ball off the flagpole in dead center. Once he pounded a pitch over the roof in left-center that sailed past Somerset and bounced off a building on Woodstock, the street running parallel to Twentieth that intersected Somerset. The kids on Twentieth Street who waited for balls that would get them into a game could guess the provenance of a blast hit over the roof in left or left-center field. They would nod knowingly at one another and say: "Jimmie Foxx. . . . Who else?"

The exuberance that money brought to North Penn and to Shibe Park blended with a significant social development in the 1920s. The passage of the Eighteenth Amendment to the Constitution, the Prohibition amendment, stopped the sale and consumption of alcoholic beverages by 1920. The Volstead Act enforced the amendment. In North Penn the working-class saloons went out of business. Prohibition turned a crucial form of socializing, particularly for the Irish, into crime. Closing down North Penn's bars not only took away the livelihood of some small businessmen but legally stigmatized a community institution.

The high point of the temperance movement, Prohibition soon spawned a series of evils that many experts believe were greater than alcohol itself. Impassioned about drink, moralistic, often rural Protestants wanted to protect the nation from the scourge of liquor. They linked it to urban districts populated by foreigners and their foul saloons. But no one could effectively ban a product in such demand in the United States in the 1920s. Illegal distillers and salesmen of booze multiplied to meet the demand, as did warehouses, speakeasies, and violent mobsters protecting one or another of the competing enterprises. One old-timer recalled how even kids participated when they combed the Square for empty pint bottles to be reused for illegal alcohol. Ordinary citizens who wanted and got a drink consequently involved themselves in and sanctioned an enlarging criminal system. Some historians have argued that Prohibition caused organized crime in the United States. Making alcoholic consumption a legal offense led to worse abuses than drunkenness and its accompanying behavior. One need not go that far, however, to note that in North Penn Prohibition ensnared many Irish young people, typically the sons of immigrants, in a web of illegal acts. The era drew them into bootlegging (the sale of liquor) and various forms of gangsterism—hijacking, intimidation, bribery, and murder. In Philadelphia in the twenties officials turned their eyes from many of these vices. Then, in 1928, bootleggers shot down Hughie McLoon near his café at Tenth and Chestnut streets, the middle of downtown. McLoon, who ran a speakeasy of sorts, was not the first victim of what was the start of a major flareup of gang warfare that killed ten to twenty Irish bootleggers. But McLoon's shooting could not be easily ignored.

It is not hard to fathom why the murder had such repercussions within the liquor trade and then outside it. In 1916 McLoon succeeded Louis VanZelst after the death of the Athletics' mascot. At fourteen, McLoon was a gnomelike, fifty-eight-pound hunchback who lived at Twenty-fifth and Lehigh. As with VanZelst, A's players thought that rubbing McLoon's back brought them luck. After he left the team, he remained a favorite with sentimental fans and a popular figure in the city's night life. His death could not go unheralded. As one later writer put it, imagine the outcry if the Phillie Phanatic—the Phillies mascot in the late twentieth century—"were gunned down in the center of the city."

Among bootleggers, who were no less subject to sentimentality than the fans, deadly attacks stepped up around the city. The first attempt to get even was an assassination on the edge of North Penn. Another day the cops sped into the neighborhood itself to arrest a suspect. Retaliation and counterretaliation occurred. More significantly, the civic outcry generated a grand jury investigation of illegal liquor sales in the metropolitan area. The grand jury exposed the links between Philadelphia politicians and police corruption in the manufacture and distribution of alcoholic beverages. A judicial report sketched out the business network of the "beer barons" and shook the Republican city machine. Although North Penn was of minor importance in Philadelphia bootlegging, the gang war and the subsequent investigation revealed the complexity of the community's culture and its complacent prosperity.

As authorities empaneled the grand jury in August of 1928, the A's were burning up the American League in pursuit of the Yankees. The home team gained first place at the end of the first week in September. Although the Philadelphia drive faltered, New York clinched the flag only two days before the end of the season. The fate of the Athletics absorbed the city. In the frenzy of an exciting race many Philadelphians could put out of their minds the unpleasant images of McLoon, gangsterism, and official deceit.

A year later, in 1929, the Athletics ran away with the pennant, but interest in baseball was unabated. The A's had a ten-and-a-half-game lead by early August, yet the largest crowd in Shibe Park's history turned out for an August 7 doubleheader with the Yankees. Although the locals finally finished in first place by eighteen games, the World Series generated even more communal pride and brought the city's baseball to a pinnacle of fame and popularity. Sixty years later some Philadelphians would remember October 1929 not as the time of the stock market crash but of the Athletics' magnificent series victory.

Earlier in the year Mack had met with his aging pitcher Howard Ehmke in the tower office and made Ehmke a surprise starter in the first game against the Cubs in Chicago. The largest crowd ever to assemble in downtown Philadelphia watched the *Bulletin*'s electric scoreboard and listened to an announcer with a direct wire to Wrigley Field. With necks craned upward, fans jammed City Hall Plaza and the streets around the Bulletin building; they hung out the windows of City Hall and its annex; bootblacks and millionaires, said the newspaper, stood packed together talking baseball. Expecting one of Mack's fast ballers, the Cubs were befuddled by Ehmke's control and off-speed pitches. When he fanned the last batter to win the game, the public address man officially proclaimed that the thirteenth strikeout was a new series record, and the crowd went wild. The next day, after Earnshaw and Grove teamed up to strike out thirteen more, the A's returned to Shibe Park with a big advantage. Nonetheless, Chicago won the A's home opener 3–1.

In the next game the visitors built up an 8–0 lead. The Cubs' bench began to ride Mack. Every time a run scored, pitcher Guy Bush threw a blanket over his head and did a mock Indian war dance. Then the A's came to bat in the bottom of the seventh.

Simmons led off with a home run onto the roof of the left field stands, ruining Chicago pitcher Charlie Root's shutout. Foxx, Miller, Dykes, and Boley singled before the first out, and Bishop followed with another single. Score: 8–4, men on first and third. Now the Cubs really had some bad luck. Facing reliefer Art Nehf, Mule Haas hit a fly to center that Hack Wilson lost in the sun. It went for an inside-the-park home run, and the score was 8–7. Mickey Cochrane walked. Up for the second time, Simmons and Foxx each singled, and the game was tied. The fourth Cub pitcher, ace Pat Malone, hit Bing Miller with a ball. Dykes doubled with the bases loaded. The Athletics led 10–8. Malone fanned the next two batters, but the A's had taken the heart out of the Cubs. One young Philadelphia fan never forgot "the sight of so many adult males with tears of joy running down their cheeks."

The next day was Sunday, and there was no baseball in Philadelphia. Intrigued by the excitement of Saturday's contest, President Herbert Hoover and a political entourage entrained from Washington on Monday to see the game. A party of dignitaries squired the president across the Shibe Park field to the special box he would occupy with Philadelphia's mayor, Harry Mackey. The city's rooters cheered the new president, but also responded in a time-honored way. It was still Prohibition, and they screamed at Hoover, "Beer! Beer! We want beer! . . . Beer! Beer! We want beer!"

Pitching a two-hit, 2–0 shutout against the A's, Pat Malone was having his revenge for the previous game. But with one out in the bottom of the ninth, Bishop singled over third, and left-handed Mule Haas hit a two-run homer over the right field fence to tie the game. After a second out, Simmons doubled off the scoreboard, and Malone intentionally walked Jimmie Foxx. But Bing Miller hit another to the scoreboard, scoring Simmons, winning the game 3–2, and completing the series victory, four games to one.

Mayor Mackey jumped out of the presidential box to congratulate Miller and cavort before the A's dugout. He joined Hoover only later when the president left for the train station and Washington. Overcome with emotion and well-wishers, Connie Mack quietly left the dugout, returned to the tower office, and lay down on his leather couch, fingers pressed to his throbbing temples. Always a gentleman, he said the Philadelphia fans were guilty of a "regrettable occurrence" in heckling President Hoover.

Four months later Mack received the Philadelphia Award, established in 1921. A "concrete expression of the city's honor," the award went to the individual who, during the preceding year, had advanced "the best interests of the community of which Philadelphia is the center." Prior winners included many of the city's luminaries in science, the arts, and university education. New York writers complained that someone like Mack diminished the award. On the other hand, the *Sporting News* editorialized that it was better to recognize something near to the hearts of the average American than "the discovery of the demi-metazoon, the kangaroolike bacillus, or what not."

The year 1929 was not a time to bring a baseball dynasty to fruition. A winning team cost money, and by 1930 and 1931 the Depression was affecting attendance. Unemployed workers or those with falling incomes were less likely to spend money at Shibe Park. Increasing expenses and declining income pinched the Shibes and Mack. Economics aside, the promotion of the sport was complex. Mack believed that .600 baseball was more popular than .700. He did not believe that a dominant team might possess such style and class that it might continue to win and to draw customers. In any event, after 1929, his great team did not overwhelmingly attract Philadelphia rooters. The A's won the series again in 1930 and the pennant in 1931—they lost the series to Pepper Martin's Cardinals. Attendance fell, however, and the decline continued into 1932, when the A's dropped to second place, again behind the Yankees.

Sportswriters implied throughout 1931 and 1932 that Mack would break up his Athletics, as he had in 1914; and the destruction started in October 1932. The A's sold Dykes, Simmons, and Haas to Chicago for $100,000. In December 1933 Grove, Walberg, and Bishop went to the Red Sox for $125,000; Cochrane to Detroit for $100,000; and Earnshaw to Chicago for $20,000. In 1935, in two separate transactions, Miller and Foxx also went to the Red Sox for $200,000. The A's were third in 1933, fifth in 1934, and last or next to last thereafter.

The experiences of 1910–1914 and 1929–1931 shaped Mack's belief that Philadelphians would not support a successful team. Each time winners had brought declining patronage. Mack was, however, so obsessed with a seasonal balancing of the books that he could not acknowledge that more factors might have been at work. Other regularly victorious franchises—the Yankees, the Cardinals—did not satiate the fans. World War I and the Federal League, or the bottom of the Depression, could have caused a decline in the Athletics' attendance. But once gate receipts and the A's themselves were on a downward slide, Mack could not afford to build up the club. He deeply invested in the view that the city would not come out to see a champion.

At the time and later Mack gave so many conflicting accounts of his motives that it is hard to make sense of what was going on. When Dykes, Simmons, and Haas left, the owner-manager said he made the deal "on the spur of the moment" and emphasized that he did not intend to destroy his team. Fourteen months later, when he got rid of Grove, Cochrane, and the other players, the *Bulletin* reported that he was "pale and trembling," but he again emphasized, "I am not breaking up my ball club." Neither had debts forced him to sell off the players, he explained, but he could not afford to pay the high salaries of some and wanted to give others a bigger chance. Then, at the end of 1935, after he sold Jimmie Foxx—a crushing blow to Philadelphia fans— Mack said debts forced him to sell.

What is astonishing about these revelations is not that Mack wrecked his Athletics. One might argue that his judgment was poor, and that in attempting to produce a competitor and not a machine, his "adjustments" were inaccurate and the result was a losing team. But Mack's sales did come in stages. He was apparently trying to find a team good enough to generate patrons but not so good as to leave potential customers saying "ho-hum." Moreover, he sold to weaker franchises. The point was to distribute talent in the American League. But although the 1932 club did not win the pennant, neither did it draw fans. Mack did have to meet expenses and apparently did have debts. Although he could not escape the disastrous interplay of high costs and declining profits, manipulating the strength of his A's was potentially a wise tactic.

Some may find it offensive that during this period Mack was, at fifty thousand dollars a year, the highest-salaried manager in the majors. He dealt his players from a plush red leather chair in the tower office, a three-room suite that, as one impressed commentator wrote, "would do credit to any corporate president." But this, after all, is American capitalism. In short, while Mack could not control his strategy, it was coherent and intelligent.

What is astonishing is that Mack easily offered up doubletalk to the public to explain his strategy and got away with it. "We did not," he said at one point, "adopt a policy of selling star players because home games were not [well] attended." Then, in the next breath: "We made a survey of conditions to find out why the fans were not coming out. . . . Our club had to act in accordance with the facts." In other words, the A's did and did not sell players because of declining pa-

tronage. Mack's stature and the banality of the sports press came together during his public conferences over these years. The sportwriters
would highly praise Mack. Then he would barrage his listeners with
verbal junk. Thereafter, as the newspapers reported, "there were no
questions."

Some observers thought that Philadelphia fans would get their own
back on opening day, 1934. The traditional march to the flagpole of the
opposing franchises and the singing of the national anthem would
bring Mr. Mack out of the dugout in full view of the rooters. Now,
commentators predicted, Philadelphians would boo him as they had
hooted no man. On April 8 at 3:00 P.M., a chilly spring afternoon, Mack
gingerly stepped onto the field and, observers felt, cowed the fans. The
game proceeded without incident, a sign that Philadelphians had
grasped Mack's Depression plight. The observers were wrong. The fans
were merely holding back.

• Part II •

1929–1954

• 4 •

Shibe Park and Depression
Era Conflict

In the 1920s the Irish predominated in North Penn and in the area around the ball park. North of Cambria Street, nonetheless, an Italian community throve. No more than eight blocks square, "Little It-ley," which had started in the nineteenth century, was another country to the Irish. There were foreign cheeses hanging in the windows of old stores, women in black dresses, and, at least in the imagination of the Irish, hints of the feared Sicilian "Black Hand." With mainly Irish parishioners, Saint Columba's was the territorial or neighborhood parish with thirty-five hundred families at its peak. But in 1930 the Roman Catholic church dedicated Saint Mary of the Eternal, an Italian "national" parish at Twenty-second and Clearfield. Inferior to Saint Columba's in local Catholic eyes, Saint Mary's nonetheless served one of the city's two largest Italian enclaves outside of South Philadelphia.

Negative ethnic distinctions were intense. In addition to "the papes"—"micks" and "wops"—along Twenty-second Street "Yids" lived above their shops, a comparatively short distance from the large Jewish community in Strawberry Mansion to the west of North Penn. Sprinkled throughout North Penn in the larger houses were American-born German, Irish, and English Protestants, communicants of the churches along Lehigh. They sent their children to Pierce Elementary School at Twenty-third and Cambria and not the parochial schools attached to the parishes. At Pierce, the kids might be joined by a few "colored" boys and girls who lived along with other marginal people in the area between the railroad tracks and "the Mansion."

The Protestant minority in North Penn were the elite. It was a point of pride to many Irish and Italians that their Protestant "betters" went to school with "the niggers." On the other hand, one Strawberry Mansion Jew remembered walking to the ball park through the "cauldron" of competing ethnic and racial groups, perhaps hating one another but bound in their Christianity, he thought, by their hatred of the "kikes."

Protestants were a tiny upper middle class of large store owners, wholesalers, and the most successful professionals; and a small but central middle class of high school graduates—owners of smaller stores, salesmen and commercial travelers, schoolteachers, and contractors. The Catholic Irish, Italians, other non-Protestants, and blacks on the edge of the neighborhood formed a numerically much larger and culturally dominant lower middle and working class of small shopkeepers, skilled and unskilled workers, and lower-ranking office and sales personnel. Distinctions within these classes were apparent. For example, the Irish born in the United States, the "kiss-me-ass Irish," as one observer called them, lorded it over the immigrant Irish.

What looked to outsiders like a homogeneous "blue-collar" neighborhood mixed competing social groups and ethnic identities. Indeed, ethnic identity itself was problematic, and by examining it we can best understand North Penn. Although the small businesses on Twenty-second Street and on Lehigh stood out, the nearby industry that employed many of the community's wage earners was more crucial to neighborhood stability. Many people had jobs just outside the area. A number worked in a manufacturing belt between Allegheny and Hunting Park Avenue, which ran roughly on a west-east diagonal from 2800 to 4400 north. Penn Reel, Midvale Steel, Exide Battery, Budd Co., Baldwin Locomotive, Heintz, Steel Heddle, Hornung Brewery, Tastykake, and similar concerns employed North Penn men a short trolley ride or long walk away. The strongest memory of one resident, then a boy, was of the influx to the neighborhood bars from the north as shifts changed in the afternoon and men stopped for a drink before coming home.

The employment that businesses around North Penn offered to people restricted the location and type of housing they occupied. Neighbors banded together, faced with the same struggles for money and similar problems on the job. Children of different families grew up with opportunities that were more or less identical. A distinctive community of shops and of financial, social, and professional services met the needs of such families.

In these circumstances North Penn's typically Irish ethnicity emerged. A common culture that immigrants brought from Ireland and passed on to children and grandchildren may have partly created this ethnicity. But it also depended on the niche occupied by the Irish (and the Italians, Germans, and English) in North Penn. Perhaps, friends from Ireland, co-religionists, or a common geographic heritage in Ireland drew Irish—and not, for example, Poles—to North Penn. But Irish culture and the propensity of this culture for familial and religious ties did not alone forge the self-consciousness of being Irish. The self-consciousness evolved as well from the stable supply of jobs and the housing such jobs made affordable. The various "foreign" heritages of North Penn took shape in the United States because of the exigencies of survival in the nation, the possibilities Philadelphia offered to people with little formal education and the taint of not having grandparents born here.

To put it another way, the various ethnic groups were much alike, the likeness a consequence of the same kinds of incomes, jobs, and residences. Neighbors proclaimed their status within one ethnic group or over another through different ethnic institutions and organizations such as the Irish parish or an exclusive Sons of Italy lodge. Leaders designed these ethnic societies to promote distinctions, for example, within the Irish community and between this community and, say, the Italians as much as to preserve traditional Irish culture. An Irish organization reinforced differences among the Irish and convinced some Irish that they were better than Italians. The institutions helped to make the Irish a community with particular norms and values. Establishing competing Italian organizations heightened the sense of Irish uniqueness as well as it promoted the virtues of more upwardly mobile Italians. The attempts of groups in North Penn to differentiate themselves from outsiders partly created ethnic distinctions. Overall, the aspiring middle-class Irish (and later Italians) of North Penn who started such institutions were mimicking the dominant "mainstream" Protestant culture outside the community, with its class distinctions and minor snobbism. Ethnicity grew up in the United States by duplicating as well as fabricating the city's social structure.

The continued stability of North Penn after World War II was also a function of the "entrapment" of the ethnic job seekers. Workers still had easy access to industrial jobs and inexpensive housing in the neighborhood. With steady employment North Penn remained internally cohesive despite its age. A persistent supply of industrial jobs as well as ethnic culture sustained interdependence between friends and relatives and the local banks, stores, and professional services.

What experts have called the "ethno-cultural" approach to understanding people's lives reveals even more the complexity of ethnicity. Ethnic groups may have been similar, but the economic issues that made them so were not all important. In politics, for example, North Penn's residents identified with the party that spoke to the religious and ethnic aspect of their lives. Public figures who symbolized ethnic success attracted different groups of neighbors. When Irishman Al Smith ran for the presidency in 1928, he won the North Penn Irish over to the Democratic party, where they stayed, although not with the zeal they had displayed for Smith. Pursuing a strategy of recognizing ethnic groups, the city's Democratic party lured, at different times and in different strengths, Italian and black voters. North Penn's Protestant "upper crust" of native English and Germans remained Republican, as did Philadelphia itself. The Protestant voters often defined themselves in contrast to Roman Catholics. This political cleavage had an obvious economic dimension, as the Democrats increasingly became a working-class party. Yet issues of style remained notable. The Democratic Irish, for example, had valued their taprooms highly, while the Republican Protestants strove for quieter, more dignified leisure. One Irish Catholic put it eloquently when she said, "You could tell the Republicans . . . they always looked sad."

By the 1920s Shibe Park impinged on North Penn in a way that made the community aware of its place in Philadelphia's political and cultural life. A succession of issues was significant. The first, concerning the repeal of Pennsylvania's "blue laws," reached its high point in 1933, but had a history that long antedated the early thirties and that would continue long after.

The laws were a collection of ordinances that dated back to 1794 and regulated drinking, gambling, and various activities that might occur on a Sunday. By the late nineteenth century, geography and money divided the groups who clashed over the morality of these laws. Supporters came from rural areas or often represented the more well-to-do. Urban workers, especially immigrants or those of immigrant background, fought the legislation. Thus Italian or Irish Catholic adversaries of the bills frequently fought Protestants who had been in the United States for several generations. Politicians in Pittsburgh and Philadelphia who attempted to diminish the force of the blue laws spoke of them as "unfair discrimination of the rich against the poor" and, at other times, as "a battle between the city slicker and the country rube."

For the A's the blue laws meant that the team could not play at Shibe Park on Sundays, potentially the best day for customers. From 1911 on the franchise tried to legalize such games. In a quest for large crowds and the money that Sunday baseball generated, owners exploited their identification with democracy. Sabbath play would elevate freedom of expression over small-minded Puritanism, as well as garner a victory for the masses. They should be allowed to congregate when and where they wished. Baseball officials made the most of the affluence of blue law supporters. If the rich could play croquet, golf, and tennis at their private Philadelphia clubs on Sundays, the common people should be able to enjoy a baseball game.

While building his expensive team in the mid-twenties, Connie Mack complained that prohibiting Sunday baseball had indebted the Athletics. In 1926, in desperation, the A's tested the ban by playing a Sunday game at Twenty-first and Lehigh. Old-stock Protestant groups announced that seventy-two property owners near Shibe Park had signed a petition against Sunday ball. Who they were is hard to tell because the great majority of those in North Penn were ethno-culturally on the other side. After much squabbling, the A's played. On a drizzly Sunday in August Lefty Grove beat the White Sox 3–2. Connie Mack told the *New York Times*, "I wish all those who oppose Sunday baseball could have been here today. They would see we are not causing a lessening in church attendance." Nonetheless, the test failed, and authorities stopped the A's from further Sunday play.

The willingness of the franchise to adopt a political stand measured the seriousness of the problem. Mack and the Episcopal Shibes had implicitly allied themselves with the Democrats—to some extent a party, as we have seen, of lower-class immigrants and Catholics. But Mack, a devout Catholic, kept out of politics. In late 1930, however, he endorsed a candidate who supported Sunday baseball. Jack Shibe worked in state Democratic circles to legalize a local option that would allow Sunday sport in Pittsburgh and Philadelphia.

To put pressure on city politicians, Shibe ostentatiously searched for a site for Sunday games in Camden, New Jersey, just across the Delaware River from Philadelphia. Liberal leaders in Jersey assured Shibe that the franchise could play there all the time. The Athletics did not want to move, however, and hoped to fuel opposition to the Sunday ban. Dickering over the Camden site continued from 1927 to 1933. By that time the state had passed a local option law. In April 1934 the A's started to play on Sundays at Shibe Park between 2:00 and 6:00 P.M. As Connie Mack put it, Sunday baseball would "not hurt religion" and would help "the morale of cities."

In addition to the religious and cultural differences highlighted in this dispute, the finances of sabbath sport threw into relief Mack's frugality. He blamed the trade of Al Simmons, Jimmie Dykes, and Mule Haas at the end of 1932 on the blue laws. The lack of Sunday baseball had forced him to sell off some of the stars from his great dynasty. "We cannot meet our payrolls," said Mack at the start of 1933, "playing on seventy-seven weekdays at home." Mack promised that with Sunday play he would keep his teams intact. Then the legislature approved Sunday baseball, and the next installment of the dismantling of the 1929–1931 pennant winners occurred.

Mack's change of mind became a weapon in the struggle over the blue laws. William B. Forney, head of the Lord's Day Alliance and a longtime prominent proponent of Sunday observances, made the most of Mack's tightfistedness. The fans, he said after Sunday baseball commenced, knew about Mack's hypocrisy and his "lemon" of a club. Poor baseball and "the desecration of Sunday," added Forney, would combine to make patrons refuse to go to Shibe Park even on weekdays.

Forney's thundering had little effect on Mack, although fans periodically reminded him of his unkept promise for the next twenty years. The A's played without class, and lavish gate receipts never materialized from sabbath baseball. Sunday hours, however, slowly expanded. In 1935 play was allowed from 1:00 to 7:00. By 1959 the laws disallowed only the start of games after 5:00 P.M.

The blue laws also regulated drinking, and the sale of beer at Shibe Park suffered more than play on Sunday. Drink was a major source of revenue where laws permitted it before Prohibition. After it ended in 1933, the A's tried unsuccessfully to get a beer permit for the park. In the late forties another movement to sell the brew in the stadium gathered force. Management pointed out that even if it did not sell beer in Shibe Park, many fans brought bottles (and later cans) to games. From time to time the club initiated search procedures to stop drinking, but these were ineffective. Indeed, the A's were able to discourage beer consumption only because the bottles and cans made nasty missiles to throw at players and umpires. At that point Shibe Park concessions sold all drinks in paper cups, but many fans had stories of the ways they could smuggle bottles into the stadium. Mindful of profits and safety, the A's (and later the Phillies) urged that if they sold beer in the park, they could stop excessive drinking. By dispensing beer in cups, they could also take dangerous projectiles out of drunken hands.

Nonetheless, Pennsylvania legalized ball park beer only after the A's left the city and Connie Mack died. A number of instances of rowdyism involving brawls and bottle throwing motivated beer advocates in the mid-1950s. By the end of the decade an unholy alliance of temperance leaders and bar owners opposed beer licensing in the stadium. Around Twenty-first and Lehigh, taproom people growled that licensing would hurt sales since people stopped off at the neighborhood bars to purchase beer for the games. Antilicensing lobbies succeeded till 1961, when beer sold in cups at long last became legal in the park. Even then beer licensing was part of a plan to raise money for a new stadium. Indeed, the sale of beer on Sundays did not occur till 1972, when baseball was being played in another park.

The 1935 "spite fence" was another significant issue for Philadelphia fans. The financial exigencies of the Depression propelled the building of this wall, but the project had its origins in the 1920s.

The 2700 block of North Twentieth Street was more intimately connected to baseball than any other part of North Penn. Across the street from the bleacher entrance was the obvious place for ballplayers to live. They also frequented the taproom at the corner of Twentieth and Lehigh, Kilroy's until 1935 and later Charley Quinn's Deep Right Field Café. Relief pitchers would leave the right field gate near the bullpen to tilt a few during the early innings of games in which the Phillies piled up a big lead. The stories of many home runs involved these houses. From the very early days people on North Twentieth and on Somerset watched games from their second-story windows. This practice ended for the Somersetters when the A's constructed the grandstand in left-center field in 1913. But on Twentieth, from the right field foul line to the center field corner where the grandstand began, residents grew accustomed to looking at games over the twelve-foot out field wall. When fans jammed the park from 1910 to 1914, they also jammed the front bedrooms and roofs of the homes, where owners charged admission to supplement their incomes. During the World Series games of that period police sold seats for homeowners on a commission basis. Neighbors would remove all the windows on the second floor for better viewing for patrons, who also stood on the porch roofs. Ladders took even more customers to pews or stands set up on the flat second-floor roofs.

In the late 1920s business, which had been almost nonexistent during the period of losing Athletics teams, picked up when Connie Mack had his second dynasty. Owners opened the skylights in the sec-

ond-floor bathrooms of the houses. In addition to depositing themselves wherever else possible, fans climbed up on ladders to the roofs.
Through these portals at 2739 North Twentieth, Pathé, Universal, and
Fox Movietone News hoisted their equipment to film the 1929 series.
Neighbors hired lusty barkers to advertise the attractions of their seats
over Shibe Park bleachers. Mothers made lemonade to sell to thirsty
rooters and dispatched the kids to buy hot dogs from street vendors for
a nickel. Back in their houses, the kids would sell them for a dime to
eager customers.

By 1929 the "rooftop stands" produced substantial income for the
block and raised its real estate and rental values. Residents wanted the
A's to win the series but also wanted a contest that would go for seven
games, with four played at Shibe Park. In 1930 North Twentieth had
wooden bleachers erected along most of the street as homeowners took
advantage of Mack's continuing triumphs. A block committee fixed
prices. During the World Series estimates were that three thousand
people per game collected in the houses, paying from seven to twenty-
five dollars per head.

Throughout this period residents fought local bureaucrats. The block
paid off the amusement tax officials and the police. When neighbors
built the stands, trouble came from the Philadelphia director of public
safety and the chief of building inspection. Still renting a room on the
block, Al Simmons spoke out in favor of his neighbors. "It's none of
[the city's business]," said Bucketfoot Al, "they should keep their nose
out of it." In a happy compromise the politicians allowed construction
if the walls between each house supported the stands and if residents
put up ten stairways from backyards to the roofs. Later the fire marshal
prohibited seating on the roofs, and for a time the police turned against
the residents and enforced the ban.

On many occasions money in the pockets of the people living on the
block would otherwise have profited the A's. Neighbors claimed that
the political contacts of Jack Shibe caused the constant harassment
from officials. Homeowners placated him. They would not sell seats
unless the A's filled Shibe Park and would not entice fans by undersell-
ing the A's. But solidarity broke. Charles Harvey, an absentee owner,
did not even rent his house because he thought it was more profitable
simply to use it as adjunct ball park seating. Harvey would not limit
patronage. His next-door neighbor thwarted him by erecting a fence
that blocked much of the view from his roof, but authorities ordered

the fence removed. Others joined Harvey in search of a quick buck. During the Depression money was in short supply. After Mack broke up the team in 1932 and 1933, the A's rarely sold out the park. In need of cash, neighbors would offer cut-rate seating even when Shibe Park was largely vacant, soliciting would-be patrons in the bleacher line.

At the end of 1934 Jack Shibe acted. The Depression and poor teams *had* cut down attendance. The A's believed that the franchise could not lose further revenue to North Twentieth. Shibe added thirty-eight feet to the original twelve-foot wall and by March 1935 completed framing a new fence from the right field line to the flagpole. The franchise used corrugated metal and green paint to finish the job for opening day.

Paul Durkin of 2731 North Twentieth stayed on relief that summer because he lost income from the rooftop stands. Other home-owners lamented that real estate values would fall because the new fence blocked the sun. Actually, however, the lack of baseball income hurt housing values. Rentals in the tenant-occupied houses declined. In the aftermath the neighbors, again sticking together, tried to have the spite fence removed. Richardson Dilworth, an outstanding lawyer and friend of Philadelphia sportsmen who was on his way to a career in Democratic politics, successfully defended the rights of Mack and the Shibes.

In 1928 John Rooney of 2739 North Twentieth took his son Jack up on their roof and pointed to the grassy sweep across the street. "For the rest of the your life," he said, "you can always say you saw Ty Cobb, Tris Speaker, and Al Simmons playing in the same outfield." Seven years later, even if the father put a chair on the roof and stood on his tiptoes, he could not see the entire infield. The residents never forgot. Despite their allegiance to the Democratic party, they voted against Dilworth fifteen years later when he ran for citywide offices. Memories died hard for North Twentieth.

When the Phillies, who played in Shibe Park after 1938, won the pennant in 1950, neighbors were still bitter and remembered the World Series home games of the past and the profits they had made. Bill Miller, the block patriarch who had moved into 2757 North Twentieth before Shibe Park was built, said, "They took all the golden eggs."

On the field itself, in some practices, players enjoyed lining up in front of the wall, throwing in unison against the corrugated metal, and rousing the neighborhood. More often the players cursed the fence as one of the hardest to play in baseball. The "Great Tin Monster" could bounce line drives into the bullpen, back to second base, or just drop them straight down on the grass at the edge of the field.

The idiosyncrasies of the wall made it easy for the fans to remember. Fathers would point to the green expanse of iron and tell their sons, "Connie Mack built that spite fence so you couldn't see the games from across the street. He was that cheap."

The North Twentieth residents thought that their unofficial stands compensated for the unruly fans who periodically rampaged along their street or for the baseballs that hit their homes. They did endure much aggravation, but their complaints often covered up a pride in the location of their housing and enjoyment in living so near the park. Four years after the fence went up, the franchise tried the loyalty of its neighbors again when the team proposed putting up lights for night games.

Major league baseball owners resisted evening baseball until 1935, when the Cincinnati Reds began to play after dark—Franklin Roosevelt pressed a button in the White House to turn on the lights. These games drew on a different crowd and, as matters turned out, a larger group than attended games played during the day. Because of the possibility of profit, the A's, so often administratively unimaginative, were first in the American League to embrace night baseball. Both Mack and the owners of the Phillies, now also playing in Shibe Park, thought that more customers and greater dinnertime concession sales would outweigh additional costs.

The North Twentieth Street neighbors who protested feared the late-night noise and disruption, even pointing to the possibility of evening Peeping Toms, aided by the bright lights. With little ado, however, Philadelphia's Zoning Board overruled the protest and permitted construction of eight 146-foot light towers, two on the wall. In 1939 the A's and the Phillies each played seven night games. Inside the park Mack built a restaurant, Café Shibe, to serve patrons who wanted a real meal with their supper-hour sport.

Failing in its attempt to curtail night baseball, the neighborhood more effectively mobilized itself against assaults on the parkland across the street from the field. In addition to Reyburn Park (the Square), the city had established Funfield Recreation Center on its land immediately to the south. In 1936 the community fought off efforts to replace Funfield, although here an entire outraged North Penn assisted North Twentieth. Similar outrage occurred in 1939 and 1940, when the baseball owners made the first two of many moves to take over the Square for automobile parking. The insistent neighborhood uproar about the few but precious amenities in the district forced the city and the A's to back off. The Depression-weary community hardly felt that the building of the prestigious Dobbins High School at Twenty-second and Lehigh in 1938 made up for these attacks.

Throughout the 1930s the Depression underlined the connection between the baseball business and North Penn. The collapse of the stock market occurred shortly after President Hoover saw the A's triumph in the 1929 series. He presided over a drastic downturn in the economy. The local Lehigh National Bank folded. Farther up Lehigh Avenue the branch of the larger Bankers Trust collapsed. After this failure, Albert M. Greenfield, the bank's leading figure and the city's most prominent Jewish banker, contended that the Protestant financial community rallied behind other larger banks. But the rally was too late for the city's economy as joblessness rose to 30 percent. Many small businesses in North Penn closed. Large employers cut back on help. North Penn residents found employment scarce. The Depression sometimes forced grown children, often renters of houses, to move back in with their parents, who were more likely to own their houses.

Connie Mack personally helped one family hurt not only by the economic decline but by the death of the husband. Mack hired the mother, Josie Hart, to clean his offices and guaranteed her four boys jobs at the park. "Shibe Park raised those kids," said one neighbor, and baseball continued to provide part-time, seasonal, employment for many people in the immediate environs of Twenty-first and Lehigh. The *Chat* editorialized that "lack of money, clothes, . . . and cultural surroundings" handicapped North Penn kids, but "in their association with baseball," families were "extremely lucky." Some persons, of course, were less lucky. Work was at times nonexistent, and one neighbor, broken by his inability to meet responsibilities, committed suicide.

Yet in some ways the Depression benefited communal life. Bad times retarded movement out of the neighborhood and intensified family ties. Economic deprivation created solidarity in North Penn, giving it a sense of cohesiveness against the outside world. The district remained vigorous and close-knit.

When voters elected Franklin Roosevelt president at the bottom of the Depression in 1932, he quickly repealed Prohibition, in part to stimulate business, in part to assuage the immigrant drinkers in the Democratic party. The saloon, now cleaned up, reappeared as a tap-room. Package stores providing beer and eating establishments selling liquor also returned to North Penn. Many of them catered to the ball park trade. But in the community repeal had more than an economic effect. The end of Prohibition "decriminalized" the selling of spirits, and bootlegging automatically vanished. At the same time the decade of Prohibition had given crime a foothold in North Penn. In the 1930s the existence of various questionable activities combined to reinforce the district's image as a poor, tough, although family-centered area.

The first form of organized crime in the United States was illegal gambling and betting on "the numbers," whose history went back to the nineteenth century. After Prohibition ended, ex-bootleggers did not go straight but, rather, often used their experience to help gamblers and numbers men with the logistical aspects of running an up-to-date illegal setup. The bootleggers provided political protection, financial backing, and legal representation for racketeers. Criminals naturally branched out to loan sharking when collecting on gambling debts. More impor-tant, crooks eventually involved themselves in commercial entertain-ment, in Philadelphia's nightclubs and bars, liquor distribution, prosti-tution, and, later, drugs.

Shibe Park focused such activity. Boxing matches there brought pro-moters, often big-time bootleggers or ex-bootleggers and gamblers, to the stadium. Gambling on ball games, however, was also a pervasive problem that the Shibes and Mack ignored again and again. Groups of gamblers regularly provided betting facilities to interested fans in cer-tain parts of the park for at least forty years. The lower right field stands were known as "Gamblers Patch," and little groups of bettors regularly occupied various parts of the grounds. One famous clique sat right above the "No Gambling" sign painted on the left field wall. Irritated by the owners' laissez-faire attitude, Commissioner Landis stormed at one point that Shibe Park gambling was the worst in baseball.

Outside the park, leadership of illegal activity shifted from the Irish to the Italians, the heart of illicit dealings being Toronto Street, between Twentieth and Twenty-second, where Italian social clubs and lounges, a pool hall, and bars were located. Kids started out stealing cars, and North Penn gave the city some of it best-known car thieves. Slightly drunk "young punks," as a more proper resident called them, careened through the streets in stolen vehicles, waking sleepers, endangering lives, and keeping the police busy. There were also a number of fighting toughs in the neighborhood, and some professional boxers. Danny Russell and John Dougherty represented the Irish. Among Italians Sammy Novea, whose father had a clothing store on Twenty-second Street, was a featherweight challenger. The papers wrote up Billy Passamonte, who boxed for a Teamsters local, as "the fighting truck driver."

The Italians established themselves in Philadelphia neighborhoods with difficulty. Some recalled that only the stigma of criminal activity and a reputation for violence gained them respect. In North Penn some Italians went from car theft and street fighting to being "the muscle" for illegal enterprises. Around Twenty-first and Toronto this method of gaining respect was notoriously exemplified by the Traitz family, which had a long history of fighting in the ring and in the streets.

In the 1920s Jimmy Traitz—then pronounced "Trait-zee"—led the family. His fists stopped the Irish from bothering the Italian girls. In the 1930s Lou Traitz, who ran a neighborhood cigar store, was a well-known Philadelphia lightweight whose cousins shared his prowess. In the fifties young Steve Traitz had a reputation as a boxer. Gamblers and numbers men rewarded him and his friends for pushing around people who did not pay up. Steve worked for the roofers union in the 1960s, and his agility with his fists strengthened the union. He beat up non-union roofers or those who resisted the roughhouse tactics he brought to bear on labor relations. Traitz and his associates had drifted from being brutal "enforcers" in the world of petty crime to a strong-arm strategy in the roofing trade. Although no longer living in North Penn in the 1960s, Traitz still embodied its strong familial sense and closely identified with the working-class union roofers, whose standard of living he helped to better. His affectionate loyalties were narrow, however, and he was callous toward people outside his circle, using or abusing them as circumstances warranted. As a roofers' business agent in the late sixties Traitz had what the federal courts later called "a creed of violence, unlawfulness . . . defiance of authority . . . force, fear, and intimidation." The "hired goons and trained boxers" that Traitz employed to control the roofers were often from his own family (his two sons and a son-in-law) and friends from the old neighborhood. Despite the fact that North Penn had become a black community in the 1960s, one nasty boxer who worked for Traitz, Michael "Nails" Mangini, still lived at Twenty-first and Toronto in the 1970s.

In 1980 gunmen murdered the roofers' union leader, John McCullough. Traitz made a deal with Nicodemo Scarfo, a man influential in the Philadelphia and southern New Jersey criminal world. Traitz got suport in his takeover of the union in a contest with another faction. In exchange, Scarfo relied on Traitz and his fighters to solve labor problems that touched on the "mob's" activities. Only in the late 1980s did various law enforcement agencies catch up with Scarfo and Traitz. For over twenty years the roofers had terrorized many an independent worker. They had bribed court and prison officers, Philadelphia police, and at least fifteen judges, while often receiving tributes from various other public officials. Such was old North Penn's contribution to what was known as the Mafia.

Back in the early 1940s more law-abiding people in the neighborhood had a better friend in another Italian, young foot patrolman Frank Rizzo, who was to become one of the more famous twentieth-century U.S. police chiefs. Rizzo was "a large powerful man with the build of a professional football line-backer." He joined the force early in World War II and was first stationed at the Thirty-ninth Police District, which served North Penn at Twenty-second Street and Hunting Park Avenue. His corner was Broad Street and Erie Avenue, some distance from North Penn, but he also walked a beat on Twenty-second Street in the heart of the neighborhood's shopping district. As one resident put it, Rizzo delighted "in battling . . . tough guys when he worked the neighborhood." "His big fists . . . owned the street."

Two more affable men of affairs were Elmer Kilroy and Jim Tate. Kilroy was a son of Matt Kilroy, who had the taproom at Twentieth and Lehigh. Elmer helped run the café but was also active in the construction business and Democratic politics. A leader in Philadelphia's Thirty-eighth Ward, where North Penn was located, Kilroy served in the Pennsylvania State House in the 1930s and became speaker in 1941. But a series of defeats for city and statewide offices in the early 1940s ended his electoral political life, even though he remained an influential person. Living on North Twentieth, Kilroy also tussled with Richardson Dilworth over the spite fence. As Dilworth's star rose in the Democratic party, Kilroy's sank. His basic problem, however, was that he ran for office slightly before the Philadelphia Democratic party came to power in the city in the late 1940s and early 1950s.

The same sort of ethnic politician as Kilroy, Jim Tate was a few years younger. Although he did not live in North Penn but rather in the nearby Forty-third Ward, he represented the neighborhood in the state legislature in the 1940s. Attuned to his urban constituency, Tate would brag that he hailed not from a Republican home on one of the large avenues, but from "a small street." By the time Tate ran for bigger offices, the Democrats controlled the city, and he had not made an enemy of the now powerful Dilworth.

Kilroy was a Shibe Park figure. Dilworth, Tate, and Rizzo had careers that only briefly intersected with North Penn. Yet they would later deal with the stadium's problems when each, in turn, became mayor of Philadelphia.

• 5 •

Tenants and Renters

From the time baseball businessmen constructed their parks until the 1960s, the buildings were central to community activity in the United States. Because few large public facilities existed, entrepreneurs frequently selected baseball stadiums to house civic functions.

In the 1940s Shibe Park held large political rallies. Wendell Willkie spoke there in 1940 as part of his presidential campaign, and Franklin Roosevelt visited four years later. In 1948 Henry Wallace, who had a notorious run for the presidency on the third-party Progressive ticket, delivered his acceptance speech at Shibe Park. Less formally, Cubans against Castro rallied at the stadium in the early sixties.

The park repeatedly hosted the crusades of Billy Graham and meetings of the Jehovah's Witnesses. The baseball owners welcomed this development because the Witnesses left the park immaculate. Rodeos and jazz concerts also took over the building. The damage the rodeo did to the playing field upset officials, however, and music lovers complained that the park was "not intimate enough" for jazz. In 1955 the Ringling Brothers, Barnum and Bailey Circus arrived for a stint after politicians denied the Big Top all the sites used in previous years.

The stadium was essential to sports other than organized baseball. In the first half of the century, the antipathy of white Philadelphia to black baseball was striking and contributed to the small number of black fans in Philadelphia. But professional Negro League teams or all-stars played exhibitions in Shibe Park. Eddie Gottlieb, the premier white promoter of "colored athletics" in the city and later financer of basketball as a major sport, monitored blacks' use of the stadium. For a time Gottlieb had stock in the Negro Philadelphia Stars baseball franchise and negotiated with Mack and the Shibes for special events that brought black players into Shibe Park. These occasions were rare, although Shibe Park did host parts of the Negro Leagues World Series in the 1940s, and at times black colleges played football there.

Amateur white baseball teams used the grounds more frequently when the "big leaguers" were not in residence. The city high school baseball champions played there every year. Some of the largest and most boisterous crowds in the park's history saw the Philadelphia High School Catholic League annual championship football game. Villanova University and its great Bob Polidor played football there. In 1946 the Associated Press voted Polidor's 109 3/4-yard punt return against Miami University the most spectacular play of the year. Professional wrestling took place in the park. In the early days the great Jim Londos performed there when wrestling was still a genuine contest of skills. Later fans saw Argentina Rocca, Haystack Calhoun, and a midget tag-team match. On other occasions, "the King and His Court," the fast-pitch softballers, entertained.

The Shibes and Connie Mack donated use of the park to the schools, but made money renting the facility to politicians and evangelists. The customary renters were other professional sports promoters. Three groups stand out—boxing promoters, the owners of the Philadelphia Eagles football team, and from 1938 on the Philadelphia Phillies, the National League baseball franchise.

Soon after his father built the park, Jack Shibe organized some fights. His interest was short-lived, but he worked briefly with Bob Gunnis, a prominent promoter in the city between the two world wars. Gunnis himself had a long partnership with Herman "Muggsy" Taylor, who managed fighters for so long in Philadelphia that he lost his nickname and became, in the 1960s and 1970s, a patriarch of professional sports.

In 1917 Gunnis and Taylor moved to the forefront of their profession when they arranged a bout in Shibe Park, one of the first at a baseball stadium. Taylor promoted boxing there for the next forty years. Fights at the ball park strengthened the link of baseball to the gambling prevalent in boxing. More important, the fights connected professional baseball more strongly to crime. Fixers, gamblers, and hustlers of various degrees of crookedness were associated with boxing. The overlap increased during the Prohibition era, when promoters often doubled as bootleggers. The North Penn fighters who later drifted into crime did not box in the park, but bouts at the stadium were a form of commercial entertainment that fostered seamy activities in the neighborhood.

The fights satisfied a primitive urge in those who attended. Philadelphia had many "blood pits"—dirty places saturated with violence—and a few larger indoor facilities. Most held considerably under twenty thousand people. At the other end of the scale was Municipal Stadium, built in 1926, which held over a hundred thousand. But because it was so large and viewing any event was difficult, entrepreneurs rarely used it, although the stadium did host the first Dempsey-Tunney contest.

Philadelphia boasted many noteworthy fighters from low-income neighborhoods. Some of these toughs became famous professionals, and their bouts attracted thousands more than the blood pits could accommodate. Although ball parks were not ideal facilities, their capacity was perfect during a period when promoters could woo up to twenty thousand to some main events and calculated profits as a percentage of "the gate," the cash taken in admissions.

Ike Williams and Joe Walcott came from nearby towns in New Jersey. Battling Levinsky, Benny Bass, and Lew Tendler lived in Philadelphia Jewish ghettos; Joey Giardello in South Philadelphia; Harold Johnson in Manayunk; Tommy Loughran in an Irish neighborhood; Percy Bassett in West Philly; Bob Montgomery, Gil Turner, and Joe Frazier in North Philly—indeed, in areas close to Shibe Park. And most of these men fought at the park.

Working-class fans also welcomed favorites from outside the city. The Irish loved Billy Conn from Pittsburgh. The Philadelphia black community adopted Harlem's Sugar Ray Robinson after his spectacular nontitle victory at Shibe Park over lightweight champ Sammy Angott in 1941.

Back at the first fight in early July 1917, seven thousand turned out to see Johnny Dundee and George Chaney in an unexciting six rounds that evoked, one writer said, the excitement of "Frank Baker . . . fanning with the bags filled." But subsequent bouts confirmed the promoters' shrewdness about using Shibe Park for contests. Later in July 1917 Benny Leonard retained his lightweight championship against Johnny Kilbane. The twelve thousand in attendance was the largest fight crowd Philadelphia had seen. Police could not stop bleacher fans from rushing across the field to better seats. A 1918 contest between Leonard and Jack Britton took place while cops seized World War I draft dodgers in crowds outside the park. In comparison to the sweaty, smoky blood pits, said Herman Taylor, Shibe Park was "grand opera" for fight buffs. Every year the park regularly drew the largest boxing crowds in the city.

Because promoters could only stage outdoor boxing in mild weather, they used Shibe Park sporadically. Between April and October the A's had first claim. Moreover, although in the 1950s a canopy over the ring protected fighters from the rain, before that time bad weather could cancel bouts. In a disputed fight of 1925, Tommy Loughran and Jack Delaney fought in a howling storm, with some of the rounds shortened because of the downpour.

The ring originally stood on the pitcher's mound, with the fans seated along first and third base. Later, promoters set up the ring at home plate and removed the screen protecting the stands behind the plate. Spectators sat in the front boxes upstairs and downstairs, flanking and behind the plate. Usually there were no ringside seats, except for officials, dignitaries, and the press. If promoters put on a fight after the baseball season and damage to the playing field was immaterial, the Shibes allowed metal folding chairs around the ring. Searchlights illuminated the stadium before the owners installed the lights for night ball games in 1939. Before Jack Shibe built the spite fence in 1935, management trained these searchlights on the Twentieth Street houses to prevent anyone from watching without coming to the park. In 1935 Taylor and Gunnis were paying a thousand dollars or a percentage of the gate to hold their matches in the park.

Fight crowds were rougher than the ones that attended baseball, but also included a high-society element. Socialite Anthony Drexel Biddle, who began the practice of wearing evening clothes at ringside, was a fight fan. Richardson Dilworth, lawyer and budding politician, was an acquaintance of Herman Taylor. What prompted these men and others to go to fights?

A good bout produced a satisfying and savage drama. Writers thought that the 1928 Benny Bass–Harry Blitman fight was the greatest featherweight battle seen in Philadelphia. Before twenty-five thousand, Bass "butchered" Blitman with a sixth round knockout in a fight that bloodied both men. In the early fifties Gil Turner gave Shibe Park fans the same sort of excitement. In 1951 the referee stopped Turner's fight with former lightweight champ Ike Williams in a contest that left Williams "tottering on the ropes, bleeding, beaten, and unable . . . [to] defend . . . himself." A few months before, Turner had defeated Charlie Fusari in eleven rounds of mayhem at the stadium. In the *Bulletin*'s "Sports Parade" Hugh Brown wrote that the battle thrilled patrons to their "club wielding primordial roots." Brown, who usually watched bouts on television, said that a ringside seat confronted him with the raw actuality of the fight. He shivered with delight at the blood that spattered on his trousers and described how the "colored boy" Turner took the handsome blond Fusari and made his face resemble "an over-aged cantaloupe after it had been bounced . . . on a concrete floor."

Professional football, which attracted little mass interest in the first half of the twentieth century, was less brutal than boxing. In the 1920s the Frankford Yellow Jackets first represented Philadelphia in the National Football League (NFL). They played occasionally at Shibe Park, includ-ing the crucial game for the 1926 championship when the Hornets de-feated the Chicago Bears 7–6. But sports entrepreneurs could not make the team a success. Business was so bad that players, often former Uni-versity of Pennsylvania stars, sometimes had to play without helmets. In 1931 the Yellow Jackets were unable to start their season at Shibe Park because the A's, bound for another World Series, refused to allow the use of the field until after mid-October. Toward the end of the 1931 season the football team canceled its remaining home games, deciding to play them on the road, because local attendance was so bad. At the end of the year Philadelphia lost its NFL franchise.

Two years later, in 1933, sportsmen formed the Philadelphia Eagles, who often struggled financially but managed to hang on as the city's NFL representative. In their first few years they played in the Phillies ball park at Broad and Huntingdon and then in the unsatisfactory Mu-nicipal Stadium. In 1940—the Phillies park closed in 1938—the Eagles officially moved to Shibe Park, although they continued to play a few games at Municipal Stadium and also tried the facility owned by Tem-ple University.

To accommodate football at Shibe Park during the winter, manage-ment set up stands in right field, parallel to Twentieth Street. Some twenty feet high, these "east stands" had twenty-two rows of seats. The goalposts stood along the first base line and in left field. The uncov-ered east stands enlarged the capacity of Shibe Park to over thirty-nine thousand, but the Eagles rarely drew more than twenty-five to thirty thousand

In 1947, 1948, and 1949 the Eagles fielded their most popular and powerful team at the park, winning their division title three times and the championship in 1948 and 1949. Halfback Steve VanBuren, one of pro football's greatest ball carriers, led the Eagles. "His chin tucked to his chest, his great shoulders lowered to batter aside anyone in his path, his knees pumping violently . . . VanBuren was a sight never to be forgotten by Philadelphia football fans."

The team won its greatest victory at Shibe Park in the 1948 championship "snow game." During a blizzard, rooters huddled for three quarters to watch a scoreless tie with the Chicago Cardinals. Then the Eagles recovered a fumble on the Cardinal seventeen and drove toward the goal line in the blinding snow. With the fans screaming, "Give it to Steve! Give it to Steve!" VanBuren hit the Chicago line between left guard and tackle and crashed through for five yards and the game's only touchdown. The Eagles won 7–0.

VanBuren as well as such favorites as Pete Pihos, Adrian Burke, Norm VanBrocklin, and Mike Jarmoluk did much to make football viable in the city. Like the old Yellow Jackets, the team drew on area college boys whom the fans loved. Chuck Bednarik, "Concrete Charlie" from the University of Pennsylvania, was one of these. The greatest local hero was "Bucko" Kilroy, a six-foot-two, 250-pound lineman who starred at Temple University in the early forties and worked as an Eagles' official after he retired in the late fifties. Kilroy's great-uncle Matt had run the bar at Twentieth and Lehigh. Although Bucko's family resided in nearby Kensington, his cousins and Uncle Elmer still lived behind Shibe Park. North Penn residents admired Bucko as the iron man of the NFL and particularly liked him because of his reputation as a mean player. Yet even with locals like Kilroy and even during the glorious period of three division titles, with the exciting VanBuren running off tackle, the Eagles never filled Shibe Park to its winter capacity. They often drew less than thirty thousand.

Much of the problem had to with the economics of the sport and its dependence on baseball facilities. Professional teams played once a week for twelve or thirteen weeks. The Eagles used the park on Sunday afternoons or, on a few occasions, Saturday afternoons or evenings. Since they played half their games away from home, the team usually appeared in Philadelphia six times a season over three months. To be profitable the club had to draw much larger crowds than baseball teams, which played seventy-seven home games a year. And the Eagles did draw more fans per game. Once-a-week contests did produce more excitement than the almost daily, more leisurely rituals of baseball for six months.

But Shibe Park discouraged football fans. The position of the fixed stands created an awkwardly placed playing area. The temporary stands were physically unpleasant and unprotected from the cold weather. They added to seating capacity at the expense of even minimal comfort. On one occasion fans vacated the seats because they were in danger of collapsing. Indeed, many Eagles patrons went to Shibe Park as much for the masculine thrill of braving the winter outside as for witnessing the team. On the other hand, September football games might leave the field unsuitable for late-season baseball and thus drew complaints. The grounds keepers considered football unacceptably destructive to the diamond.

The problems of parking at the stadium that would bedevil baseball executives in the 1950s and 1960s began earlier for the Eagles. Parking at Twenty-first and Lehigh was troublesome when baseball drew over ten thousand people. In the late 1940s, when twenty-five to thirty thousand turned out to see the championship Eagles, these troubles were impossible to solve and were made bearable only because the fans appeared once every other week for a few months.

Despite their titles, the Eagles failed financially. Their owners put them up for sale in 1949. To keep them in the city, a syndicate of one hundred sportsmen bought them for $250,000. In the next several years the team earned a small profit but still suffered in cramped quarters designed for another sport. By the late fifties, astute entrepreneurs sensed that football was about to spurt in popularity, but having to play in made-over baseball parks still crippled the sport. Although the Eagles wanted to stay in Philadelphia, other cities offered larger quarters and spacious parking lots.

At the end of 1957—and on the brink of the growth in the mass appeal of football—the Eagles left North Philadelphia. Their new home was Franklin Field, the stadium of the University of Pennsylvania in West Philadelphia. As tenants at Twenty-first and Lehigh, the Eagles paid about sixty thousand dollars in rent a year, 15 percent of their gate receipts. The agreement with the university probably required the expenditure of more money in an informal arrangement to pay Franklin Field maintenance costs. At the same time Franklin Field held a maximum of sixty-eight thousand, as opposed to the thirty-nine thousand salable seats in North Philadelphia. Sportsmen widely agreed that it was one of the best places in the country to watch a football game. The university also had attractive surroundings that crowds of fans, nonetheless, would not disrupt; close proximity to major transportation arteries; and if not adequate parking, at least more than was available in North Philadelphia. The Eagles obtained a playing site that had, as the *Bulletin* reported, "seating capacity, accessibility, parking facilities, and other factors lacking" at Twenty-first and Lehigh.

Increased interest in football undoubtedly helped the Eagles in their new home, but people were also motivated to come to Franklin Field in a way they were not to the club's old quarters. Attendance jumped from 130,000 in 1957 to 175,000 in 1958. By the early 1960s the Eagles were drawing well over 400,000 fans for seven games as opposed to their 1947 record of 187,000 for six games at Shibe Park. The team now regularly filled Franklin Field.

There were perhaps a hundred fight cards at Shibe Park in forty years, and the Eagles played there some one hundred times over eighteen years. Connie Mack's more important tenant and the most important user, however, became the National League baseball franchise in the city. The Philadelphia Phillies rented Shibe Park from the late 1930s to 1954. From 1954 to 1961 the franchise owned the park and thereafter resumed tenancy until 1970.

Both before and after its time in the stadium the club was known as one of the weakest, if not the weakest, in baseball. The franchise was founded in 1883. Baseball men immediately called it a "humpty-dumpty" or third-rate club. During World War I the Phillies began a thirty-year stay in the National League's second division. Called the "futile Phillies" in the twenties and thirties, they were "the *lumpenproletariat*," "the laughing stock," of the league. In the late thirties the fans dubbed Hugh Mulcahy, defeated twenty times in 1938 and twenty-two times in 1940, "Losing Pitcher" Mulcahy. In the mid-forties their owner described the Phillies as "the worst team ever to play in the major leagues before or since." A later Phillies yearbook said that this mid-forties club went into games "with the hangdog reluctance of a team . . . inured to beatings." One baseball writer called the players "a collection of tailenders and misfits."

Even brief victories in the later 1940s and early 1950s did not change the team's long-term reputation. Historian David Voigt wrote that the Phillies pennant in 1950 was "as believable as a socialist presidential victory." The 1950 team was a sentimental favorite in Philadelphia history but, as Voigt said, "a one shot phenomenon" that did not recur. By the late 1950s and early 1960s the Phillies were back to their old tricks.

They finished last four seasons in a row. One boy growing up at the time remembered that "the cellar" was never the basement in his house; the cellar was where the Phillies always were. In 1969, the year before the team left the stadium, one West Coast ballplayer remarked that he would rather quit the game than be traded to Philadelphia, "the grave-yard of baseball."

Thomas Boswell noted that the Phillies occupied the park for thirty-two years without winning a world's championship. The field (and two of its predecessors) had long been torn down before the franchise produced a champion. "You measure failure," Boswell wrote, "not in seasons, but in buildings crumbled under the weight of defeat, parks that lasted longer than the lives of men and now are gone."

From 1887 to 1938 the Phillies played in what came to be known as Baker Bowl, the last specimen of the nineteenth-century parks where fans had an intimate relation with players. By the mid-twenties Baker Bowl looked neglected and in the mid-thirties was dilapidated, like the team that occupied it. For many years the Phillies had considered moving. In 1927, after the collapse of some stands forced the bowl to close for a time, the franchise played a dozen games at Shibe Park. In 1933 Jack Shibe built an office and clubhouse for the Phillies on the ground floor of Shibe Park in the furniture warehouse on Lehigh. They sat empty because the Phillies could not break their Baker Bowl lease.

In the middle of the 1938 season the Phillies finally departed the bowl, becoming tenants of the Athletics. The new occupancy meant complex scheduling for Shibe Park from April through September, almost precluding events other than baseball games. The Phillies added marginally to the site's profitability. They made a simple agreement to pay Mack ten cents per customer as rent and to arrange for their own park help. The move may have done something for the morale of the Phillies but had little impact on their won-and-lost record. In 1938 they finished last, twenty-four and a half games behind the seventh-place Dodgers.

William Baker, who owned the club from 1913 to 1930, began the practice of selling good players. This affected the quality of play and, thus, attendance. The flow of cash from sales nonetheless made the franchise minimally profitable. Gerry Nugent, who succeeded Baker from 1932 to 1942, ran things similarly. In *The Kid from Tomkinsville* (1940) John R. Tunis portrayed the Dodgers as desperate for a pitcher in their bid for the pennant. They could get a good left-hander from the last-place Phillies, but "the Phils wanted money: plenty of it." The franchise consequently brought to Shibe Park a tradition of eighth-place teams and, as one writer said, "a few defenseless baseball writers, the park help, and mere handfuls of patrons."

One nationally syndicated columnist wrote that the Phillies did not deserve to be in the same place with the franchise that had produced the dynasties of 1910–1914 and 1929–1932. The Phillies did not fit "at Shibe Park, home of the Athletics." "There . . . where the ghosts of Bender and Plank and Baker and Collins and Cochrane still cavort in their brilliance, where every retrospect is pleasing, there you see the Phillies." The Phillies, wrote Frank Yeutter, a senior Philadelphia sportswriter, had "a perpetual lease on last place," whereas in Connie Mack's Shibe Park there was "a parade of heroes and winners . . . [and] household names."

In truth, however, the A's had become as bad as the Phillies. Mack's ownership style in the 1930s and 1940s did not differ from that of Baker and Nugent. At times the frustrations and even anger of the fans would surface not only about the Phillies but also about the venerable Mack. A joke of the time captured his cheapness and the quality of his teams. Not recognizing the grand old man, a cabbie picks him up at Shibe Park and drops him at North Philadelphia Station. Connie pays the driver and walks off to the train. "Hey pop," shouts the driver, "how 'bout a tip?" "A tip?" says Mack. "Young man, don't bet on the A's."

One analyst wrote that during this period Shibe Park was "the unhappiest of major league locations." With a small captive audience of the city's diehard fans, the management of both clubs fielded the least expensive and worst teams. The A's and Phillies finished last in their respective leagues in 1938, 1940, 1941, 1942, and 1945. The 1944 Phillies had the best record of either club in over a decade when they tied for sixth place. That year the Phillies sponsored a contest to give themselves a new nickname. The winning name, the Blue Jays, did not take but prompted a sportswriter's brevity in capturing baseball highlights in the city: "A's, J's Bow." A year later, in 1945, *Stars and Stripes* printed the American and National League standings in reverse order one day to pep up Philadelphia servicemen. From 1930 to 1950 the two clubs competed with each other for the lowest average finish and attendance among all the major league franchises.

The affections of the fans stayed nonetheless with the Athletics, who easily remained the more profitable team. By 1942 Gerry Nugent was heavily in debt to the National League and owed rent money to Mack. The National League owners—long suffering because their receipts from playing in the city were minimal—had the league buy the club. After much dickering the league then sold the franchise to William Cox, a New York businessman. Cox agreed to pay the back rent on Shibe Park as well as to lease it in the future. He did not have much money, and his 1943 team finished seventh. Yet the Phillies paid their debts, and Cox's colorful and controversial ownership doubled attendance and made the club profitable. Still, he feuded with fans, other owners, and the National League president. His end came when his gambling on the Phillies enraged Kenesaw Landis. In November 1943 the commissioner banned Cox from baseball.

A year before, in November 1942, when Nugent was running the team, sportswriter John Lardner wrote that the Phillies needed "a handsome millionaire to come to the rescue." A year later, with the removal of Cox and the franchise again in disarray, this is exactly what occurred.

Robert Carpenter, Sr., was a vice president of DuPont Chemicals and married to a DuPont. Their son, Robert, Jr., was a wealthy young man with little interest in the family business. After dropping out of college, he pursued sporting activities near his home in Wilmington, Delaware. In his early twenties, he became Connie Mack's partner in a minor league Wilmington team. The junior Carpenter was president, and Mack used the Wilmington Blue Rocks as an A's farm club. When Landis drove Cox off in 1943, Carpenter's father offered to buy the Phillies. Mack assured Landis that the family would stabilize the floundering franchise. The sale took place, and Carpenter, Sr., turned over the presidency to his twenty-eight-year-old son.

At his first press conference the young man confessed that he did not have much experience. "But I'm not worried," he added. "I think we can all have a good time."

In many ways Carpenter's ownership was unexceptional. He was a decent, pleasant man of ordinary abilities. His distinguishing characteristic was that he was *very* rich. He had a sporting interest in the club. One of his executives recalled that what "Bob loved doing most was signing Robin Roberts," his star right-handed pitcher of the 1950s. Carpenter himself said that he best liked sitting "in my box seats and talking to great old players." He approached the club as an uncritical fan. Owning a franchise was also a civic duty or public service for him. "Inherited wealth," he said, "carries with it responsibility. I think an heir has an obligation to put his money to work." This combination of executive capacity and sentimentality meant that during the thirty-year period of his ownership the franchise never produced a sustained contender. Philadelphia sportswriter Sandy Grady defended Carpenter for a long time, but near the end of the Carpenter period even Grady described him as "a meddlesome, soft-hearted owner," unable to help the franchise.

At the same time Carpenter's critics insufficiently appreciated the dramatic improvement he wrought. As Connie Mack had hoped, Carpenter stabilized the Phillies. He ran the team from 1943 until 1972, and his son carried on, far more successfully, for another nine years. The Shibes, Macks, and Carpenters were the three families that shaped Philadelphia baseball in the twentieth century.

The Phillies had previously been operated on five-and-dime-store principles. After Carpenter took over, the business immediately became more complicated and financially sophisticated. The new owner put into place a new accounting system, in part necessary because far more money was being spent, much of it in novel ways. As writer Stan Baumgartner pointed out, the Phillies were at long last "a big time operation doing business with big money." Carpenter poured dollars into the farm system, engaged marketing consultants, and investigated ways to promote ticket sales. As matters turned out, he proved conservative in his single-minded concentration on the sport, but he surrounded himself with professional administrators who quickly modernized his franchise.

Carpenter sometimes said that anyone could lose money at baseball and that the object was to make a profit. But he also believed that money was not the main issue. It was easier to make more, he claimed, in other enterprises. With his sense of noblesse oblige in sports, he wanted to expand Philadelphia's civic consciousness in baseball. He worked hard and enthusiastically at his job, refused a salary, and was steadfastly committed to the survival of his Phillies in the city. The franchise was usually not in the black year-to-year, but Phillies financial executives showed Carpenter how to "write off" his entire way of life. The dollar value of his club increased dramatically over the years. In the end Carpenter transformed the team from a sort of joke into a substantial, although mediocre, major league franchise.

His most significant accomplishment, however, was more complex. During the early period of his ownership, Carpenter achieved his greatest triumph. His club of 1949 to 1953, known as "the Whiz Kids," won a pennant. Although they were not a great team, they also won the love of fans in Philadelphia. More important, despite the sustained mediocrity of the Phillies, they won that love at the expense of the Athletics.

Mack and his A's had been the city's premier franchise since the turn of the century. The A's were sometimes great; the Phillies never. Even when the A's were bad, and that was often, the Phillies were predictably worse. Even in their darkest hours, the A's could point to their tradition of glory. By the mid-1940s memories of this tradition had grown dim for fans as Mack managed loser after loser. Even so, the Athletics held sway at Shibe Park.

In 1943 the A's finished last and the Phillies seventh, and Cox's Phillies outdrew the Mackmen, 447,000 to 373,000 This was the first time this had happened at Shibe Park, and perhaps signaled that the rooters had had enough of Mack. In 1944 and 1945, however, the A's once more outdrew the Phillies by 135,000 and 150,000, respectively. Carpenter recalled that during these early years he was thrilled if the Phillies defeated the A's in "the city series" that preceded the regular season. Then Carpenter's 1946 team, a harbinger of the Whiz Kids, finished fifth. The Phillies drew over a million, a first in Philadelphia baseball history, attracting 400,000 more customers than the last-place A's. A writer at the time noted that this was "a bitter pill" for Connie Mack to swallow, as he often met with Carpenter in the tower office at Shibe Park to advise the young man. The humiliation continued the next year, when the Phillies, with only a seventh-place team to the Athletics' fifth-place team, again outdrew the A's by a slight margin.

Three years later, 1950, was the fiftieth anniversary of Mack's career in Philadelphia. His teams in the preceding three years had had a marginally positive record. He predicted a pennant. The club finished last, while the Phillies came in first. Their attendance was four times the Athletics', 1.2 million to 300,000.

Carpenter's monied operation was more successful than Mack's "mom and pop" store. Carpenter said people loved seeing someone else, especially a rich man, spending large sums of money. But along with receipts went something less palpable, the loyalty of the city. In the decade after the war, baseball had gone against Mack. In Philadelphia affections also altered. Carpenter oversaw a crucial if intangible shift for which the Athletics would pay dearly.

• 6 •

Baseball and Business

After 1932, when Connie Mack broke up his team, A's fans had little to cheer about. The Phillies' arrival in 1938 only added to the won-and-lost blues at Twenty-first and Lehigh. Mack continued tryouts on a grand scale at the park in the hope, once more, of finding inexpensive stars. After the A's left, this practice continued with the Phillies through the late 1950s. Much mediocre talent thus passed through the city. Hal Kelleher pitched for the Phillies while on the local police force. Lawrence "Crash" Davis, a utility infielder for the A's in the early 1940s, wasn't even good enough to last through World War II, when the Athletics were especially abject. Rumors said that Mack kept third-string catcher Tony Parisse on the Athletics' payroll during the war because his father owned a butcher shop in North Penn: the Parisse family procured the club the best meat available. Later the Parisses were involved in various criminal activities, and Davis went on to a minor league career that was the basis for the movie *Bull Durham*.

Ballplayers who were truly minor leaguers or involved in cops and robbers did not attract customers to the park. The patrons seemed, rather, to come to be entertained or to vent anger. Manager Joe McCarthy waited till his Yankees played in Philadelphia to pitch Walter "Jumbo" Brown, at 295 pounds the largest man in baseball. McCarthy said only Brown could draw fans to Shibe Park. The rooters nicknamed A's pitcher Lynn Nelson "Line Drive" because opposing teams hit him so well. When Phillies pitcher Walter Beck was on the mound, the crowd, in ragged unison, cheered, "Boom, *Boom* . . . Boom, *Boom* . . . Boom, *Boom*." Hence, "Boom Boom" Beck got his name for his inability to get anyone out. In the thirties and forties home teams that were easy targets for heckling reinforced the now legendary contentiousness of Philadelphia rooters.

Sometimes the ongoing traditions of baseball attracted people, as 1941 exemplified. In May the city and state proclaimed Connie Mack Day in honor of Mack's forty years in Philadelphia (Elmer Kilroy introduced the bill). On May 17 dignitaries held a ceremony at City Hall and then paraded up Broad and out Lehigh to Shibe Park. Among the many celebrants was Mack's old friend George M. Cohan who sang—with accompaniment—his own composition, "Connie Mack Is the Grand Old Name." Old A's stars, including Eddie Collins, Lefty Grove, and Al Simmons, participated. Shortly afterward Dobbins High School, across the street, had its own Connie Mack Day for the "always . . . loved and welcome figure" in North Penn. On the seventeenth Mack had roped off the outfield to house the expected overflow crowd, a condition unnecessary since the pennant-winning days of 1910–1914. A heavy rain cut attendance to fifteen thousand, still a great turnout given the Athletics' performance in 1940 and 1941, when they finished last each year. That afternoon the rooters saw more of the same when the Detroit Tigers completed a three-game sweep of Philadelphia.

Stars on other teams drew when the A's did not. In June 1941 Joe DiMaggio came to Philadelphia during his fifty-six-game hitting streak. A's pitcher Johnny Babich bragged that he would stop DiMaggio. When DiMaggio lined a ball through Babich's legs for a double in the third inning, however, even the "notoriously hostile" Philadelphia fans stood up to cheer. At the end of September the Red Sox were in town for a season-closing doubleheader with the A's. Ted Williams was batting .3995, which would have been rounded up to .400 had he sat out the last two games. But after nervously walking the city's streets the night before, Williams played and went six for eight in the two games, raising his average to .406. Between the games, Philadelphia fans presented Lefty Grove, then forty-one and still playing for the Red Sox, with a silver chest for winning his 300th game that July. Grove started the second game, but the A's knocked him out of the box in the first inning. It was his last big league outing. "I started with Connie Mack," said Grove, "and I finished at least in the same ball park with him."

When the United States entered World War II at the end of 1941, baseball adjusted dramatically as the able-bodied players went into the service. The war, however, offered opportunities for owners to associate the sport with patriotism and for fans to display their love of country in the ball parks. Shibe Park became a center for community activity that downplayed diversity and conflict and accentuated a vague Americanism.

Baseball under the lights received a lift. In the "green light" letter, in which FDR sanctioned play during wartime, the president mentioned his interest in evening ball. Workers on shifts that conflicted with afternoon games could relax at night. The floodlit parks, however, might violate "dimout" regulations designed to protect coastal areas from enemy attack. But in Philadelphia the army decided in early 1942 that the lights were not hazardous to shipping. Evening baseball became routine, although Mack closed the recently opened restaurant Café Shibe because meat was so difficult to obtain. Test blackouts interrupted some games, but fans responded positively to these inconveniences. Andrew Aloysius "Babe" O'Rourke, Shibe Park's public address announcer, led songfests during these "intermissions" and told customers that they should douse cigars and cigarettes "if you are American."

Management now began each game with the "Star Spangled Banner," a convention previously reserved for special occasions such as opening day. The A's and the Phillies sponsored games whose profits went for servicemen's relief and admitted uniformed personnel free. Military bands performed at the park. At one game an American Legion post supplied poppies to decorate the uniforms of ballplayers. The franchises auctioned off autographed balls at games, with money going to the war effort. One ball, signed by Connie Mack and Franklin Roosevelt, brought fifteen thousand dollars in war bonds.

Ballplayers in the service made appearances, and Mack made the most of the Athletics' ties with those players fit for duty. When the military inducted A's shortstop Al Brancato in 1942, Mack, then seventy-nine, witnessed the ceremony. He denied stories that authorities would give Brancato a special assignment so that he could continue to play with the A's in off hours.

The most striking publicity stunts were elaborate "nights" for heroic serviceman–ballplayers, which were both emotional and profitable. Baseball owners exploited the commitments of Americans to their soldiers, beginning a practice that would characterize the late 1940s and 1950s. Before one game in 1942 officials brought former Phillie Hugh Mulcahy from his military base to pitch batting practice. His old teammates presented him with a war bond, and the American Legion gave him a silver platter. Phil Marchildon, a young Canadian tail gunner shot down off the coast of Denmark in August 1944, lost thirty pounds in a Nazi POW camp. Returning to civilian life in 1945, he was too weak to pitch. Connie Mack coaxed him into an outing for a "Phil Marchildon Night." The show raised attendance for the returned hero. Marchildon went three innings and received a thousand-dollar bond, while the A's had a big evening.

Mack made the most of other serviceman heroes. After losing one game for the A's in 1942, Bob Savage became the first major leaguer injured in action. He received shrapnel wounds in Italy and wrote Mack from a hospital bed, "I hope they will be able to dig it out because more than anything else, I want to pitch." With suitable fanfare he briefly played with the A's immediately after the war.

A bigger and more publicized hero was Lou Brissie, who failed a teenage tryout with Mack and subsequently joined the army. Shell fragments also hurt Brissie in Italy, breaking both feet and his left leg, smashing his left ankle, and wounding both hands and shoulders. After twenty-three operations he turned up at the Athletics' 1946 training camp with a whittled-down catcher's shin guard on his left leg and a rubber sponge underneath to protect bones and nerves exposed by injuries. The A's promoted this genuine hero, a symbol of courage for veterans. He was 14–10 in 1948 and 16–11 in 1949, before he left the majors in 1953 with a 44–48 record.

Customers who went to the ball park during the fighting kept up with the great issues of the war. In addition to leading songfests, Babe O'Rourke relayed the news of major Allied victories. In this way fans learned the latest details of the surrenders of Italy, Germany, and Japan. On June 7, 1944, Shibe Park hosted a light heavyweight fight between champion Ike Williams and former champ Sammy Angott. Before the bout fans listened to President Roosevelt's prayer to the nation for the success of the Allied second front in Europe, which had begun the day before. Promoters also announced the progress of the landings on the French beaches of Normandy during the show and between rounds of the main event.

After World War II ended a year later, Shibe Park baseball flourished. The general ebullience of the period raised the sights of everyone. A postwar attendance jump benefited the owners of both the A's and Phillies and brought employment and prosperity to many connected with the park.

During the first third of the century Jack Shibe supervised not only the Athletics' finances but also park maintenance. A fastidious man, he detested the dirt from the sale of food and drink. Although the franchise sold peanuts, ice cream, sandwiches, soda, and (by 1915) hot dogs, the A's hawked them only with Shibe's grudging and late consent. Gradually, however, sales grew under the aegis of Bob Schroeder, who had worked for the team since 1902, when he began selling peanuts at age twelve. Later, as personal secretary to Jack Shibe, Schroeder kept the Athletics' books. After Shibe died in 1937, Schroeder figured crucially in finances. Called an accounting "genius," he upped the sale of food and therefore profits. The only member of the franchise's board of directors who was not a Mack or a Shibe, Schroeder motivated the construction of Café Shibe in 1939. At the same time he introduced mobile equipment, "the traveling kitchen" from which a vendor could dispense hot dogs, soup, and coffee. World War II food rationing prompted Schroeder to discover different sorts of snacks for the fans to eat. After the war he carried on his profitable ways.

Growing concession sales went with postwar prosperity. After Schroeder's death in 1950, Pennsport Service and later the American Restaurant Association (ARA) made concessions even more businesslike. Logan Parker, another habitué of Shibe Park, represented these businesses for twenty years. Under Parker, fans eventually could buy chicken, shrimp, pizza, and roast beef sandwiches at the ball park. He did taste tests of foods. More important, Parker plotted sales figures and predicted consumption accurately. In purchasing supplies he anticipated the weather, advance sales, starting pitchers, and the performance of both home and visiting clubs. Parker also knew, overall, how much each fan consumed—one hot dog for every three-quarter customer in 1959; $1.05 spent per customer in 1967.

The teams also earned money from the print shop, a low-risk enterprise located under the stands along the third base line. The only two bosses the business had in over fifty years, Leon Gumpert and Joe Friedlander, knew that every other fan wanted a scorecard. When Friedlander took over after the war, Shibe Park distributed athletic program books in the city, selling mainly to high schools, colleges, and professional football teams.

Soon after the war, too, management redid the park. In what Mack planned as the first installment of a series of major changes, the A's spent three hundred thousand dollars in renovations for the 1949 season. The owners had long since exhanged the original metal folding chairs for wood-and-steel-frame chairs embedded in concrete, and now added additional expensive seats. On the upper deck beyond third base, Mack put an "annunciator" that flashed the at-bat number; ball, strike, and out count; hit or error; and the score. Prior to 1949 the only water was in the dugouts, but finally the A's put water coolers elsewhere. Ramps replaced the old grandstand stairways. Finally, in a new concourse under the stands along first and third base, Mack upgraded dreary rest rooms. A short time later, in the mezzanine behind home plate, the franchises installed Dot Langdon with her electric organ. She played customers' requests before the games and, during the games, rewarded exciting feats with appropriate music. Langdon most enjoyed applauding a victory by pitcher Robin Roberts with "When the Red, Red Robin Comes Bob, Bob Bobbin' Along."

The teams got new quarters. In the early fifties Philadelphia's unpleasant fans made life difficult for opposing players when they walked from their clubhouse on the ground floor to the dugout. At the end of the 1952 season the A's built a tunnel so visitors could avoid hometown "wolves." The franchise planned similar tunnels for the home team clubhouses.

Schroeder, Gumpert, Friedlander, and many others—including members of both the A's and Phillies ground crew, the chief clubhouse attendants, and Connie Mack's office staff—were longtime employees. Most of them lived in the neighborhood. The record holder was visiting clubhouse attendant Theodore "Teddy" (or later "Ace") Kessler, who spent almost sixty years in Philadelphia baseball. The most important employee, however, was Andy Clarke, head of stadium maintenance by the 1950s. He started at the park in the 1930s, out of high school, and did not retire until the late 1970s, long after the Phillies had moved from North Philadelphia. More powerful than other employees, Clarke oversaw minor political relations in addition to running the park. One old employee recalled that Andy "knew every cop in the city and every City Hall politician." He used his association with baseball and the lure of free passes, as well as an engaging personality, to obtain security and public transport services, repair contracts, help in smoothing over difficulties in the neighborhood, and aid with the tax and assessment department and the licenses and inspections bureau.

Clarke dispensed patronage. By the 1950s he had at his disposal more than two hundred jobs as ushers, ticket takers and sellers, grounds keepers, and cleaners. An additional two to three hundred concession people were separately controlled and unionized, as Clarke was aware when he informally mediated disputes that put hot dog hawkers on picket lines outside the park. But even the vendors were subject to his indirect prerogative.

Clarke lived at Germantown and Allegheny. In the 1940s, when he ran the Phillies ticket sales, he met and married a North Penn girl employed as an usher. Clarke's ties to the community increased, and he often went to friends and neighbors to hire his workers. In providing jobs that gave residents a common interest, baseball illustrated how the business system contributed to the area's stability.

Connie Mack himself got work for Sam Crane, who played with the A's at the end of 1914 and thereafter with other clubs in a nondescript career. In 1929, long out of the big leagues, Crane killed his former sweetheart and her new boyfriend in a drunken rage. The courts sentenced him to a term at the then new Gratersford Prison, which housed many small-time criminals from North Penn. Again and again Mack wrote letters of endorsement for Crane in the hope that he would be paroled. Finally, in 1944, the state granted Crane's request for clemency. He took a Shibe Park job.

Clarke himself hired the bluecaps—ushers with minimal police duties—and other seasonal and part-time employees. These workers could vividly recall their experiences long after they had left the job. One bluecap, given his job through one of Clarke's friends, remembered his troubles in handling unruly fans. A vendor, a low man on the totem pole selling soda, reminisced about his hike from the Shibe Park dispensing area to the upper tier in right field with two ice buckets. It took twenty minutes to trudge to a part of the stadium nicknamed "Siberia." Another young man lasted at his job only a day because he did not have the energy to do his work properly. Years later he wrote "The Sweeper," a short story detailing the trials of trying to clean up a section of the stands covered with the usual litter.

Because of the money involved and the technical complexity, broadcasting was an area outside of Clarke's direction. As matters initially stood, the baseball enterprise had fixed costs in any given year and one source of revenue, the fans. The growth of concessions taught management that it could extract money from patrons at someplace other than the ticket window, but ticket sales were still the focus of attention. The salaries for players and other personnel and the cost of Shibe Park maintenance remained the same whether one thousand or ten thousand people showed up. Above ten thousand, perhaps more help was necessary to put on a game. In general, however, the club needed a certain number of paying customers to break even. Above that number each admission and the concessions income it meant were pure profit. The "marginal utility" of extra fans, as it was put in economic terms, was very great. Because of these factors, as we have seen, the Shibes and Mack used various devices to boost admissions during the season and, like other owners, feared anything that might diminish attendance.

From the 1920s on radio presented a delicate issue. Afraid that "free" broadcasting of games would encourage people to stay away from the parks, management only slowly saw radio as a means of promoting a team. In the two-franchise cities such as Philadelphia owners worked out a simple scheme. They would broadcast the game of the team playing at home but not that of the team playing away. The owners thought that transmission, say, of the A's at Shibe Park would attract customers but that of the Phillies on the road at the same time would detract from the Athletics' gate, and vice versa. So each team got the nod for half of its games.

After Bill Dyer began announcing contests from Shibe Park and Baker Bowl in the 1930s, the two teams had many "voices." The one that counted most was By Saam, who broadcast continuously for the A's from 1938 to 1954 and for the Phillies from 1938 to 1949 and again from 1955 until 1975, five years after the park closed. Saam was not without his problems, but popular in the city anyway. From his press box perch high up in the park, he called more losing games than any other announcer. As one critic put it, Saam did his "overblown best" to tout mediocre baseball on Philadelphia radio stations WIP, WCAU, WPEN, WFIL, or WIBG. "Plenty of good seats still available," he would start out, "under a Lehigh Avenue moon."

The coverage of away games increased slowly. At first, Saam would broadcast them if no home game competed or in case rain prevented a home game. Later, he covered away games if they were in the afternoon and the home game in the evening, or the other way around. When owners saw that radio did not hurt attendance and even publicized interest in baseball, broadcast of all away games became possible. Still, it was too expensive to send a sportscaster with the team on road trips. Announcers broadcast these games through "re-creation."

One writer called this transmission baseball's imaginative "theater of the mind." It was an activity that found the sport receptive to the imposition of drama and color. In, say, a Brooklyn radio studio Saam's opposite number would receive an abbreviated report, sent by Morse Code, of a game the visiting Dodgers were playing in Philadelphia against the Phillies: AB Mueller . . . B1 H [high] . . . S1 L[low] . . . B2 W[wide] . . . 2B, line drive RF . . . AB Bragan . . . S1 S[swinging] . . . B1 I[inside]. With these meager data and sound effects such as a record of crowd noises and a hammer on a piece of wood, the announcer would construct a game for Dodger fans.

"AB Mueller . . . B1 H" might become "Owen tosses the ball back to Swift, and Heinie Mueller stands in at the plate. . . . If you've just tuned in, this is Red Barber sittin' in the catbird seat. It's the bottom of the eleventh in a long game here at Shibe Park, tied at five-five, and the crowd is thinning out on a warm and languorous night in Philly. . . . Swift in the stretch . . . ball one, high and outside, and Mueller's not taking." "2B, line drive, RF" was translated: "Mueller laces the pitch. It's a line drive off that corrugated wall in right field. The Cherce is having a little trouble playing it. . . . The throw's good and Reese is on second. He's out . . . no, too late . . . the ump calls him safe. Mueller slides under Reese for a double. Mueller stands up and dusts himself off. Peewee didn't like that call, and it looks like a little rhubarb out there." In Philadelphia itself Saam would be announcing the same game from the press box at Shibe Park. Not until 1950, however, did he actually attend the A's and Phillies away games that he broadcast.

The franchise finally transmitted all games live because the sale of rights to stations, which then charged advertisers to sponsor the games, became a lucrative source of income. Owners began to perceive baseball not merely as a game played before a large but limited number of "fans" but as entertainment appealing to a casual but indefinitely large audience.

This perception came about in Shibe Park itself in the mid-1940s. "PA" announcer Babe O'Rourke, the man who conducted songfests early in World War II, usually had limited duties. Jack Shibe first installed primitive loudspeakers in the 1920s to aid O'Rourke, who had announced the battery and any substitutions with a megaphone. Then Shibe introduced a more sophisticated public address system, although it was used primarily to report emergencies or to inform fathers about lost sons rather than to give information about games. As one Shibe Park regular wrote, it was ridiculous to announce that the next batter was "number 4, Bobby Estalella, centerfielder." But Sherry O'Brien, O'Rourke's successor at the Shibe Park mike—located in the home team dugout—took a different approach. He introduced each player as he came to bat for the first time and offered up various bits of information about both the home and visiting clubs. Some fans cracked that O'Brien would soon be announcing age, weight, height, and hometown! Overall, however, as Ed Pollock wrote in "Playing the Game," "In these days of fluctuating attendance . . . not all the patrons are regulars," and they wanted the commentary. Pollock, indeed, liked the "touch of theater" and advocated more patter.

By the mid-1950s, along the third base upper deck, the Phillies were piping to fans the radio broadcast of their games. This brought complaints from some customers, who claimed that, as a captive audience, they did not want their baseball mixed with ads for Ballantine beer, Phillies cigars, and Tastykakes. By this time, however, the most important medium was not radio but television.

In 1937 Philco Radio and TV Corporation interviewed Connie Mack in its factory a short distance from Shibe Park. Transmitted several miles to two hundred editors of newspapers and magazines at the Germantown Cricket Club, the telecast introduced baseball to TV. Ten years later Mack televised the first game from Shibe Park from a converted refreshment stand under the sloping tier of the upper-deck seats, first level, behind home plate. One camera, mainly focused on the pitcher, batter, and catcher, did the job. Connie Mack and Bob Carpenter, again, feared that TV would cost them fans but soon saw the possibilities of television as a sales gimmick and money-maker. By 1950 management went to two additional cameras at first and third bases. By the late 1950s the Phillies led the National League in securing a profitable radio and TV package for broadcasting and sponsoring games.

Radio and televison forced the Philadelphia franchises to rethink their understanding of baseball. Broadcasting became a form of advertising. Yet the teams did not have to pay for it. Instead, people paid them. One marketing firm that dealt with the Phillies in the late 1940s and the 1950s noted the "extremely selfish" and "entirely new" ideas that transmission now embodied. The Phillies no longer sold rights to games; rather, they "merchandised" a "commodity," just like Buicks, breakfast foods, soap, and cigarettes. Baseball, however, was in the uniquely lucky position of being able to command dollars for the merchandising and not having to make an outlay for it.

As telecasting grew in importance, the club moved to insure even more positive "reporting" than it received in the newspapers. Executives met with the announcers each month, explaining "their weaknesses and the little points we . . . [want] them to stress during the game." The broadcasters seldom "knock[ed] the organization," even when the Phillies were in "reverse conditions" but still needed "guidance from their superiors." Nonetheless, By Saam and his colleagues did not always please management. They occasionally had to be "reprimanded" when they got out of line. In one period when the Phillies were particularly bad, the owners still blamed the announcers for lack of "enthusiasm" in "selling the product to the fans."

From the 1930s to the 1950s the baseball business altered. It had started as a spectator sport in which each team drew its money directly from a committed group of patrons. Now owners creatively enhanced baseball's human drama and displayed it to enormous audiences. Most of these people were not fans in the old sense of bugs or kranks but instead valued the sport as an occasional diversion and only indirectly paid for the costs of individual clubs.

For all of baseball, attendance leapt after the war, but both the A's and the Phillies produced exciting teams. Although he overestimated its abilities, Connie Mack cheaply put together a competitive and likable club by the late forties. The A's boasted one of the great all-time double-play combinations. Shortstop Eddie Joost, second baseman Pete Suder, and first baseman Ferris Fain had fans writing 6-4-3 on their scorecards and beaming over "Joost to Suder to Fain." In addition, Fain won two American League titles in the early fifties. He complemented hard-hitting third baseman Hank Majeski. In the outfield Mack played a number of men popular with the customers. Sam Chapman, Wally Moses, Barney McCosky, and Elmer Valo came first. Later Mack added Dave Philly and Gus Zernial, a home run hitter lustily booed for his strikeouts.

The pitching staff was not as prepossessing, but patrons recognized the pitchers by the unique system Mack used to call them without a telephone from the bullpen to the mound. He ordered a coach to stand in front of the dugout in view of the pen. Then the assistant might pantomime a man shoveling coal to produce Joe Coleman. Or he would beat his fist against a wall, and the bullpen would think: man pounding on Shibe Park wall—Shibe—Carl Sheib. When Mack's coach stooped as if he were picking flowers, regulars knew the manager was exhibiting his well-known tendency to misremember names: Mack wanted "Mr. Flowers," Dick Fowler.

Bob Carpenter's Phillies were more expensive and more successful than the A's. Rebuilding the Phillies farm system and using bonuses, Carpenter assembled a clutch of young talent known as "the Whiz Kids." In 1948 he hired Eddie Sawyer to manage them. Sawyer constructed the team around two starting pitchers. Curt Simmons was the left-handed ace. The right-hander was Robin Roberts, one of the dominant pitchers of the 1950s. He won twenty games or more a year, six years running, including a 28–7 season in 1952.

The Phillies had an excellent shortstop in Granny Hamner. At first base was Eddie Waitkus, who was nearly killed in 1949 when a disturbed girl shot him in a hotel-room tryst. The Waitkus affair was the stuff of fiction and film and became such in Bernard Malamud's *The Natural* and the Robert Redford movie of the same name. When Waitkus came back, in 1950, to start for the Phillies, his suitably whitewashed sexual escapade assured his heroic stature.

Offensively the Phils had third baseman "Puddin' Head" Jones and catcher Andy Seminick. Two noteworthy outfielders also gave punch to the lineup. Del Ennis was one of the great home run hitters in the club's history, although the fans hooted this slugger, like Gus Zernial, for his popups and strikeouts. In center field was Richie Ashburn, who turned out to be one of the most popular and durable players to wear a Phillies uniform. Rookie of the Year in 1948, he won two batting championships in the 1950s and consistently hit over .300. A speedster, Ashburn played excellent defensive baseball, roving widely over the outfield. At bat he was a threat to hit straightaway but often walked or beat out infield grounders. On base he did not hesitate to steal. Ashburn also bunted adeptly, and to keep his bunts fair the Shibe Park ground crew built up the third base foul line, "Ashburn's Alley."

The Whiz Kids lacked depth. In 1950 second baseman Mike Goliat and left fielder Dick Sisler had their only years as successful starters. The regulars played most games without replacements. The strain on the pitching staff was unrelenting. Simmons and Roberts won 40 percent of the club's victories between them. Their primary aid was an outstanding relief pitcher, Jim Konstanty, whom Sawyer had brought up in 1948. Konstanty was one of the first pitchers used exclusively in a nonstarting role. Fans regarded him as superhuman, cheering his every step from the bullpen to the pitching mound. For every Phillies difficulty the sages in the bleachers said, "Better bring in Konstanty." In 1950 he appeared in a record-setting seventy-four games, posting a 16–7 record and winning the National League Most Valuable Player award.

In the late 1940s and early 1950s the A's wound up in the first division twice, the only times they had been there since 1933. In 1949 the Phillies, who had finished in the first division once since 1917, finished third. It was like Mardi Gras, reported the *Bulletin*. Fans flocked to see both teams and long after recalled their trips to the park. They could take the R bus to Twenty-ninth and Allegheny from where the old number 33 trolley went directly to the door of Shibe Park. From East Oak Lane, the O bus went to the subway, and the subway to Broad and Lehigh. Then, strolling up Lehigh, groups of people would come together, the excitement building as they discussed baseball. Others rooters took the route 54 bus on Lehigh. Adult males stopped in at a taproom for a couple of beers and a sandwich, and would buy more beer to take into the park. Matt Kilroy's old place at Twentieth and Lehigh, now Charley Quinn's Deep Right Field Café, was still the most notable of the many small businesses serving the ball park trade.

After World War II, more and more people drove their cars to the park but, to avoid traffic problems, might park as far away as Twenty-first and Allegheny. They would then walk down Twenty-first toward the stadium, where they might buy a "water ice," scraped from a block of ice and flavored with a sugar syrup. Some, after the war, came in buses from "Jersey," "upstate," or "the Northeast"—with the American Legion, a volunteer fire department, or, if they were younger, the Cub Scouts.

Art Hill wrote about a "hypothetical" A's fan who lived in Philly when he was a kid and followed the team by newspaper long after leaving the city. Other avid rooters never went to a single contest. In *North toward Home* Willie Morris recalled that, in Mississippi in the 1940s, radio broadcasts "from all the big-city ballparks" set imaginations churning "for the glory and riches [of] those faraway places." Geography did not determine the "home team" of fans like Morris. Something intangible might solidify allegiance. For the A's and Phillies it might be identification with the underdog, or a cousin's residence, the memories of a neighbor, a Del Ennis home run. One distant boy rooted for the A's because the local barber implied that Dario Lodigiani, a utility infielder in the late 1930s, was remotely related. Another kid from New York City periodically visited relatives in Washington, D.C. The height of the trip was a view of Shibe Park, flag flying, the scene visible as his Pennsylvania Railroad train snaked through North Philadelphia en route to Washington.

For those who actually got there the first sight of the park stuck in memory forever, just as it had for preceding generations. Youngsters felt the great size of the stadium in comparison to the row houses around it. If they were outside the park early, the crack of the bat during practice was a thrilling sound. Inside, they remembered the push and noise of the crowd. As they walked up the runway, more of the field came in view with each step. Few could forget the look of the green lawn juxtaposed against the dirty concrete.

The kids were often absorbed by the baseball in progress, but that was not essential. More important, the conventions of the park brought children into the grownup world. A set of rituals began the game. When the umpires jogged onto the grass, Dads would note the hooting: "You always boo the umps, son." Then a hush would fall over the stadium immediately before the national anthem. People would quickly rise, the men removing their caps. Children would be told, "Get up! It's the 'Star Spangled Banner.'" Following their fathers or uncles, the youngsters would sing in a low, embarrassed voice and applaud afterward. "After the umpire calls 'Play ball,'" explained the adults, "it starts." Throughout the game the kids were schooled in the intricacies of the sport. They would watch Elmer Valo or Richie Ashburn "fouling them off," "waiting for his pitch." A grown-up would tell a boy why the infield moved to the right when Ted Williams came to bat, "the Boudreau shift." A man sitting next to a family would discuss batting stances—Al Simmons, Stan Musial, Stan Lopata—with a precocious nine-year-old girl. Later in the game, one man recalled, "I learned about the seventh-inning stretch. What was that? I'd never heard of it before." Some groups would leave in the eighth inning "to miss the traffic," especially if the A's or Phillies were losing. Children would come to see that the problems of urban transport took precedence over witnessing the outcome of a contest. For other kids who stayed till "the game broke," a final treat was running onto the field and circling the bases.

By the 1950s the often-renovated park had nooks and crannies in strange places, and regulars had their favorite spots. Powers Gouraud, the Philadelphia radio personality, insisted on sitting in the right field stands just off first base, but others favored left-center, the third base upper tier, or behind the plate. One writer of a doctoral dissertation argued that a single memory of the stadium captured the essence of ball parks: "a muggy North Philadelphia night . . . [with] the smell of stale beer and cigars . . . leaning to see beyond the column support."

Fans of the forties and early fifties no longer had the Huckster or Bull Kessler to lead the razzing. But Pete Adelis, known variously as "Leather-Lungs," "Foghorn," "Loud Mouth," "the Iron Lung of Shibe Park," or "the Voice of Shibe Park," continued the heckling tradition. Weighing in at 279 pounds, Adelis sat in the upper tier along third base. He was so effective that a frustrated umpire stopped one game for fifteen minutes in a vain attempt to have Adelis ejected.

Shibe Park home runs continued to thrill rooters. After Jack Shibe put up the spite fence in 1935, fewer batters aimed for the new wall, now fifty feet high. Twentieth Street residents breathed more easily. But the higher fence also heightened the awe a prodigious clout inspired. Big left-handed Johnny Mize, playing for both the American and National leagues in the 1940s, relished visits to Shibe Park, where he rapped home runs over the wall. Stan Musial also hit a memorable one into the Twentieth Street houses. Author John Updike wrote of a Ted Williams shot rising "methodically along a straight line" as it cleared the right field fence, and one fan remembered the longest hit, foul, when Williams cleared the roof at the right field line with a ball that eventually landed in Nineteenth Street, a block east of Twentieth. In the late forties the Phillies hit a record-setting five home runs in one inning.

Stan Thompson, onetime city editor of the *Bulletin*, deployed reporters at the Deep Right Field Café to get an individual account of many home runs for local color stories. Once, the paper reported, Bill Nicholson of the Phillies hit the windowsill of Otto Gessner's house on the near side of Opal while Gessner was sitting down to apple pie. Another time Willie Mays hit one that made it into a Twentieth Street bedroom; Helen Flowers was there, too, ready to give birth. The ball landed on her abdomen, and she was rushed to the hospital. Or so the paper said.

In 1950 the Phillies captivated the city by winning the pennant on the last day of the season. Without strong reserves, the club had suf-

fered debilitating injuries in early September. Curt Simmons had reported for active duty in the armed services. Then a long losing streak
cut the Phillies' first-place lead to nothing. Even Konstanty could not
help. Robin Roberts started three of the last five games, including the
final contest against Brooklyn for the pennant at Ebbets Field.

In the bottom of the ninth with the score tied 1–1 Ashburn saved the
game for the Phils by throwing out Cal Abrams in a play at the plate. In
the next inning, in an equally exciting moment, Dick Sisler hit a three-
run homer that won the game when Roberts blanked the Dodgers in the
bottom of the tenth. Although critics point to the discussion of Joe
DiMaggio in Ernest Hemingway's *Old Man and the Sea*, Hemingway also
had the old man speak of "the great Sisler," who hit "the longest ball I
have ever seen."

Philadelphia surged with pride. The crowd at the North Philadelphia
station that hailed the champions overshadowed those that used to
greet the pennant-winning Athletics. The prospect of another Philadelphia World Series, the first since 1931, excited North Penn through
September. Even when the Yankees swept the Phillies in four straight
games, the affection and pride remained. At the end of the January
1951 Mummers Parade on Broad Street, Konstanty got an ovation that
to one commentator dwarfed even those Connie Mack had received.

One fan remembered the time as the last era of absolutes. There were
nine planets, forty-eight states, sixteen major league teams, and no one
would ever hit more than sixty home runs in a season. But Philadelphia,
in one revolution, seemed finally to have climbed out of its baseball
doldrums.

The Whiz Kids, however, could not repeat, or even remain in con-
tention. They dropped to fifth in 1951 and played no better than .500
baseball for the next several years. Carpenter fired Eddie Sawyer in
1952, then rehired him six years later. But Sawyer quit in disgust after
opening day, 1960. By the end of the decade, as *The Phillies Encyclopedia*
put it, the club was again "wretched." In 1961 the team lost twenty-
three straight games, setting a major league record and confirming its
ancient status as one of the more pathetic franchises.

The A's were worse. In 1950 they plummeted to last place, and after
briefly reviving went on the skids again. As attendance in the majors
tapered off, noncompetitive teams exacerbated the Athletics' inability to
scare up customers. Fans came only to jeer. When Gus Zernial fell and
broke his collarbone chasing a fly ball, they booed him as he was car-

ried from the field. The financial troubles connected to the lack of customers forced the Athletics to leave the city at the end of 1954. In a few
years the promise of the A's and Phillies in the postwar period had
come to little and dramatic change was about to occur.

The Yankees' World Series rout of the Phillies in 1950 began with two
home games. The Phillies lost the opener 1–0. In the top of the tenth
inning of the second game the score was tied at 1–1, with DiMaggio due
to lead off for New York. Frank Rizzo, a motorcycle cop soon to be
promoted to sergeant, was protecting the Yankee dugout. In a story
he recounted again and again with awe, he recalled that DiMaggio
was smoking a Lucky Strike. DiMaggio said, "Hold this cigaret for
me, Frank. I'm going to hit one out." A few moments later DiMaggio
homered against Robin Roberts into the upper left field stands. Rizzo
refused to return the butt to DiMaggio. Soon after the Phillies had lost
2–1. It was October 5, 1950, and this was the last series game played
in Shibe Park. Rizzo kept the butt in an envelope until it disintegrated.

The Mack Family and Shibe Park, 1946–1954

When Ben Shibe died in 1922, the Shibe interest in the Athletics passed into the hands of his four children, but primarily to his two sons, Tom and Jack. They administered the business while Mack stayed on the field. Tom Shibe performed ceremonial duties during his father's later years and was president from 1922 until his death in 1936. His younger brother, always in charge of finances, then briefly became president. Connie Mack took over at the beginning of 1937, shortly before Jack's death. Mack bought Jack's share of the Athletics from his widow and with this block of stock controlled the A's and Shibe Park for the first time, although the Shibe family still had considerable holdings in the franchise.

Mack set about dividing his shares among his heirs. He had first married in 1887. His wife had three children before her death in 1892. Mack long thought that the two sons from this marriage, Roy and Earle, would carry on the business. Earle had played with the A's for a short time and managed in the minor leagues before assisting his father, sitting next to him on the Shibe Park bench. Connie assumed he would serve as manager, while Roy, like the Shibes in the earlier period, would run "the front office," where he had been for some time.

Connie, however, had married again in 1910, eighteen years after the death of his first wife. He had five children by his second spouse, including a son, Connie, Jr., some twenty years younger than his half brothers. Because the father had laid his plans when Connie, Jr., was a child, Connie, Sr., did not know how his youngest son would fit into the business. In the 1930s the young man learned the sales end of Shibe Park, now an essential part of the franchise, and worked with Bob Schroeder, head of the club's concessions. Connie, Sr., envisioned the three male heirs ruling the franchise in concert.

To this end he split his majority holdings. He kept a block of shares for himself and apportioned the rest among his wife and his three male children, giving nothing to his four surviving daughters. Perhaps having in mind the Shibe stock, held in part by Ben Shibe's daughters, Mack did not want the affairs of the franchise "muddled." He would not include a group of women in ownership. The club, Mack said, would go to his sons so that "the name of Mack, the House of Mack," would go on.

His wife had other ideas. Mack's plan would ultimately give power to Roy and Earle, the surviving children of the first marriage. The second Mrs. Mack proposed that her husband distribute stock in equal shares to her, to each of her five children (four of whom were female), to Roy, to Earle, and to the children of Mack's deceased daughter from his first marriage. Controlling interest in the club would then go not to the men but to the family of the second marriage (and, indeed, to the women).

So adamant was Katherine Mack that the couple separated, her husband leaving the house when they could not agree. Well over eighty, Mack's humiliating estrangement become public knowledge in the winter and spring of 1946 and 1947. The Macks were reconciled after several months, although Connie did not compromise on the stock allocation. The feud, however, was just the sort of family quarrel Mack wanted to avoid.

Undistinguished men, Roy and Earle lived in the shadow of their father. Roy was a mediocre executive, given to talking too much. Earle was better known as his father's field lieutenant but without motivation of his own. The older brothers fought between themselves "like cats and dogs," one observer said. Yet a generational bond and a lengthy baseball association that antedated Mack's second family united them. Their stepmother's plan crystallized an alliance between the two. Connie, Jr. and his mother *needed* allies and turned to the Shibe heirs, who among themselves owned some 40 percent of the Athletics' stock. Now failing, Connie, Sr., was unwilling or unable to settle disputes between the first family and the second family *cum* "Shibe faction."

The prosperity of the postwar period initially masked the problems of the franchise. Baseball attendance soared. Before World War II 10 million patrons for all of major league baseball signaled a banner year. In 1946 attendance climbed to 18.5 million, and topped 20 million in 1948 and 1949. The Philadelphia franchises profited. In 1946 over

600,000 saw the A's, in 1947 and 1948 over 900,000, and in 1949 over 800,000. The crowds were comparable to those in the great twenties era of Athletics prosperity when the franchise first revamped the grounds.

Connie, Jr., in particular, seems to have wanted to move the franchise more surely in the direction of the most successful major league clubs. He pressed to refurbish and enlarge the park in the late 1940s and sought new managerial and promotional skills for the A's. The latter goal went unfulfilled, but the Macks did renovate the stadium. The most grandiose part of the design called for a new ten-thousand-seat grandstand on the west side of Twentieth Street along the right field wall, untouched since the erection of the spite fence in 1935. The Macks wanted to build the new grandstand by extending the park to the curb of Twentieth Street, with an archway fifteen feet high over a footwalk. This and other modifications costing $2.5 million would increase capacity from 31,500 to nearly 50,000. Neighborhood opposition and zoning problems ruled out the new grandstand. Eventually the franchise altered the park only minimally to expand seating. Nonetheless, the A's spent $300,000 on remodeling.

Roy and Earle had not adequately factored their aging father into the franchise's equations. From the 1930s the public doted on Mack, "the Grand Old Man of Baseball" or "Mr. Baseball." Local sports commentators sponsored a yearly celebration of his birthday at Shibe Park. Writers and players spoke of him and to him as "Mr. Mack." Writing in the *Atlantic Monthly* in 1940, John R. Tunis described Mack as "an institution . . . the first citizen of Philadelphia." During the war GI's trapped disguised German soldiers passing through their lines by asking if they had heard that "Connie Mack pitched a shutout against Brooklyn." What American would not know this was nonsense? In rare disputes on the field umpires would respectfully come over to the dugout for discussion with the old manager. Later, in the early TV age, when Mack might view a game from his tower office, A's officials would bluff umps by saying that the elderly owner had seen a play on television and disagreed with the ruling. Mack was, said one analyst, "one of the most popular figures sports has ever known . . . unique in the game's annals."

But the public approbation could not hide from insiders, and in time from the fans, the deterioration of Mack's mind. In 1946 he traded future Hall of Fame third baseman George Kell to the Detroit Tigers. Wish Egan, who made the deal, stated that "I was a little ashamed of myself for taking advantage of the old man." On the field players would ignore incorrect signals. The coaches would override obvious mistakes. "My goodness, yes," Mack would say in acknowledgment. Things got worse. His memory failed, and by the late forties he would call out the names of stars of bygone days—Baker! Foxx!—to pinch-hit.

Sportswriters commented euphemistically on these "mental lapses." Mack refused to quit. "If I did," he said, "I'd die in two weeks." In a widely read sympathetic article in *Life* magazine in 1948, Bob Considine wrote that both players and coaches noted their manager's errors of judgment. The same year Mack exploded in public and fired pitcher Nelson Potter in front of the dugout as he came off the mound. He now occasionally broke into stormy emotions, reduced to tears. The manager was "off the beam." Historian David Voigt described him as "an anachronism." Mack's downward slide and the bickering of his family, wrote a commentator, began to accustom fans "to sudden, sometimes calamitous moves." Many people no longer ignored his senility.

At the same time Mack had constructed a curiously interesting team, assembling draftees, waiver players, and promising youngsters in his usual fashion. In 1945 and 1946 they finished last. In 1947, 1948, and 1949, however, these bargain counter discoveries, though they wound up only fifth, fourth, and fifth, respectively, were in the thick of the American League race for much of the season. They collapsed in August and September as their lack of reserve strength became critical. To some extent their modest prowess accounted for the high attendance. Nonetheless, Mack overestimated their talents and his ability to make up for their deficiencies by clever strategy.

The year 1950 was Mack's fiftieth as the Athletics' manager. He was eighty-seven, but baseball in April is a siren, and the spring of the sport is a season of eternal youth. Should Mack retire? He would not. His team had shown some mettle. As one writer put it, "The will o' the wisp that danced ahead each spring" captivated the old man. Mack would manage and predicted a pennant for his "Ath-el-etics." Roy and Earle agreed, and squelched the doubts of their half brother. The *Elephant Trail*, the A's newsletter, expected the club's attendance to pass the million mark for the first time. The magazine urged fans to send in ideas to boost the gate to that figure but asserted that patrons would come out in any event. The A's would be contending for the pennant, and Mack would be receiving nationwide honors throughout the season. Honoring Mack's golden anniversary as manager, a motorcade from City Hall to the park began the festivities on opening day.

Things went downhill from there. The year proved disastrous as the A's tumbled deep into the second division and stayed there. Bill Veeck, a notable professional baseball figure, was asked if a rumored purchase of the A's involved him. "They haven't got a ball club," he said. "All you get is the ball park." In June the family's internal squabbling, intensified by bad baseball, became more serious and more public. The youngest son and the Shibes failed in their attempt to force Mack's retirement. They did succeed, however, in removing the indifferent Earle as assistant manager. Voting his faction's stock against his father for the first time, Connie, Jr., made his brother take a job with the franchise's farm system.

The crisis came later in the 1950 season when the A's were in last place. The youngest son agreed to a plan that would permit Roy and Earle to buy out the other shareholders. If they could not come up with the money, Connie, Jr., had the right to buy them out. In either event the senior Mack would remain as titular head.

Both sides competed to raise money. Local businessmen wanted to buy stock in the team. The newspapers reported that Phillies owner Bob Carpenter refused a half interest in Shibe Park and its concessions. Connie, Jr., talked to James Clark, president of the Eagles, and the press said that wealthy builder John McShain wanted a piece of the franchise.

Roy and Earle triumphed. They needed approximately $1.75 million to buy the 60 percent of the stock owned by the other side. To finance the transaction the brothers took a portentous step. They mortgaged Shibe Park, the franchise's single real asset.

Appraisers valued the park at $436,000 and the land at $250,000. But the stadium made money, including $40,000 from the Eagles and 10 cents per head from the Phillies' gates, which in 1950 would generate over $100,000. Concessions were also important. "Following a careful analysis of the value of Shibe Park and its earning record," Connecticut General Life Insurance Company issued Roy and Earle a $1.75 million loan over ten years. In addition to the mortgage on the park, the A's turned over to Connecticut General the rent they got from the Phillies. A representative of the insurance company joined the A's board. To raise more cash Roy and Earle leased the concessions to Jacobs Brothers, a pioneer food service organization, who called their new operation Pennsport Services. Thus the Athletics' dependence on outsiders increased. Leasing also occurred because concessions head

Bob Schroeder had died in May 1950 and because his assistant, young Connie, no longer worked for the franchise.

These steps changed the club's business. Concessions made big profits and had expanded beyond Shibe Park. A separate Athletics corporation sold wares at the ball park, at the stadium of Temple University, and at other places. Now the A's got a pared-down amount from concessions and at the same time gave to Connecticut General some of their other income. Thus, in mortgaging Shibe Park, Roy and Earle took on a $250,000 interest burden at a time when their cash flow was declining. Much hung on the elder brothers' ability to draw people to Shibe Park. The A's had based their 1950 budget on 800,000 admissions from which they estimated earnings of $800,000. But when Roy and Earle took over in August, the A's were thirty-five games out of first, "locked in a death battle," the *Bulletin* wrote, "with the St. Louis Browns for last place." The A's won, finishing eighth and drawing 310,000 fans, 500,000 off their budgeted number, 700,000 off the million patrons they had wished for.

Worse, Bob Carpenter's Phillies won the first Philadelphia pennant in twenty years, drawing over 1.2 million. While Roy and Earle sat in the oval office figuring out how much they were in the red, applications for World Series tickets poured into the Phillies' Shibe Park headquarters. In mid-September Carpenter announced the rules his club would use to accept ticket requests from "the general public." In two days the Phillies received 500,000 applications from all over the country for a maximum of 92,000 available tickets. The post office sold 18,000 money orders made out to the Phillies and shipped thirty bags of mail to Shibe Park.

Part of the Athletics' problem, though not the Phillies', was that baseball attendance began to fall off in 1950 after the postwar rush and did not stop until the latter part of the decade. The consequences for the A's were dire. At the end of the season, the Athletics were deeply indebted and Shibe Park heavily mortgaged.

The most knowledgeable commentator on the family's fortunes wrote that Roy and Earle forced Connie to retire in October 1950. As the abysmal year unfolded, patrons proclaimed, with Connie, Jr., that the senior Mack should go. In the seventeen years prior to 1950, the A's had finished in the first division only once. "He should know the parade has passed him by," said one. "Why doesn't he step down and give a younger man a chance?" Philadelphians voted with their feet. Roy and Earle totaled the books and recognized that their younger brother had been right. Their father must retire. "The fans would never be content with any other move." After fifty years Philadelphians finally lost patience with Mack.

Sportswriters who had snickered in private about his failings now flooded newspapers and magazines with platitudes about the octagenarian manager. Only the communist *Daily Worker* criticized Mack, a fact that highlighted the vapidity of sports journalism.

The franchise was sick, but the elder brothers tried to restore its health. Connie remained the nominal president. Roy and Earle did everything they could to capitalize on his name. In 1951 they opened the Elephant Room under the Lehigh Avenue stands behind first base. The Macks wanted to attract "baseball men" and filled it with memorabilia from the Athletics' great days. To replace Mack as manager, the older sons appointed the popular Philadelphia figure Jimmie Dykes, a stalwart of the dynasty of the twenties and early thirties. Arthur Ehlers, a crafty baseball executive, took over as general manager. In 1951 the results were marginally better, with the A's coming in sixth. Then in 1952 they finished a surprising fourth and drew over six hundred thousand. As Roy Mack later commented, however, the middling prosperity of the team did not depend on management. Robert Clayton Shantz made the A's solvent.

"Little Bobby" Shantz was a left-handed pitcher, five foot six, 140 pounds. Born in Pottstown, Pennsylvania, he played semipro ball in the Frankford section of Philadelphia after the war. In the late 1940s, he recalled, for the price of "maybe a few car tokens to Shibe Park and home," he signed with the A's. In 1949 and 1950 he compiled so-so statistics and labored under Connie Mack's suspicion that he was too small to win. In 1951, however, Shantz displayed real ability and had an 18–10 record when managed by Jimmie Dykes. The next year he won twenty-four games and lost only seven. The American League named him its Most Valuable Player.

Shantz was a likable and modest young man whose "diminutive stature," as the sportswriters put it, gained him the affection of fans everywhere, but particularly those in Philadelphia. Ray Kelly of the *Bulletin* wrote:

> Atop the Shibe Park pitching tee
> the village hero stands . . .
> the shrimp has muscles in his arms
> as tough as rubber bands.

The Year the Yankees Lost the Pennant, later made into the hit musical *Damn Yankees*, was an early 1950s novel about middle-aged Joe Boyd, who signs a baseball pact with the devil. Set in the then future of 1958, the novel has Boyd win the pennant for the Washington Senators. In one scene at Shibe Park the Senators face Shantz in "the late afternoon of a great career." In the ninth inning Boyd homers over the right field wall to ruin "the diminutive portsider's" no-hitter and win the game for Washington. But Shantz is such an icon that Boyd spends a sleepless night, agonizing about what he has done.

Shantz's crowds in Philadelphia in 1952 averaged almost eighteen thousand. When he did not pitch, the A's drew under eight thousand. His sixteen Shibe Park appearances accounted for almost 44 percent of the Athletics' home gate. In the 1952 All-Star game at Shibe Park Shantz pitched the fifth inning against the National League and struck out the side—Whitey Lockman, Jackie Robinson, and Stan Musial. The hometown crowd, said Shantz, cheered as if he had won a World Series game. Then, the inning over, the umps called the game because of rain. The rainout left the city's fans believing that Shantz would have gone on to duplicate or overshadow Carl Hubbell's 1934 All-Star feat of striking out five batters in a row. Later in 1952, on August 5, Shantz won his twentieth victory before a packed Shibe Park house. The *Inquirer* editorialized that the triumph brought to "countless Philadelphians . . . the comfortable assurance that, no matter what else was happening, the world was a pretty good place to live in. Something about Shantz moved thousands to have some minor part in the occasion." The editorial concluded that "there'll not be another such time in Philadelphia for many days."

The *Inquirer* was right. Shantz won four more games, and then in late September a pitched ball fractured his wrist. He never had another successful year in the city. In 1953 the A's dropped to seventh place and drew 362,000. In 1954 they were last with 305,000. If only Shantz had stayed healthy, said Roy Mack later, the club would have remained in the black. After a few years of precarious profits, the Macks were broke once more.

The problem, again, was not just the team but more family squabbling that hurt the franchise in public. Allied so long as they competed
with Connie, Jr., and the Shibes, Roy and Earle now feuded openly.
When Earle and his wife separated, he moved into the small suite that
the franchise provided for him off the A's clubhouse in the stadium.
Still in charge of the front office, Roy turned the water off so that his
brother could not bathe or use the toilet. They sniped at each other
from different Shibe Park offices, to and from which reporters scurried
in their quest for stories.

As early as the fall of 1951, after they took over, the brothers denied
tales they would sell the team. In truth, however, only Roy wanted to
stay. In the middle of the poor 1953 season he countered rumors of a
sale by saying, "We have been here for fifty-two years and will be here
for fifty-two more." The club was "part of Philadelphia . . . as much a
part of the community as Fairmount Park." But Earle wanted to get out.
The brothers never had a united front, and conflicting stories attributed
to their father worsened the situation. By the fall of 1953 lack of money
and internal strife were tearing the Macks apart. Pressure also came
from the American League. The Athletics' tiny attendance affected the
receipts visiting clubs got from trips to Philadelphia. As had happened
with the Phillies ten years before, other owners demanded change. The
powerful voice of the Yankees pushed for the transfer of the A's to Kansas City, where New York had a farm club.

At the start of the 1954 season knowledgeable sportsmen talked
about the Athletics' debts and their failure to meet their Shibe Park
mortgage. Then, in the middle of June, the Macks advised Philadelphia
mayor Joseph Clark that they would have to sell or shift the franchise
unless the Athletics' attendance leapt dramatically. Roy and Earle hoped
that they could turn public feeling to the Athletics' advantage, but the
mayor was an insubstantial friend.

Clark was not interested in baseball. Professional sports in the city
were a low priority for him. He did form a Save the A's Committee in
July, but it had one hundred members and fifteen subcommittees. The
mayor also said that he personally rooted for the Phillies and that he
was "no socialist"—government would not subsidize sports. Clark
thought that his committee might come up with some long-term solu-
tions to the Athletics' woes. But publicists immediately attempted to
encourage more people to turn out to the park. The Macks needed

550,000 patrons to meet their obligations and stay in the city. The committee tried to boost attendance for the remaining games.

As Save the A's mobilized its forces, the newspapers asked Philadelphians to express their views. The torrential response surprised the papers and provided arresting insights into the fans' minds.

Appropriately enough, a few letter writers recalled better days. "As a small boy," said one, "we saw the opening of Shibe Park, and we remember the fans, like swarming bees clinging to the outside of summer trolleys." "I learned to love baseball and the A's as a boy following Connie Mack's great team of 1929–32," said another. "I don't want the A's to move from Philadelphia." "Save the team," wrote still another, "that so often brought a thrill of pride in being a Philadelphian." "It would be like losing something very dear." The most poignant mail noted how significant baseball was "for the kids." "My son is an A's fan," wrote one father now too ill to go to the park. "I took him to his first game when he was five years old to see Babe Ruth. The future of all things is in children."

More often, however, letters displayed the rage and frustration that loyal rooters felt about the franchise. For the first time the public commented on the park and neighborhood. The *Inquirer* reported that parking stirred "bitter complaints." Driving to Twenty-first and Lehigh "exhausted" patrons. One said, "Get out of that undesirable neighborhood and get a bigger home, where parking will be no problem." Fans wanted "spacious acreage." Motorists did not want to endure "intimidation" or "gangster mob damage" to their cars. Inside the stadium, they demanded "modernistic improvements," escalators, better lighting, roomier seats, more rest rooms, and drinking fountains. Finally, fans complained about the concessions, angry about the "ridiculous" price of hot dogs and soda.

To the extent that the stadium and its community were an issue Mayor Clark did not help. The city at this time was collecting land and generating construction capital for projects that would revitalize Philadelphia's industrial base and central business district. Other towns interested in the Athletics—Kansas City, Minneapolis, and San Francisco—proposed bond issues to finance new playing fields. But Clark did not think that such bond issues should assist sports facilities. Although he came to accept the principle, he evinced little enthusiasm.

In any event the stadium was not really an issue. As the Athletics' publicity director asked: If parking kept people away from the A's, why didn't they desert the Phillies (who were drawing twice the fans)? Letters emphasized that the real problem was the Macks and the teams they fielded. The impatience with Connie Mack that had surfaced in 1950 now turned to rage, mainly directed against Roy and Earle. "Get rid of the Macks," said the letters. Connie Mack had "surrendered to the years" and a new generation could not "rest on memories" or listen to "sentimental drivel about . . . past glories." The Mack dynasty had "overstayed its welcome by about twenty years." For the preceding two decades the Macks had run "a bush league circus." One man wrote that he was "tired of watching a franchise made up of second string ball players." Another said the Macks had done little "to earn the fans' support," consistently fielding second-division teams and selling off good players. Under Bob Carpenter, said one writer, "the Phillies star" had risen, and Philadelphians need not accept the Macks' "take it or lump it" attitude. To the Macks' repeated statement that fans "will not support a winning team," wrote one exasperated rooter, let them compare "the cellar years to the pennant years." "The Macks," concluded one perceptive citizen, "are on the same path as all venerable one-man family businesses." "Family expansion" proves ruinous. A disgruntled father who had faithfully gone to see the A's through good times and bad and had made fans of his children was more blunt: "Roy and Earle Mack ain't worth a shit."

These sentiments affected the Save the A's campaign. In early July the club needed a turnout of thirteen thousand per game, as opposed to the approximately six thousand it was then drawing. But as each home date passed with much ballyhoo in the papers, the average draw required at Shibe Park for the remaining games climbed, as a mere three, four, or five thousand patrons turned out. By the end of July the Save the A's effort neared collapse. The committee reported apathy toward the franchise in the business community. The Mack family had "a public relations problem to solve," and "a struggle in the family for power" accentuated the problem. The Macks rejected the committee's advice that well-to-do sportsmen be permitted to buy into the franchise and that the team search for playing talent.

The 1950s were an era of change for baseball as franchises shifted for the first time in over half a century and expanded to the south and west. Many patriarchal sports businesses crumbled. A simple pattern emerged as the weaker team in the two-team cities moved elsewhere and people questioned the facilities built between 1910 and 1920. The Browns left St. Louis, the Braves left Boston, the Giants and Dodgers left New York. Attendance problems heightened the owners' concerns about the old ball parks in declining neighborhoods with antiquated features, poor parking, and bad transportation. Shibe Park survived longer than most of these stadiums, but the A's would leave Philadelphia.

Urban areas without franchises easily stirred up the civic pride and public funding necessary to entice teams. This combination was equally necessary to rescue existing enfeebled clubs, but it was not apparent in many cities with established franchises. The willingness of cities to aid the teams they had was minimal. Early on in the debate over the A's, the *Bulletin*'s Hugh Brown analyzed the club's "deeprooted" miseries. The stadium needed "a complete refurbishing" inside, and outside "swifter and more direct transit" and "extensive parking." In examining the Athletics' specific problems, Brown said that "no city, no matter how large and charitable, can be whipped or cajoled into suppporting a team that has finished in the cellar eight times in the last thirteen years."

In early August Chicago businessman Arnold Johnson, who was connected to the Yankee farm team in Kansas City, offered to buy the A's for $3.375 million and move them to Kansas City. As completed in early November, the deal paid the three Macks—Connie, Sr., Earle, and Roy—about $1.5 million. In addition, Johnson assumed the team's debt, estimated between $400,000 and $800,000, mainly to the Jacobs Brothers concessionaires, who had taken over park sales and lent the Macks money. Finally, Johnson liquidated the stadium mortgage, standing at about $1.2 million. The A's had paid off $500,000 of the mortgage, but at the cost of indebting themselves to the vendors.

The transfer of the franchise honored the ability of baseball capitalists to profit from the American commitment to the sport. One cannot help but remark on the contrast between the attraction of the game for millions of ordinary people and the avarice and imperfection of those who ran it. What is striking is not that the institutions of baseball were part of an acquisitive society, but that in the affection of fans the game transcended American culture.

Roy and Earle Mack took over a weak franchise in 1950 for $2,000 a share. In four years they had run it into the ground, dismissed advice that might have helped them, demanded that someone else save them.

Assisted by a spiritless Mayor Clark, however, their incompetence was self-serving. When they sold out to Johnson, they did so at an effective price of $2,250 a share.

Arnold Johnson's even greater gain demonstrated adeptness at joining civic pride to his real estate manipulation of the Philadelphia and Kansas City ball parks, the latter of which was Johnson's major asset. He purchased the Philadelphia A's with little or no outlay of cash. Stock in the new club paid off Roy Mack. Connie Mack's money came from Johnson's sale of the minor league Kansas City park, to Kansas City. (The city then rebuilt the facility to meet major league standards and leased it back to Johnson.) The new franchise's profits gradually liquidated the Athletics' debt to the Jacobs Brothers.

Bob Carpenter of the Phillies put up the cash in the transaction. After a series of negotiations he bought Shibe Park for $1.7 million. The money satisfied the mortgage on the ball park and paid off Earle Mack. Carpenter recalled that Johnson was a slick speculator surviving by the skin of his teeth. He picked up the Athletics' franchise on the strength of Kansas City's willingness to underwrite a major league baseball team.

In the summer of 1954, before Johnson made his purchase, Carpenter said he did not want "to buy the park under any circumstances." He let it be known that the stadium was a dubious real estate investment and elaborately looked for land for a new field in West Philadelphia that would have six thousand parking spaces. No one, said Carpenter, could renovate the present stadium. It would cost $1 million to modernize, and enlarging the seating capacity was impossible. At one point, when it looked as if the A's sale would not go through, he said that purchasing a stadium had not interested him but that he "wouldn't have had any alternative."

The Phillies were leasing the field until 1957, which gave them a short breathing period. Apparently Johnson suggested a new lease. It called for twenty-cents-a-head rental, double the old rate, plus payment of maintenance expenses that the A's had previously carried. Staying in the park without buying would be very expensive. In addition, the value of Carpenter's franchise would rise if the Athletics left. If Johnson would not take the Athletics unless Carpenter bought Shibe Park, was it worth sabotaging the move? He did not covet a ball park but had few options. Indeed the price of the property was just what Connecticut General had figured four years before, appraising the site as valuable and income-producing. Later, as part of the franchise shift, Carpenter bought the property from the Philadelphia American League franchise.

Johnson's initial offer to the Macks energized Philadelphia business and sports leaders. Harry Sylk, head of Sun Ray Drugs, pointed out that "what we stand to lose is not only the A's but the whole American League." Prominent realtor Albert M. Greenfield added that the "loss of the team would be a blow to Philadelphia's prestige."

In August and September 1954, before Johnson concluded the transaction, various local businessmen tried to purchase the Athletics. They focused on Roy Mack, a weak man who yet seemed determined to keep the team in Philadelphia, as opposed to Earle, who saw no alternative to leaving. No Philadelphia plans had panned out, however, when the American League owners approved the sale of the franchise to Kansas City in mid-October. But Roy Mack was not sure. The day before the deal was final, the Macks sold the A's to a local syndicate. Two weeks later, amid a flurry of rumors, charges and countercharges by various members of the Mack family—including Connie, Sr., and his wife—the American League met again in New York and vetoed the move to keep the A's in the city. Led again by the Yankees and conscious of their profits, the owners turned down a plea from Connie Mack himself, whom a chauffeur had taken up from Philadelphia. "The Grand Old Man" was a useful symbol for the sports entrepreneurs, but not a person to listen to in his dotage. Sentiment did not govern the league. The Kansas City move stood.

Ten days later a remnant of the rejected syndicate raced Johnson to the senior Macks Germantown apartment to buy Connie's share of the club. Apparently this group wanted to obtain his stock and force the American League to keep the Athletics in Philadelphia. Whether such a move would have worked is doubtful, but Mack refused four proffered checks from the locals in favor of a single check and some smooth talk from Johnson. "There must be some less excruciating way to spend money," said one of the rejected principals, "than trying to buy the A's." In the end all the Macks broke down and wept.

New York Times columnist Art Daley wrote that Connie Mack "gave Philadelphia fans a pride in the Athletics. Without him there is nothing left but a dwindling force of habit." The new Athletics spent thirteen years in Kansas City before they picked up again for Oakland, California. Although they drew large crowds and enriched their owners, the

Athletics performed worse in the Midwest than they had in their last twenty years in Philadelphia. The Kansas City A's were nicknamed the "Yankee Farm Club," as Johnson scandalously traded with his friends in New York. The transfer assisted the dominance of the Yankees through the 1950s and also upped the American League's income.

The removal sealed the ascendancy of New York over Philadelphia during that part of the century when they were the two leading U.S. cities. In defeating McGraw's Giants and the Yankees of Ruth and Gehrig, the A's had established Philadelphia's credentials as an urban competitor of New York. But by the time the Yankees swept the Phillies in 1950, Philadelphia was less significant. The transformation of the A's into a midwestern affiliate of New York ended an era of great rivalry between the two towns. New York writers had good reason for their comfortable, smug feeling that the transfer was an unmixed blessing.

Back in Philadelphia in early 1955 two trucks carried off memorabilia to Kansas City from the Elephant Room at the stadium. Johnson planned to display them for a couple of years. For the time being Connie Mack was driven to and from his old tower office with the benign consent of Bob Carpenter. But Mack was going downhill rapidly and died just over a year later.

Another less noticed death more fully embodied the minor tragedy of the Philadelphia Athletics in the 1950s. "Yits" Crompton lived in the neighborhood and came to the stadium as an A's batboy when he was fourteen. Later he was a fixture in the park as clubhouse custodian. He followed the A's to Kansas City in 1955 but returned to North Penn a year later, disconsolate and unemployed. On August 23, 1956, he killed himself in his home around the corner from Shibe Park. He left a note: "I can't get baseball out of my life."

Some time afterward, two years before his own death, Roy Mack reminisced: "People always say to me 'I wish the A's were still at Twenty-first and Lehigh.' " Years later many old-time fans agreed, as they tried to figure out how Philadelphia lost the franchise of the hundred-thousand-dollar infield and of Simmons, Foxx, Grove, and Cochrane and got stuck with the worst team in baseball.

• Part III •

1953–1976

• 8 •
Connie Mack Stadium,
1953–1970

In 1940, around the time Connie Mack bought majority stock in the A's, Philadelphia judge Harry McDevitt, a baseball fan and friend of Mack, thought about changing the name of Shibe Park. At the beginning of the 1941 season, McDevitt hung a large sign bearing the words "Connie Mack Stadium" over the main entrance. The alteration marked Connie Mack Day, the May celebration of the manager's fortieth anniversary in the city. Mack resisted because the Shibe family still participated in the franchise. The building officially remained Shibe Park. The sign stayed, however, and some people referred to the field by the new title. In 1953, with the Shibes out of the picture and Mack himself only a figurehead, his sons formally renamed the park, desperate for any favorable publicity that would raise attendance. With a public flourish at the opening of the season, they put a new foot-high plate—CONNIE MACK STADIUM—over the original inscription. Under the plate, however, SHIBE PARK was still written in stone. Old-timers refused to acknowledge the new name.

A year and a half later the A's and the Macks had gone. Reporters said that new owner, Bob Carpenter, might change the name again, to Phillies Ball Park. But "in deference to the Grand Old Man of Baseball" Carpenter kept Mack's name. When Mack died at ninety-four in early 1956, prominent sportsmen sought suitable tributes to him and reinforced Carpenter's sentiment. The city council proclaimed a Connie Mack Week and urged all Philadelphians "to play a part in perpetuating his memory." A Connie Mack Memorial Committee decided to erect a statue and asked fans to contribute to make Connie Mack "live for more than a hundred years . . . in memory."

The drive prospered. A year later in Reyburn Park, still affectionately known as the Square, across the street from the stadium bearing Mack's name, officials unveiled a ten-ton monument on opening night. Connie

Mack stood in a familiar pose, waving a scorecard in front of his dugout. On the base of the statue was inscribed a series of homilies about good sportsmanship, Mack's "Sportsman's Creed." At the same time the city council renamed the park and adjoining Funfield Recreation Center "Connie Mack Park and Recreation Center." Forgetting the scandals that beset the end of Mayor John Reyburn's term in 1910 and 1911, one Republican councilman protested that the change unfairly "discredited" a former mayor. People persisted in calling it "the Square." But few complained about the city's "lasting tribute to its most famous baseball personality." The dedication occurred, the newspapers said, "in an air of reverence." Various dignitaries and members of the Mack family attended. The *Inquirer* reported that "to future generations" Connie Mack's pose would be as distinctive as the statue of Billy Penn that sat atop City Hall.

In the stadium itself the Phillies built some new offices, moving from their former headquarters in downtown Philadelphia. George Harrison, the Phillies' treasurer, occupied the tower. Carpenter, however, did not know what to do with his recently acquired grounds, whose defects, from parking to rest rooms, fans had vigorously attacked when the A's left. Ten years earlier, when he bought the Phillies, Carpenter had talked about building his own stadium and had looked at a parcel of land near Fairmount Park, at Thirty-third and Columbia, west of Shibe Park. When dickering with Arnold Johnson about the purchase of the property in 1954, Carpenter considered West Philadelphia. But his primary concern was the team. Carpenter did not much care about where it played, or about the park, which he later described as "just another piece of real estate." He would not pick up and leave but rather would be content to let inertia take over. Because of his wealth, he was not overly troubled that the Phillies might lose money playing in an aging facility.

After Carpenter arrived in 1954–1955, the Phillies painted the stadium, added some box seats, and completed repairs that the Macks had deferred. Expenses totaled some four hundred thousand dollars. In 1956 the franchise replaced a 1941 scoreboard in front of the wall in right-center field and topped the new one with a large Longine's clock. Carpenter also began to sell outfield wall space for advertising, the first time billboards appeared at the park. These changes aside, Carpenter altered his building little. He did think about the grounds and imported his grass seed and sod from Kentucky. In 1955 he restricted fans to the outfield after a game and prevented them from trespassing on the diamond. As one writer put it, the "age-old custom of hundreds of kids running the bases after the game" had ended. As late as 1969 he shortened the distance to the center field wall to 410 feet by constructing a fence between the scoreboard and the left field fence. A shorter center field would help his hitters, chief among them slugger Dick Allen.

In the long run, Carpenter recalled many years later, he was conscious that the Phillies could not be "a paying proposition" in Connie Mack Stadium. He recollected three issues. An unspoken or euphemistically stated complaint was first: the "undesirable" neighborhood. "Undesirable" and "unattractive" were code words for "black." Powerful demographic changes occurred in northern cities in the postwar period, as working-class whites moved to the suburbs and black families replaced them. Around Connie Mack Stadium this transition came in the mid-1960s, but had begun much earlier. If one can attribute obvious motives to the Phillies in the absence of direct evidence, they feared that their patrons would not come to a black neighborhood. Whatever the legitimacy of qualms about safety, the franchise in a larger sense did not want itself linked to an old, "low-class" community. "Let's just say," said Carpenter, "we knew things weren't getting any better."

The second issue was that he could not significantly increase Connie Mack Stadium's capacity. Carpenter worried that a thirty-three-thousand seat park was not enough in the modern era.

Finally and most important, the franchise thought about urban transport. Years after the demise of the park, everybody who went there could tell a story about cars, crowded streets, and parking. These matters constantly troubled Phillies executives, if not Carpenter, whose chauffeur brought him to and from the park from his home in Wilmington.

The street congestion, pollution, and other difficulties that went with the automobile's popularity had distressed city planners since the early part of the century. But experts also urged that cheap, mass-produced vehicles might alleviate some urban troubles by more rapidly moving commuters around and might solve problems of overcrowding by decentralizing the population. The car moreover eliminated worries about horse manure, a major sanitary hazard. As the automobile spurred the growth of suburbs, many officials argued that it was quieter than the trolley and were happy to free municipalities from the extortionist hold of transit companies.

This did not happen all at once. The trolleys carried most people until after World War I. Then the bus emerged as a significant mass transit adjunct. More flexible than the trolley, the bus demanded street maintenance identical to that for the automobile. When the streetcar gave way to the bus, it often demonstrated the power of the automotive industry but also indicated that the public preferred mass transit closer to the individual car. People could tailor the use of buses and hire them for specific outings. Even so, by the late twenties the auto was replacing all mass transit as the desired way to travel. Then the car again became something of a luxury during the Depression; and World War II suspended automobile production and rationed gasoline. For a time dependence on the car slowed. In the postwar era, however, autos brought more and more customers to the stadium. The growing number of night games and the longer time of games may have contributed to the use of the car: an afternoon trolley ride from the office was no longer convenient. But fundamentally, people were using their cars for all their travel, and at the ball field they wanted a place to park. More than anything else the nation's commitment to the automobile determined the future of the field.

A large five-hundred-car lot, Sports Parking, operated across the street from the stadium between Twenty-first and Twenty-second on Lehigh. Smaller lots sprouted up wherever they could. But these ancillary businesses were inadequate in comparison with the ten-thousand-space garage that the franchise wanted even in the mid-fifties. As time went on, the demand increased and existing resources became less adequate. Moreover, Connie Mack Stadium was near none of the limited access arteries, particularly the newly constructed Schuylkill Expressway. Frustrating travel over busy streets irritated fans even before they got to the stadium and began to search for "a spot."

Nonetheless, Carpenter concentrated on his ball club and temporized about these varied problems during a period when everyone was discussing a new location. The Phillies did try to meet the immediate demand for parking. For years baseball entrepreneurs had coveted the Square, now Connie Mack Park. From the late thirties on, the A's had attempted to secure its use for automobiles. But the Square, the local civic association argued, was the last remnant of the spacious ground once surrounding the area from Huntingdon to Lehigh. Time and again united neighborhood opposition put down plans to turn it into a lot. "Blacktopping" three acres of the park would make spaces for four hundred cars, and the Phillies pushed this idea again in early 1959, even though it would have encircled Mack's statue with automobiles. Although the maneuver failed, the team continued to seek space in the area.

The franchise negotiated for the square block between Twenty-first and Twenty-second, Lehigh and Somerset. A parking garage on this parcel would accommodate seven thousand vehicles and resolve the parking problem. But the Phillies could not agree with Penn Fruit, which had a large store there, and the deal fell through. Minor adjustments occurred. In 1959 a small piece of land expanded the 500-car lot to 850 spaces. Some neighborhood businesses, friendly to the Phillies, opened their customer lots to fans during nonbusiness hours. Neighbors eager to make a buck rented as few as three, four, or ten spaces on small bits of ground.

The slow transformation of the community into something resembling a vast open-air garage had its own irony. The incremental growth of spaces did not answer the automobile question but did contribute to the undesirabilty of the district. The immediate neighborhood more and more resembled a land of vacant space periodically filled up with cars. Its appearance confirmed the view that the Phillies ought to give up Connie Mack Stadium.

Politicians rejected as too costly a proposal to construct parking facilities at the Pennsylvania Railroad yards at the nearby North Philadelphia Station. Then some Fairmount Park acreage near Thirty-third Street in Strawberry Mansion was suggested for "hard surfacing" for automobile spaces. Shuttle buses would take fans to the park. Officials vetoed this idea, just as they had the one about the railroad yards, but made parking available at the Robin Hood Dell concert center in Fairmount Park, some fourteen blocks from the stadium. Express buses went from the Dell to Twenty-first and Lehigh. This plan foundered when only nine motorists used three buses, and three other buses were sent back to the car barn. People wanted to park their cars *and* to walk to the game.

For fans intent on this last sort of automobile travel the franchise circulated clear maps with the location of parking lots. The Phillies played up the advantages of "on street" parking "almost everywhere" in the stadium area, but also emphasized the virtues of mass transit. In the early 1950s the team promoted group sales and transportation to the stadium. A Phillies official contacted industrial firms, businesses, clubs, and fraternal organizations. The franchise worked out seating and ticket plans, planned rail or bus service, and looked after a party's needs at the game. In the early 1950s buses on the "Whiz Kids Express" made round-trip runs regularly from Camden, New Jersey, and Upper Darby, a "near" suburb and central transportation node. The buses enabled anyone to get an inexpensive ride to the park and back. After the time of the Whiz Kids, the buses simply became the Phillies Express. Busing also appealed to private groups in the suburbs. American Legion Posts, lodges, and community associations all liked baseball but wanted to avoid the private parking system. They frequently put together their own mass transportation, and the Phillies arranged parking.

The franchise also ordered special buses at the end of games to take fans to the Broad Street subway (at Broad and Lehigh) and other connecting points. The city rerouted traffic and created one-way streets in the neighborhood to expedite bus service as well as auto traffic. Inevitably the buses, the bus parking, and the network of one-way streets added to North Penn's unattractiveness.

For most people the unattractiveness evidenced itself in on-street parking adventures. These began in the 1930s when neighborhood children, for a fee, jumped on the running boards of automobiles and directed motorists to parking places. Or the kids stationed themselves near some open curb space and charged motorists who parked there to "guard" their vehicles. From the 1940s to the late 1950s fans paid first ten cents and later as much as one or two dollars to have their cars "watched." "Hey, mister! Watch your car?" the refrain went. Customers dug into their pockets, afraid that if they did not comply the youngsters would slash their tires. The cops regularly arrested "watchers," and the papers just as often, to no avail, lambasted the "shakedown fee" extorted by the "leeches."

By the late 1950s politicians, baseball men, and the press agreed that no one could salvage the area for baseball. Attempts to make a trip to Connie Mack Stadium pleasant had failed. Negative sentiment gained credibility from a 1957 "Municipal Sports Stadium Study" that the city commissioned. The study concluded that Connie Mack Stadium had no future because of its age, parking problems, and location. In April 1959, on the fiftieth anniversary of the park, Ed Pollock celebrated the event in his column, "Playing the Game," by saying that Shibe Park was "outmoded" and "inadequate." Five years later the *Bulletin* editorialized that the stadium had "some hopeless aspects about it, notably its poor

parking facilities and the lack of attractive forms of public transport."
That same year Phillies outfielder Wes Covington spoke to local civic
groups of the Phillies' need to leave Connie Mack Stadium. Interviewed
from what the reporter described as "the dungeon called the Phillies
clubhouse," Covington argued that Connie Mack Stadium was worthy
only of a minor league club. In agreement, the *Greater Philadelphia Magazine* called the stadium "a relic," an "ancient park" on "its last legs."
Four years later Sandy Grady, in his column, "Man About Sports," described opening night 1968 as being "brutish and cruel." The crowd
was "surly," and the ballplayers had a "desperate edge." Connie Mack
Stadium looked "dusty and disreputable." Fans "shuffled [in] . . .
grandstand corridors . . . [that] look like they haven't been swept since
Connie Mack left." In another part of the ball yard a kid mugged a
newsman calling in his story from a phone booth. At the end of the year
another *Bulletin* editorial theorized that the second worst attendance in
twenty-three years resulted from "the inconveniences of Connie Mack
Stadium [that] discourage all but the hardiest fans."

Where would the team go? As early as 1922, writing about comparatively new parks, the *Sporting News* remarked on parking and maintenance problems. The *Sporting News* also grumbled about cramped
seating and primitive rest rooms, annoyances that though less frequently mentioned later also provoked the wrath of Philadelphians. But
management did not replace the ball parks built in the second decade
of the century. Construction and real estate costs mounted with the
prosperity of the twenties, and franchises avoided revolutionary improvements. Then the Depression and war reduced the owners' ability
to refurbish their playing fields. By the 1950s stadium costs had increased nearly beyond the reach of private capital. Locating a suitable
piece of property had become almost impossible. The only quick answers to these concerns came in cities that did not have major league
teams and, in the 1950s and 1960s, eagerly subsidized professional
sports and assembled land for modern playing fields. But in cities
where professional sport was a tradition, the owners, who later came to
show a mind-boggling greediness, only slowly learned how to use their
control of franchises to get government subsidies for their businesses.
Urban politicians later came to respond with alacrity to the most outra-
geous demands of sports entrepreneurs. But in the fifties cities like Phil-

adelphia, with established teams, shrank at the notion of municipal financing for sports and fought over sites; and men like Carpenter were relatively ungrasping. The Phillies might have to vacate Connie Mack Stadium, but no one knew who would pay for a move, where a new park could be built, or what it would look like.

Sports entrepreneurs in baseball and football first met with civic authorities about municipal funding for a new stadium in 1953. They got nowhere. When the A's left a year later, Mayor Joseph Clark evinced little interest in public financing, which he used, for example, for a new food distribution center. The city-sponsored "Municipal Sports Stadium Study" of 1957 clarified the need for civic money, but practical funding was another matter. As late as 1959 Jim Tate, then city council president, announced that although he "desperately" wanted the Phillies to stay in Philadelphia, he could not recommend public financing of a ball park.

Carpenter was frustrated, but his geniality, his immunity from financial concerns, and his exclusive interest in the team made him appear unswervingly patient. He was also undecided about what he wanted to do in the long run, when it is clear that he recognized his team could no longer play in Connie Mack Stadium. The city might not have responded in any case, but Carpenter's indecision perhaps permitted politicians to dally even more. On the other side, as Carpenter put it, he was "a rich man from out of town" and believed it would have been "counterproductive" to push officials.

Carpenter got a boost when voters elected Richardson Dilworth mayor in November 1955. Dilworth and his predecessor, Clark, were wealthy Democrats who ousted an entrenched and corrupt Republican machine. In the early 1950s, when Dilworth was district attorney, the Democratic patricians had quickly involved a group of reformist administrators, urban planners, and educated liberals in municipal government. By and large these men were intent on the city's economic base and its "high" cultural institutions; they looked down on professional sports. Clark's bloodless view of the A's was typical. Dilworth, however, was different. A talented, outspoken, and flamboyant man, he was the most impressive Philadelphia politician of the century. He also believed that professional sports brought an irreplaceable zest to the city.

Mayor until 1962, when he resigned to make an unsuccessful bid for the governor's office, Dilworth remained prominent in civic life thereafter. Right from the start of his tenure as mayor, in late 1955 and 1956, he spoke out in favor of a municipally sponsored stadium. In 1957, however, the *Inquirer* published a series of articles arguing against a city stadium. Less devoted to sports than Dilworth, the mayor's advisers convinced him that voters would not approve a bond issue for new grounds.

This opposition delayed a vote on public funding, which did not come until 1964, after leaders tried and failed with other strategies. The delays upset Dilworth, who feared that the Phillies would leave and that other professional teams would follow. The town, Dilworth said, would be "creepy" without major league sport. The Phillies also upset Dilworth. In the late 1950s and early 1960s Carpenter fielded dreadful clubs. In early 1961 they lost twenty-three games in a row and could not, the mayor thought, generate enthusiasm for themselves. "You don't build an air-conditioned stable for a worn-out horse," commented Richie Ashburn, one of the last of the Whiz Kids. The Phillies were "dogs," said Dilworth, but still needed another field.

Dilworth wanted a large multipurpose facility that might house conventions as well as many sports. His model was the all-weather Astrodome then being proposed in Houston, Texas. At several points in the late fifties and early sixties Carpenter offered essentially to share with the city the cost of a new forty to forty-five-thousand-seat park for baseball. Dilworth rejected these plans because cost-benefit analysis dictated a huge complex, amorphous enough for at least baseball and football. Andy Clarke, Carpenter's park supervisor, prudently observed these struggles at the "upper echelons." He believed that the franchise had to move but detested the idea of a "sports complex." When Carpenter's plan did not come off, Clarke reminisced, it was "the fatal error" for Philadelphia baseball. Thereafter, discussion presupposed complete public funding, concomitant political control, and, as Clarke put it, a "bisexual" stadium.

As early as the 1910s, local planners imagined a municipal sports complex at Thirty-third and Oxford streets in Fairmount Park. Throughout the 1950s John B. Kelly, Commissioner of Fairmount Park, again proposed such a building, seating one hundred thousand in his domain. But these dreams went unrealized.

By the late 1950s and early 1960s functionaries were more serious. They considered and abandoned a site Carpenter suggested in Cheltenham Township just outside the city. Then he nudged politicians. First, after rejecting an offer to move to Minneapolis, he talked to Mayor Robert Wagner of New York City, which had lost its two National League teams. Perhaps the Phillies would go north where Wagner would build a stadium for them in Flushing Meadow. Second, Carpenter purchased land in Camden, New Jersey, where a new park might house the Phillies. It was not far from where the A's had threatened to move thirty years before, when Pennsylvania prohibited Sunday baseball. Carpenter later recalled that he never intended to move to New York because he "hated that city," but allowed that Camden was a viable option.

After the New Jersey deal collapsed in 1959, Carpenter reversed course in a last attempt to make do at Connie Mack Stadium. The Philadelphia Eagles had played football in the park in the winter since 1941, although their fans were few. In 1957 a *total* of 129,000 watched the team play, and the franchise hinted that it might leave the city. When the club decamped to the University of Pennsylvania's Franklin Field in 1958 and attendance shot up, however, the Eagles facilities were no longer a concern. Carpenter was not unhappy with the Eagles' move from Connie Mack Stadium, for their maintenance expenses were high, as was the cost of rehabilitating the baseball field after the football season.

Nonetheless, commentators long noted that Carpenter liked football better than baseball. He correctly predicted that the 1960s would bring the sport the mass appeal it had previously lacked. At the end of 1959 and in early 1960 he negotiated for a franchise in the new American Football League. The key was Connie Mack Stadium. The Phillies "have offices, a sales-staff, and a park with nothing in it after the baseball season closes," said Carpenter. "For that reason alone, a football franchise has merit." While Connie Mack Stadium might be a loser if it supported baseball alone, Carpenter believed it could survive as a truly multipurpose stadium. When the American Football League negotiations failed, he again changed course.

At the end of 1960 the Phillies proposed a move to Torresdale, in the northeast section of the city. As civic leaders debated this idea, Carpenter sold Connie Mack Stadium in 1961 to New York developers. In the 1954 deal with Johnson, Carpenter, trading as Twenty-first and Lehigh Realty Company, bought the park himself. The Phillies then paid him, as they had previously paid the Athletics, for rental of the stadium. In 1959 the franchise and its owner drew up a new and complicated lease to maximize the tax benefits for each. By 1961, however, Carpenter had had enough of his accountants' maneuvering and simply wanted to divest himself of legal responsibility for the property. The sale and the future ones that occurred were purely real estate deals. Money and mortgages changed hands and so did formal ownership, but the franchise ran and maintained the park. The Phillies got a three-year lease and the option to extend it for four more, from year to year. Thus, the club had till 1967 to find a new Philadelphia home but expected to be in Torresdale within three years. After the team left, the developers were to tear down Connie Mack Stadium. The out-of-towners, who immediately transferred the stadium title to another New York real estate group, were supposed to build bowling alleys and a retail discount store on the site.

Carpenter lost over $1 million on the transaction. He paid $1.7 million for Connie Mack Stadium and sold it for $600,000. As his treasurer put it, with a new stadium coming, the value of Connie Mack Stadium would decline each year. "In 1954 we just had to have a stadium. This year we had a stadium for sale. How many people do you know who are in the market to buy a stadium?" One commentator wrote that the transaction was "a time bomb" for the city: the Phillies would have to move somewhere in seven years. Yet more than anything Carpenter did not want the headache of owning a park.

In any event, the sale had little effect. The first years of stadium debate bewildered commentators, but the next several years confused them even more. One writer described the negotiations as "chaotic wrangling" and a second as "endless political bickering, bureaucratic bungling, and the pressures of commercial interest." Meanwhile, another writer said, Connie Mack Stadium sank "deeper into decay." Parking troubles at the old park worsened. By the early 1960s the police reported an average of five complaints per game about auto damage near Connie Mack Stadium. Vandals broke into cars and took accessories or, for spite, damaged cars with paint or sharp objects. One fan complained that "the kids who used to watch a car for 25¢" were now "punching windows and walking away with hubcaps." Another said that "one hundred cars parked in the street . . . unattended, owned by 'Whitey' from the suburbs, was like Christmas every day."

Back at City Hall matters were no better. Politicians vetoed Torresdale. The Citizens Council on City Planning recommended three other centrally located parcels. Their development would replace urban

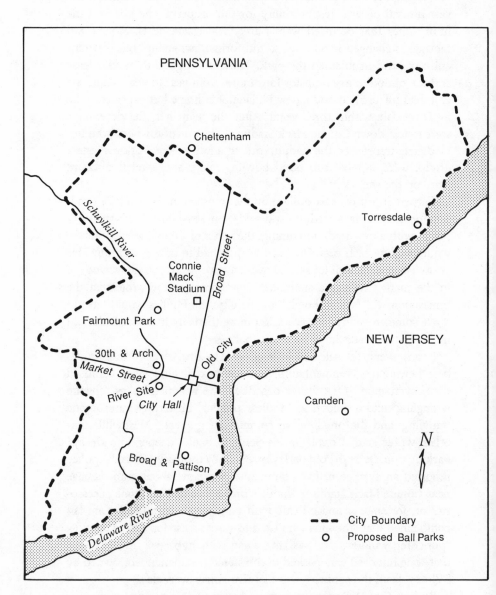

Map 5. Proposed ball park sites, 1950s–1960s

"blight": Old City north of Market, Twenty-second Street near the Schuylkill River, and Thirtieth and Arch streets at the home of the Pennsylvania Railroad. Shortly after these proposals a committee appointed by Dilworth backed a stadium at Broad Street and Pattison Avenue in South Philadelphia. In 1962, shortly after the city rejected this last site, some groups mobilized strong pressure for the parcel at Thirtieth and Arch streets. Intense lobbying from the Pennsylvania Railroad and support from Dilworth's successor, Jim Tate, aided this plan for a facility "on stilts" over the railroad yards.

Carpenter had park supervisor Andy Clarke check all of the possibilities. Clarke and his wife drove from City Hall and timed a drive to each place noting traffic conditions and surroundings. Carpenter compared these reports to his sense of a similar trip from City Hall to Connie Mack Stadium. The Phillies liked the site in Torresdale best. Yet by 1964, when Thirtieth and Arch became the front-runner, Carpenter said he would be happy with anything. Then entrepreneur Jerry Wolman arrived in Philadelphia.

Wolman was a wealthy Chevy Chase, Maryland, contractor interested in sports and speculation. In his mid-thirties, he was as enamored of real estate as Carpenter was disdainful of it. In February 1964 Wolman acquired the Philadelphia Eagles. In May, as part of a larger transaction, he bought Connie Mack Stadium, whose value was set at $757,000. Wolman's love of intrigue complicated his dealings. He announced that he purchased the stadium to help the Phillies and to insure them a place to play when their 1967 lease ran out. This was "help" the Phillies could do without. Wolman also said his Eagles had no need to move from the satisfactory Franklin Field to Thirtieth and Arch. If, as Wolman allowed, the Phillies could stay where they were and the Eagles were happy at Franklin Field, Philadelphia did not need another stadium. He thus single-handedly frustrated the Pennsylvania Railroad idea and put any new facility in doubt. Actually, problems with funding and opposition of crucial interest groups also threatened the Thirtieth and Arch site, but Wolman wanted to pressure the city to build a stadium of which he approved. Or, as he suggested at other times, he may have wanted to have the city redevelop Connie Mack Stadium and its environs for baseball and football, and move the Eagles back to a modernized park that he owned. If Wolman genuinely wanted to overhaul Twenty-first and Lehigh, the fracas that followed his announcement was Connie Mack Stadium's last stand.

Wolman was on a collision course with the new mayor. Jim Tate was an unlikely successor to the wealthy Ivy Leaguers Clark and Dilworth. From an Irish neighborhood near Shibe Park, he had worked his way up in Democratic politics in the 1940s through a combination of brains and hard work. His ethnic maneuvering contrasted even with Dilworth's rough-and-tumble politics. Tate disliked Wolman from the start not the least because Wolman had outbid a friend of Tate's for the Eagles. Some of Tate's friends were also interested in the new American Football League. In pushing for his pet stadium at Thirtieth and Arch, the mayor wanted to deny the Eagles unrestricted rights to play there, or at any other new complex. When Wolman bought Connie Mack Stadium, he wrecked Tate's plan.

One problem with Thirtieth and Arch streets was that its proponents hoped to get federal money for urban renewal of the site. But Washington would not certify the area as appropriate. National largesse for the "inner city" during the presidency of Lyndon Johnson was significant. In June 1964, turning its back on Thirtieth and Arch, the Urban Renewal Administration in Washington reported that the reconstruction of Connie Mack Stadium and its neighborhood was conceivable. In a related move two weeks later, Wolman offered to sell Connie Mack Stadium to the city for fifty cents, contingent on Tate's rehabilitation of the park and the area.

Tate did not think the offer a bargain. He told one press conference that buying the park was a "bad investment" for Wolman and not "in the public interest." Tate argued that no solution existed to the problems of automobile access to the old stadium. Several city studies had made clear that rehabilitation of the stadium and provision of parking would require a great outlay of cash and much destruction of property. Playing up his sensitivity to demolition and neighborhood integrity, Tate noted that renewal at Twenty-first and Lehigh would require wiping out two to six hundred homes and eight to ten industries. Urban renewal politics gave the mayor power to designate the final sites. Tate said that no one had approved Connie Mack Stadium. He concluded by calling for positive action on Thirtieth and Arch.

Three weeks later, at the end of June, Wolman stated for the record that the Eagles would not play at Thirtieth and Arch. Tate retorted that the city would purchase Connie Mack Stadium "from petty cash" for fifty cents. Wolman refused the offer because the city would not follow up the purchase with modernization. In August the city withdrew the

Thirtieth and Arch idea from consideration, weighed down as it was by various problems, conspicuous among them Wolman's resistance. Simultaneously, exhausted by the fighting, civic and political leaders coalesced around the previously rejected choice in South Philadelphia at Broad and Pattison.

This proposition had a comparatively easy time. The Phillies and Eagles bargained over rental agreements, and full municipal funding did not come until May 1967. During this period both clubs rejected alternatives should the voters disapprove city financing. The Eagles negotiated exclusive rights to play in the new complex, and the Phillies rejected an initial seating design as "monstrous" for baseball. But consensus existed on what came to be called "Veterans Stadium." Philadelphia's leaders broke ground for "the Vet" in October 1967. Long before its completion, they touted it as "the finest sports stadium in the United States," a "magnificent dream," "the model for any stadia of the future," "the greatest thing that ever happened to sports in the City of Philadelphia."

Back at Connie Mack Stadium Carpenter redid his timetable. In 1961 he had hoped to be out of the park by 1963 or 1964, but had an option to stay until 1967. Instead of moving during that absolute last year, the Phillies prepared for several more seasons at Twenty-first and Lehigh. In 1966 they had negotiated a new lease that could extend for a decade, but Carpenter said that Connie Mack Stadium, though structurally sound, had a life expectancy of only five more seasons. Even then, after "twelve confusing years," all he would threaten was that "he couldn't say he wouldn't leave the city if there was no alternative" in five years. Yet "in no way," he said, "could I be critical of the city."

Despite his conciliatory statements, Carpenter was no longer complacent. By the late sixties the franchise felt that its home field was a major burden. Aggression at the park against property spilled over to persons, as the angry side of the civil rights era revealed itself. Gangs with knives mugged fans and attacked people going to and from games. Attendance in 1969, just over five hundred thousand, was the worst in twenty-five years. One of the reasons was the woebegone teams that played there. Another was the stadium and its environs.

The Vet was to be ready in time for the 1970 season. Delays put off the opening, however, and the Phillies spent all of that year in Connie Mack Stadium. By then the city assigned twenty-five extra police, as well as numerous plainclothes personnel to games at the park, in addition to the normal squad of foot patrol officers. Cops were to protect customers from "wolf packs of youths" in "an area of violence" around Twenty-first and Lehigh. Fans were frightened, reported the newspapers. They ran "a gauntlet of hostility," especially after night games if they walked northeast to the North Philadelphia train station or east to the Broad Street subway.

Jerry Wolman's personal fortunes declined with the price of his property. He appraised Connie Mack Stadium at $1.2 million in 1967, apparently in hopes of a redevelopment bonanza, and had two mortgages on it, totaling $700,000. Eagles stock secured the first mortgage, but at the end of the year Wolman could not meet payments on either loan. As the Phillies played out their time at the stadium over the next four years, the value of the property fell precipitously. Wolman manipulated what assets he had. Various real estate developers passed the Connie Mack Stadium mortgages from hand to hand, making money from the Phillies' $125,000 yearly rental and hoping for speculative profit connected to the site. When the Phillies finally left, Wolman himself went bankrupt.

The changing role of the park mirrored changes in northeastern cities in the middle of the century. As we shall see, the urban economy declined and racial and ethnic divisions intensified. Capitalists fought to preserve commercial investments in working-class districts. In Philadelphia the A's had proudly owned Shibe Park for over forty years. It was a piece of property and part of a business, but it had its own value. From the time Roy and Earle Mack mortgaged it in 1950, however, the place—almost entirely under the name of Connie Mack Stadium—had a different meaning for the business. The feelings baseball men and civic leaders had about it altered. Bought and sold repeatedly, it became a pawn in the struggles of sports entrepreneurs, politicians, developers, and city planners. Its worth, to repeat what Carpenter had said, had become no different from any other parcel of real estate.

1. Groundbreaking at Twenty-first and Lehigh, 1908. *From left*: first, Tom Shibe; fifth, Ben Shibe; seventh, Connie Mack. *From right*: fourth, John Shibe.

FINAL GAME WORLD'S SERIES, 1911
SHIBE PARK, PHILA.
"Athletics" 13 – New York 2 –

2. The A's won this final game of the 1911 World Series against the Giants, 13–2.

3. Mascot Louis VanZelst sat under manager Mack in this 1910 team photograph.

4. Shibe Park shortly after completion of its facade, about 1909.

5. Railroad tracks dominated the North Philadelphia neighborhood around Shibe Park in this aerial survey photograph of 1929

6. North Twentieth Street opposite right field was busy during the 1929 World Series.

7. Shibe Park and its surroundings were at one of the peaks of their vitality and prosperity in the late 1920s.

8. In August 1932 John Nolan of the Baseball Writers Association of America presented Lefty Grove with the first "modern" Most Valuable Player Award (American League, 1931).

9. Franklin Roosevelt spoke at a campaign rally in October 1944.

10. Henry Wallace accepted the nomination of the Progressive party for president in July 1948.

11. This crowd assembled for an A's–Cleveland game in July 1948 during the last period of the park's prosperity.

12. Under duress Phillies manager Ben Chapman agreed to share a bat, although not shake hands, with Jackie Robinson in May 1947.

13. Philadelphia Eagles versus Chicago Cardinals in the snow game of December 1948. Eagles players included quarterback Tommy Thompson (11); left halfback Steve Van-Buren (15); right end Pete Pihos (35); right guard Bucko Kilroy (76).

14. The House of Mack in the late 1940s. *In descending order*: Connie, Jr.; Connie; Earle; Roy.

15. Connie Mack autographed a ball in 1953 for Pete Adelis, the "foghorn" of Shibe Park.

16. The last day game took place on September 25, 1970.

17. At the end of the last game, October 1, 1970, fans went on a rampage.

18. A fire gutted the stadium in August 1971.

19. Inside, by 1973, the place looked like this.

20. In 1975 the old playing field was overgrown.

21. (*opposite page*) Before completely demolishing the park in 1976, the wreckers knocked off the CONNIE MACK STADIUM plate on the facade, revealing the original SHIBE PARK inscription.

22. The site of Shibe Park in the late 1980s before groundbreaking for Deliverance Evangelistic Church.

Race Relations

In the early part of the century Connie Mack tried to smuggle talented black players into Shibe Park as Italians or Indians. He was, however, fundamentally against desegregating the sport. For the first half of the century Shibe Park was a typical place of prejudice. More than many northern cities, indeed, Philadelphia was a white baseball town. Blacks were not fans of the A's or Phillies, and the franchises did not attract blacks to the ball park. They came in any number only on infrequent occasions when exhibitions were held or when the Philadelphia Stars or other teams of the old Negro Leagues were permitted to stage contests there.

The genteel bigotry of influential leaders of opinion as well as the largely docile response of blacks permitted remarkable abrogations of civility. The stresses on baseball during World War II, however, hastened the racial revolution in the sport of the postwar period. Moreover, the weakness of the Philadelphia franchises made them a prime focus for Negro Leagues talent. Philadelphia also had a black population of nearly four hundred thousand in the 1940s, a fact noted in a treatise on conditions affecting basball attendance that was prepared at the Wharton School of the University of Pennsylvania in 1951 with the assistance of the Phillies. "Colored people," the work argued, were likely to spend their discretionary income at places like Shibe Park. It would be economically advantageous for Philadelphia teams to hire black players and cultivate blacks as fans.

Nonetheless, neither Philadelphia nor its teams responded. Earlier, in September 1942, Roy Campanella, who had a black mother and an Italian father, came to Shibe Park for a tryout. His family lived in Nicetown, some fifteen blocks away from Shibe Park. For twenty-five cents "Campy" watched his first major league game in 1932 from the Twentieth Street stands—the day Lou Gehrig hit four home runs. By the early forties Campanella, already a rising star in the Negro Leagues, heard rumors that "organized" baseball might take in blacks. He wanted to play in his hometown and so approached Phillies scout Jocko Collins. Collins recommended that owner Gerry Nugent sign the twenty-year-old. Campanella, said Collins, could help the team. Nugent agreed but told Campanella that he would have to play minor league ball in the Georgia-Florida League. As Collins recalled, Campanella, on hearing that news, "just stared at him."

In the early forties it was also suggested to Nugent that black stars like Satchel Paige and Josh Gibson could help the Phillies. Nugent would not act himself, but others had their eyes on the main chance. The black press published rumors that black religious leader Father Divine might buy the Phillies from Nugent. Around the same time, Eddie Gottlieb, an entrepreneur who promoted black sports in the city, interested two wealthy Jews, Ike and Leon Levy, in purchasing the Phillies from the financially pressed Nugent. Gottlieb would be general manager, and the idea was that he might hire black stars. But National League president Ford Frick made it clear that he wanted neither Jews nor blacks in the majors. Then, at the end of 1942, with his franchise bankrupt, Nugent agreed to sell the club to Bill Veeck, who wanted to stock the team with blacks. Apparently the Congress of Industrial Organizations (CIO) and Phillies Cigars backed Veeck financially. He thought, during the war, that he could transform the seventh-place club into a pennant winner. When Commissioner Landis and Frick learned of this plan, they thwarted Veeck. The National League bought the Phillies and quickly sold them to lumber dealer William Cox, who was chosen in desperation. Less than a year later Landis banned Cox from baseball for gambling, and Bob Carpenter took over.

As much as he could, Carpenter opposed a black presence in the majors, and certainly at Shibe Park. Although Connie Mack had claimed apologetically that he could not cross the well-known prejudices of Landis, fifty years later old-timers remembered how the elderly Mack worked to keep blacks out of his Germantown neighborhood. For the period Mack and his family were a force in baseball, they were almost as adamant as Carpenter. The Philadelphia black press reported in the 1940s that Mack was one of the owners "most bitterly" opposed to the integration of the major leagues. Both the Phillies and the A's were racist on principle. They willingly hurt the quality of their teams and, consequently, gate receipts. The city's white rooters also proved to be committed to discrimination.

World War II did make Mack relent slightly. Eddie Gottlieb apparently sold Mack on the idea that "colored teams" and their followers could be as good tenants as anyone else. In 1945 black clubs began to use the park during high summer for evening doubleheaders. The Philadelphia Stars would face two opponents, or four different teams would play. Moreover, games in the 1942, 1945, and 1947 Negro Leagues World Series took place at Shibe Park. What these developments would have meant in the long run is difficult to say because the integration of the major leagues in 1947 killed the Negro Leagues. The question then became: When would the A's and Phillies hire black players?

In the postwar years Judy Johnson, an all-time star in the Negro Leagues, informally scouted for Mack, who finally put him on the A's payroll. Although the Athletics said they were in the market for black talent, they also would "not exploit just anyone in order to draw fans." The statement was true enough. For under five thousand dollars apiece, Mack refused Larry Doby or Minnie Minoso. For thirty-five hundred dollars he rejected Hank Aaron. "If Mr. Mack had signed him, Doby, and Minoso," said Johnson, "the A's would still be in Philadelphia."

When Jackie Robinson came up with the Brooklyn Dodgers in 1947, the cruelest taunts he received at Ebbets Field came from the visiting Phillies, led by manager Ben Chapman, a native of Alabama. Before the Dodgers played their first series in Philadelphia, Carpenter urged Brooklyn owner Branch Rickey to bench Robinson. Carpenter's close friend general manager Herb Pennock phoned Rickey to tell him not "to bring that nigger here" to Shibe Park. After much pressure, the Phillies relented and publicly made the best of the integration of the National League. At the first Dodger game in Philadelphia, Robinson took a much-publicized walk to the home team dugout for a conciliatory photograph with Chapman. Nonetheless, Robinson represented a new phase in U.S. race relations. Reporters took the picture peacefully, but Robinson later said he had wanted to go over to the Phillies dugout and "grab one of those white sons of bitches and smash his teeth."

Larry Doby, who broke the color barrier in the American League, found Shibe Park equally unfriendly. At one point the A's helped fan Pete Adelis, the "loudmouth" of Shibe Park, by giving him a prominent seat just above the visiting team's dugout. Then the Athletics paid Adelis to trail Doby around the league and heckle him.

Three weeks before the end of the 1953 season and a year before they left the city, the A's brought to the big leagues the first black Philadelphia player. Pitcher Bob Trice spent two years in the majors, one with Kansas City, compiling a record of nine wins and nine losses.

The Phillies dragged their heels more than the A's. By the mid-1950s they had the only all-white club in the National League. The black press in Philadelphia described the franchise as the "most prejudiced"—perhaps flattering the Yankees and the Red Sox—and argued that the bias accounted for the low black turnout. Carpenter announced, "I'm not opposed to Negro players. But I'm not going to hire a player of any color or nationality just to have him on the team." Leaders of the black community conferred with the Phillies management, and in 1955 Mayor Richardson Dilworth told the local branch of the National Association for the Advancement of Colored People (NAACP) that the city's Human Relations Commission had been working on the team for years. The runaround finally got to the black papers. The *Philadelphia Independent* editorialized in a piece titled "Phooey on the Phillies" that it was happy to have the team lose. In June 1956 the NAACP requested an interview with Carpenter to discuss the "anti-Negro feeling" of the Phillies' front office. Carpenter told the organization that "the big club" was only the "show window" of the franchise and did not measure the club's interest in equal opportunity. He compiled a list of the forty-three black employees at Connie Mack Stadium, most of them cleaning staff and toilet attendants, and sent it to the NAACP. The head of the organization asked that in the near future Carpenter upgrade black jobs to include "ticket takers, ticker sellers, [and] ushers."

In 1957 the first black member of the Phillies arrived in the city. The performance of John Kennedy was limited to several games that May. Over the next five years an equally undistinguished group of "players of color" followed, most of them not from the United States. Blacks from Central America were less threatening to the Phillies than those from the United States. It almost seems that the club was set on hiring only mediocre black Americans to justify its discrimination. In the spring of 1962 the Phillies were one of the last major league teams to end segregated housing in spring training and did so only when the NAACP threatened to picket Connie Mack Stadium. The *Bulletin* commented that the Phillies dallied because they had no black players "secure enough to protest."

Blacks were moving into Shibe Park with the same halting steps that brought them to the neighborhood around it. As the Reverend William Gray noted, the location of Connie Mack Stadium "in a predominantly Negro area" exacerbated the irritation blacks felt about Carpenter's hiring practices. This startling and momentous demographic change had actually begun during the onset of the Depression.

By 1930 Philadelphia was losing manufacturing jobs. Technological innovation was shifting industry from northern cities to other areas. The growth of a national highway system and of automotive transport encouraged this shift. But the economic trauma of the Depression slowed these changes. Business was stagnant everywhere. The automobile and suburbs became less important to many people who were compelled to remain close to older neighborhoods. Then World World II briefly revived Philadelphia industry. Public transportation temporarily boomed due to the unavailability of new automobiles and to gas rationing. Large wartime orders vitalized Midvale Steel, Budd, Philco, Westinghouse, and Bendix. A critical defense complex existed in Hunting Park, just to the north of North Penn. The war put to work the large unemployed pool of skilled labor in the city.

After the war, however, the downward slide of manufacturing went on precipitously, accelerating the process that had started at the end of the 1920s. Some Philadelphia companies departed for outlying areas of the city, where they drew employees from the growing suburbs. Others headed to other parts of the United States where labor costs and taxes were lower, or even went out of business entirely. Industrial jobs near North Penn shrank. In quest of employment less likely to be a trolley ride or a long walk away, North Penn families moved closer to the new businesses located at the periphery of the city. The spacious, affordable housing in the growing suburbs—Cherry Hill, Havertown, Springfield—also attracted these families. By the late 1960s neighbors who had previously lived in North Penn were putting their children on school buses, chauffeuring them to ballet lessons, or raising money for expensive Little League uniforms. Parents asked themselves nostalgically what they had gained. The answer was obvious: they got more pleasant homes on larger parcels of ground, better schools, higher-paying jobs, and even greater socioeconomic homogeneity than had existed in the old community. They valued all of these benefits.

As the Irish and Italians left the environs of Shibe Park, blacks replaced them. During the Depression and the war the black population in the city grew to be the third largest in the United States. North Philadelphia below Shibe Park became the principal black residential area. Experts on urban affairs referred to it as "Lower North Philadelphia." Most white people just said "the ghetto." Increasingly crowded into substandard housing, blacks in North Philadelphia spread immediately to the north, along the Pennsylvania Railroad tracks that lay aslant

North Penn. This triangle from Twenty-ninth above Susquehanna, north along the railroad lines, had always been racially mixed, with a small population of blacks. In the years after the war this population expanded.

In the late 1930s the federal government proposed a vacant lot adjacent to Funfield Recreation Center as a site for a black housing project. White neighbors defeated this direct and early challenge, and the city appropriated the land for a playground. But in the forties blacks gradually came north. "The niggers crept up, block by block," recalled one resident. "They infiltrated," said another.

In August 1944, during the war, the national government's Fair Employment Practices Commission ordered that blacks be promoted to better jobs on Philadelphia buses and trolleys and prompted a citywide public transit strike. For a few days federal troops ran the system after Franklin Roosevelt declared a wartime emergency. It was a nervous time. One of the centers of the white strike was the car barn on Allegheny Avenue, just outside of North Penn. White motorists shot a black boy. Black gangs broke the windows of white shopkeepers in North Philadelphia not far from the baseball field.

At Shibe Park on August 4, in the middle of the strike, Connie Mack celebrated his fifty years as a baseball manager. Abbott and Costello performed their "Who's on first?" routine in baseball uniforms. President Roosevelt sent a telegram of greeting: "May your scorecard continue to wave." The packed house of white fans used their gas rations or showed their loyalty to the Grand Old Man of Baseball by walking though a racially strained neighborhood, its southern border on the railroad tracks now occupied by black families.

After the war, the bitter and complicated 1948 presidential campaign made relations between the races significant in a national election for the first time since the 1870s. For a brief moment Shibe Park played a role in this complex political drama.

In 1945 Harry Truman had become president when FDR died, and Truman wanted to run on his own in 1948. Although he eventually gained a narrow victory, his unpopularity and the fragmentation of the Democratic party initially threatened his chances. Disenchanted with Truman, prominent Democrat Henry Wallace ran against him on the Progressive party ticket. The Wallace campaign, which the American Communist party influenced, called for an end to the growing cold war with Russia. The Progressives also denounced the treatment of blacks and exhorted them to leave the Democratic party. Moderate Democrats hated the Wallace movement, fearing that it would take black and liberal voters away from Truman.

Philadelphia business and civic leaders worked hard to get all three conventions—Republican, Democratic, and Progressive—to the city that year. Delegates would spend a lot of money, and the gatherings would give Philadelphia publicity around the world. But only at the last minute did officials persuade Connie Mack to permit Wallace to deliver his acceptance speech at Shibe Park. The A's wanted no part of a leftist third-party movement.

The Democrats, also in Philadelphia at around the same time, had more problems with Wallace than did Mack. They wanted to show themselves enlightened on the issue of race, but their meeting in the city to nominate Truman split the party even more. When it adopted a civil rights plank in its platform, some southern Democrats walked out of the convention to form the Dixiecrat party.

Rebecca West, the famous English novelist, came from Britain to cover the conventions. She used her internationally syndicated essays about her trips to Shibe Park to support Truman's campaign. West defended a middle-of-the-road position on blacks and claimed that the racial radicalism of the Progressives was pro-Communist. When she showed up at Shibe Park for the Wallace rally, she was committed to a belief that the Progressives were an evil influence. She thought the Wallaceites a potential Fascist movement led by U.S. Communists. West was nonetheless relieved because the third-party Shibe Park crowd, with which she made a point of mingling, was so "soft." The elders were "woolywitted." The many young people were "stupid," with signs of "serious maladjustment." The girls were physically and mentally inadequate. The boys, "with sullen eyes and dropped chins," could never master the world's complexity. West thought the red Progressives would fail in their campaign to foment race riots and civil division, to make the blacks a discontented minority.

On another trip to the park West took a more benign view of U.S. race relations. Boxing promoter Herman Taylor hoped to cash in on the conventions and staged a major prize fight in Shibe Park to coincide with the Democratic meeting. On July 13, in the middle of an A's home stand, Taylor scheduled a lightweight bout between two black boxers, champion Ike Williams and challenger Beau Jack. West, an intellectual who liked boxing, went to Taylor's show.

In the first five rounds both fighters exchanged hard punches. In the sixth Williams took command. He stunned Beau with a left hook to the jaw and slugged him to the ropes and at last to a neutral corner, where he beat the challenger into a helpless condition. The "blood splashed" in what was a "murderous" scene of "near manslaughter." As the *Bulletin* reported, Williams finally stepped back and turned "a beseeching look" to the referee. "I didn't want to hit him around the head any more," Williams later said. But when the champion received no sign from the official, he continued pummeling his opponent, although apparently without much joy. Then the referee intervened and declared Williams the winner.

West thought the fight was "beautifully controlled and civilized." The "largely white" boxing crowd that watched one "colored" man pound another into insensitivity also impressed West far more than the Wallace radicals. The fight audience appreciatively followed the action, showing much respect for the boxers. Patrons had gone through "an experience which is the rough equivalent of reading a very good book indeed."

Walking to and from the park, through a black area south of Lehigh, further touched West. Looking into houses whose windows were without shades, she found the blacks not "simple and brutish people" but "highly civilized." The boxing and the experiences on the walk made her think about the civil rights movement. She realized that the Communist or Communist-influenced ideas about race in the United States were lies. Blacks might have a great deal to fight for in the United States, West concluded, but her evening in Shibe Park and its environs convinced her that the Communist propaganda about the ill-treatment of blacks should be discredited.

Some North Penn residents recalled the late forties and early fifties as relatively tranquil. The neighborhood was still pleasant enough to draw the white ballplayers—the Whiz Kids and Connie Mack's last winning team of the late 1940s—to reside in it. Moreover, stresses had always existed among the Jews, Italians, Irish, and English sharing the border near the railroad. Blacks added only another element. One neighbor remembered the "uneasy familiarity" of all these groups and the accommodation that took place, for example, as black children walked north to Pierce Elementary School.

By 1950 black pressure on one side and white opportunities elsewhere had shifted the neighborhood's boundaries from the tracks and York Street to Lehigh Avenue. Lehigh became a social line, which deference, fear, and, more important, the practices of real estate agents and bankers protected. Below it, as one neighbor remembered the early 1950s, was "the forbidden zone."

Farther south, however, urban renewal experts in the late 1940s and early 1950s were unwittingly destroying the older black neighborhoods and, consequently, forcing blacks to move out of them. The "blight" in Old North Philadelphia distressed liberal Democrats in the affluent Clark and Dilworth administrations. They wanted to counteract housing deterioration and carried out various schemes to prevent its spread. One idea was to demolish poor, overcrowded homes but only partly to replace them with new, less densely occupied housing units, creating in Lower North Philadelphia a suburban atmosphere that would give blacks the same sorts of amenities whites were acquiring outside the city. Government would subsidize a few examples of such renewal, a type of "public housing," and these "spores" would generate continuous rehabilitation by businessmen concerned with profits. Other reformers refused to spend precious tax money for the economically disadvantaged and instead focused energy (and government money) on downtown Philadelphia.

The result increased neighborhood destruction in Lower North Philadelphia, as planners agreed only on demolition. Fewer houses became available to a larger population. From 1950 to 1980 the government tore down 30 percent of the housing in Lower North Philadephia. Employment in local businesses diminished as some of the small commercial areas in Lower North Philadelphia vanished. The lack of commitment of liberal politicians to anything other than the razing of property matched the lack of interest of the real estate and investment community, unwilling to risk funds in Lower North Philadelphia. The homes in this part of the city were always impoverished. In the late 1940s and early 1950s the destruction of existing houses and what economists called the "disinvestment" of government and private funders aggravated the problems.

As demolition in Lower North Philadelphia proceeded in the fifties, black families with stable and modest incomes bought or rented housing to the north. In August 1954 the first such family crossed the Lehigh Avenue line, moving into a run-down storefront near Judson and

Cambria, two blocks north of Lehigh, between the Italian and Irish communities. The address would stick in the minds of old neighbors forever—2863 Judson. A white crowd welcomed its new neighbors by breaking windows and shouting obscenities. The conflict attracted city-wide publicity. The Commission on Human Relations announced that it was the most significant and far-reaching of the incidents typifying the changes in the communities in what was now called Upper North Philadelphia.

Actually, neighborhood ties and geography distinguished North Penn from the adjacent communities of Strawberry Mansion, Nicetown, Tioga, and Hunting Park. The railroad was an almost impenetrable barrier, and North Penn was close-knit. The black population made its way *farther* north more quickly by detouring around the railroad and going up Broad Street on the east and Ridge Avenue and Hunting Park on the west. By 1960 the communities to the north of North Penn were black. Some of the area's residents now called it "the white island," although the ballplayers would no longer live there and often commuted to the park from the suburbs. Black families made minor inroads, living in the less expensive houses on the smaller streets. Then the social upheavals of the 1960s—the civil rights movement, more radical demands for social reform, and the war in Vietnam—overwhelmed North Penn.

Turning against their white clientele, local real estate agents flooded the community with handbills urging owners to leave before values fell. Realtors went from door to door advising residents that they would get better prices if they sold their houses to blacks at once. In the mid-1960s bumper crops of FOR SALE signs signaled what urban historians term "white flight."

Whites harassed and bullied the blacks when they could. Racial hostility made moving into the area not just emotionally trying but physically dangerous. Blacks often bought substandard housing, vacated by families wanting only to leave. The new arrivals constructed lives for themselves in a community from which many small businesses were departing, following their white customers to the suburbs. A striking example of this sort of disinvestment was the departure of the A's, which occurred in November 1954, a few months after the first black family moved into the neighborhood.

Many of those whites who moved away were looking for other work. The blacks who replaced them found fewer jobs available connected to baseball. More important, the supply of industrial jobs within easy commuting distance lessened, and the community could no longer count on them. Nonetheless, in the short-term blacks may have stabilized or even increased housing values in neighborhoods that the exodus of white ethnics to the suburbs had imperiled.

Whites in North Penn did not see it that way. The difference between North Penn and other North Philadelphia communities showed that the "pull" of the suburbs was much less strong than the "push" of the population below Lehigh. Some older couples did not have the wherewithal to "move up" in the housing market. Others had little wish to leave a neighborhood they had lived in for forty, fifty, or even sixty years. They hoped North Penn would stay "nice" for a few more years. Some younger couples did not want to be cut off from extended families and hung on for a time, hoping that their block, at least, might remain "good." They were genuinely threatened, and although perhaps for the wrong reasons, felt beleaguered as a way of life they had known for generations altered irrevocably.

The *Chat*, the local newspaper, assiduously ignored the transformation. In 1954 neighborhood realtors advertised "junior estates" in the suburbs. Yet the newspaper maintained its white, small business orientation and proclaimed its "nonpolitical" stance as late as 1965. In early 1967, however, the paper changed hands and at once backed political change, representing the civil rights movement in all of North Philadelphia.

As North Penn went black, Lehigh Avenue remained a strategic barrier. Aided by patrician liberals wielding a wrecking ball, black communities below Lehigh disintegrated in the chaos of the sixties as abandoned housing, drugs, unemployment, and theft took their toll. The police knew this part of the city as "the black belt" or, more bluntly, "the Jungle." Above Lehigh the black communities were better off, as those blacks with steady jobs, more income, and aspiring middle-class values fought to escape the ghetto.

Conflicts between blacks and whites escalated. Violent clashes occurred in 1963 over job discrimination in the Philadelphia construction industry. Cecil Moore, the militant and charismatic head of the local NAACP, emerged as a leader in North Philadelphia. Whites called him "an agitator." In October 1963 tensions increased after police shot a black shoplifting suspect. Then, in August 1964, just ten years after the first black family moved into the Connie Mack Stadium area, Lower

North Philadelphia erupted in a fierce riot that exemplified the discontent of the sixties and finally motivated the white residents of North Penn to get out. The disorder began at Twenty-second and Columbia, spreading east on Columbia and north and south on Ridge, which intersected Columbia at Twenty-third. For four days at the end of August, Mayor Tate declared an emergency and ordered the populace off the streets in a 125-block section of the city. Looting spread through Lower North Philadelphia right up to Lehigh Avenue, the far boundary of the riot. The newspapers used Connie Mack Stadium as the landmark to show readers the extent of civic disruption. The park was perched on the northern tip of an area patrolled by fifteen hundred police.

On August 31 the mayor and his aides met to discuss the return of the Phillies from a six-game road trip the next evening. The home team had already drawn over a million in attendance. The club's performance in August put them in first place by five and a half games. Rooters looked forward to the first Philadelphia pennant since 1950. Many of the fans who turned out for the initial home stand game parked just south of Lehigh, where they normally would have worried about minor damage to their cars. But on that early September evening, as fans walked past the dozens of businesses vandalized on Lehigh, hundreds of police patrolled the streets. Fifty more ringed Connie Mack Stadium.

By the mid-sixties the Philles had picked themselves out of the National League cellar. Carpenter acquired some talented players—Johnny Callison, Bobby Wine, Tony Taylor, Jim Bunning, and Chris Short. But the major reason for the Phillies' surprising year in 1964 was their new black talent. After its halfhearted commitment to Latin Americans, the franchise signed some black power hitters born in the United States. Wes Covington, who started in 1961, was a slugging outfielder who was obviously outspoken. After he criticized manager Gene Mauch's work with the team at the end of 1965, the Phillies traded him to the Chicago Cubs. More important than Covington was a seventy-five-thousand-dollar bonus baby who started for the Phillies in 1964: Dick Allen.

Allen was a prodigious and exciting talent who played in Connie Mack Stadium for six years. During this time he batted almost .300 and hit an average of almost thirty home runs a season. Tom Boswell, a baseball analyst who developed a total average statistic, ranked "the vastly under-rated" Allen twenty-first on an all-time list. Although he never reached the heights many predicted, Allen reminded many observers of Ted Williams. In three years with the Chicago White Sox later in his career, Allen single-handedly raised the attendance and performance of the Sox. The American League named him its Most Valuable Player in 1972.

Back in Philadelphia in 1964, fans held a Richie Allen Night at the end of September. The National League later designated him Rookie of the Year. He batted .318 and hit twenty-nine home runs. Allen drew fans to the stadium. Part of his appeal was his power. Everyone who went to Connie Mack Stadium in the sixties had a story about a shot rifled off the right-center field scoreboard or, even better, an Allen home run, "those blasts," said one fan, "disappearing—still on a rising trajectory—into steaming North Philadelphia summer nights." One nonfan had been taken to the park once during the sixties and remembered only driving through "rundown slums . . . with worn out people out on their steps trying to beat the August heat" and "a home run by Richie Allen." A fan who regularly went to opening nights reminisced about "Philadelphians booing Jim Tate when he threw out the first ball, and rockets by Richie Allen." On at least three occasions he hit shots over the wall in dead center field, between 410 and 450 feet from home plate. Old-timers remembered that only Jimmie Foxx, a mythic figure by the 1960s, had equally crushed the ball. Allen was, one fan wrote, a "uniquely fearsome" batter. Twenty-five years later, Allen said, people would still recall to him their memories of home runs he hit over the Coke and Cadillac signs on the park's left-center field roof. The sight of Number 15 digging in at the plate brought a surge of excitement to Philadelphia crowds, who stayed in the park until his last at bat, no matter what the score.

Even with Allen, however, the team could not triumph. In September 1964 the franchise assembled a temporary staff and sold World Series tickets from the oval office at the stadium. But then this "young underprivileged team of have-nots," as Roger Angell described them, collapsed and merely tied for second place. It was one of the most heartbreaking finishes in baseball history. The Phillies were in first by six and a half games with only twelve to play. They then lost ten in a row. Many of the defeats took place in Connie Mack Stadium, including the first and most memorable one on September 21, 1964, when Chico Ruiz stole home to give the Cincinnati Reds a 1–0 victory over the

Phillies. Fans would always remember and, later, claimed to know that the successful steal was "an omen." The calamity confirmed for many Philadelphians that the city was one of "losers." The failure debilitated the franchise. Carpenter had been struggling to rebuild his pennant-winning Whiz Kids of 1950. The 1964 Phillies offered him the best hope in a quarter century of a victorious club. But the disaster of the "Phizz Kids" took the heart out of the Phillies for the next decade. Except for Allen, they limped along, unable to capture attention. As one writer said as early as the end of the 1964 season, without Allen "the Phils can cut off the lights . . . and board up the ball park."

They were going to board up the ball park in any event. The 1964 riot accentuated what one Phillies executive called their "vulnerability." The pressure for the new city-financed stadium mounted. Although the riot briefly cleansed North Philly, all of black Philadelphia smoldered with rage and conflict through the 1960s. The assaults on fans and their vehicles at the park expressed black hatred as whites trespassed on their turf. One white observer wrote of "the unrelieved tide of blackness," and spoke of "the isolating experience" of walking in North Philadelphia, subject to "the hostile stare of streetcorner youth, the boarded up and vandalized houses, abandoned and stripped cars . . . the white-washed injunction to 'Join the Black Guard.' "

Frank Rizzo, who first walked a beat around Shibe Park, worked his way up through the police hierarchy in the 1950s. Mayor Tate, who had been aware of Rizzo's tough, spit-and-polish image years before in North Penn, promoted him two ranks to deputy police commissioner in early 1964. At the same time Cecil Moore of the NAACP accused Rizzo of "stormtrooper tactics" against blacks. During the 1964 riot Rizzo advocated harsher tactics than his superiors. Briefly, as acting commissioner in 1966, he staged "dynamite raids" against black radicals in the ghetto. As part of his reelection strategy, Tate named Rizzo commissioner in 1967, solidifying the white ethnic voters around his candidacy. Later that year Rizzo broke up a black demonstration over educational discrimination. In 1970 he challenged "yellow" black radicals to a "Mexican shootout" on Broad Street. For many whites Rizzo was the mean cop who would deal aggressively with black troublemakers. In 1971 he became mayor himself.

The Phillies believed they had no future in North Philadelphia, where the problems of the city centered and where their team played poorly. As its commitment to alternatives far from "the black belt" grew, the franchise allowed Connie Mack Stadium to fall into disrepair, contributing to disinvestment in the area. The dirty and unkempt park mirrored the down-at-the-heels team.

Throughout this period the public attended to Allen, whose involvement with owner Carpenter and Philadelphia fans said much about the trials of the United States in the sixties. Although Carpenter was hard working and well intentioned, many writers thought him intellectually limited. "A big kid who loved baseball," Carpenter was a multimillionaire with southern roots. Even circumspect observers noted his "paternal," "aristocratic," or "feudal" values. By 1967 the unrest of the 1960s had even transformed the uncritical sports press. *Daily News* columnist Bill Conlin wrote that the owner and his general manager were racists. In the early 1970s Carpenter himself acknowledged that he was at fault in not knowing how to treat black athletes and that he was struggling to correct the problem. From the late 1940s on, his racial policies revealed an antipathy toward black people. He hardly had the moral awareness necessary to grasp the conflicts of the 1960s. The city's rooters underscored Carpenter's deficiencies. Blacks had only come to Shibe Park in any numbers to see Jackie Robinson and the Brooklyn Dodgers in the late 1940s, and continued to see the Dodgers thereafter, who were "black America's" team. Then, in the 1960s, blacks began to follow Philadelphia baseball because of Allen. But the city's fans were still almost exclusively white. Hailing from the suburbs or Philadelphia's blue-collar neighborhoods, they were less sensitive than even Carpenter. On the other side was Allen, a complicated and brooding man who developed an erratic and troubling style.

Some writers attributed the Phillies' collapse after the 1964 riot to a dark unease that overtook Allen, the effect on him of the widespread tension and his emerging racial consciousness. A native of a small town that had a tiny black community, he claimed not to have known bigotry until he got into organized baseball. In fact, before Carpenter brought him up to the Phillies, Allen spent 1963 in the minors in Little Rock, Arkansas. There, where southern whites ridiculed him, he broke the sports color line. The essential thing, Allen said, was that "I came here black . . . [and] militant." No crisis occurred, however, until the next year, 1965. That July Frank Thomas, an outfielder known as "the Big Donkey" because he said the wrong things to the wrong people, fought

with Allen during batting practice. Thomas made racial slurs, Allen
swung, and Thomas hit him with a bat. Five hours later the Phillies
placed Thomas on waivers and ordered Allen not to discuss the incident, although it crystallized his own anger about his problems as a
black baseball star. Many white fans responded negatively to Thomas's
dismissal. More and more of them delighted in jeering Allen. Some of
the hostility was explicitly racial: "Nigger! Go back to South Street with
the monkeys." Allen certainly thought that "racial prejudice and . . .
segregation" caused his troubles with the patrons.

Facts corroborate many of Allen's perceptions. After he visited a
radio talk show, the moderator received letters calling him "a nigger
lover." Fans sent Allen hate mail. Kids bothered his daughter at school.
His wife received cruel phone calls. Hoodlums stoned their home.

Yet matters were more complex. Carpenter later adamantly asserted
that although Allen was "pro black," he was not "a militant." And the
extensive public record does not show that civil rights, the political
protests of the 1960s, or social principles preoccupied Allen. Rather, he
bought some racehorses and developed a love for the track, where he
sometimes went, in expensive and exaggerated clothing, instead of to
his job. By the late 1960s Allen was periodically and predictably late for
games. He got into a celebrated barroom fight in 1967. Sometimes he
came to the park drunk or did not come at all.

When Allen did show up at Connie Mack Stadium, fans would be-
rate him mercilessly. They persisted in calling him "Richie," instead of
"Dick," as he preferred. One writer said that in six years in the city Allen
"smarted from the most sustained abuse . . . of any player in the history
of the team"; another that Allen was "the most booed man in Philadelphia from April to October." In an editorial titled "The Right to Boo" the
Bulletin said that such hooting was intrinsic to "the democratic process."
On the field Allen got the nickname "Crash" because he wore a batting
helmet to protect himself from the coins, bolts, and bottles fans would
hurl at him. In response, his opinion of the city became well known
enough to get into the *New York Times* crossword puzzle. The clue for
"Armpit of America" was "Richie Allen's epithet for Philadelphia."

Allen became a star just before the unheroic side of ballplayers became common knowledge. Some of his antics did not differ from the
activities of less notorious white players. Still, the need to hide his fears
and insecurities drove Allen to destructive excess. "I was labelled an
outlaw," he said, "and after a while that's what I became."

Manager Gene Mauch tried fining and benching his star to bring him into line. But Allen had excuses for every infraction, including his non-appearances. He missed a bus, he got caught in traffic, he overslept, someone got the time wrong. More important, in what he called "fairness" to Allen, Carpenter often overruled his manager. In 1968 Mauch told Carpenter that he had to choose between him and Allen. Carpenter wanted "this boy" to play and fired Mauch. In 1965 Carpenter had traded Wes Covington for criticizing Mauch. Three years later the manager, instead of a black ballplayer, lost his job. Reversing long-standing patterns of behavior, Carpenter went out of his way to protect Allen.

A year later, in 1969, Allen did not show up for several games—AWOL from the Phillies' "decaying old ball park," as one writer put it. Now Carpenter refused to back up Bob Skinner, Mauch's successor. Carpenter wanted to be "benevolent" to Allen and would not collect a series of fines Skinner had imposed. The Phillies owner finally asked Allen to name a charity to contribute the fines to. When Allen refused, Carpenter handed over some ten thousand dollars to the Police Athletic League. Commissioner Frank Rizzo accepted the money, and one wag wrote about "the great Allen-to-Rizzo doubleplay combination."

Two months later, in an emotional and acrimonious press conference at Connie Mack Stadium, the new manager resigned. "I'm quitting," said Skinner in the presence of Carpenter and his general manager, "because of lack of support from the front office." Everything Allen wants, continued Skinner, "he gets. . . . He's been spoiled to the point that a manager cannot handle him." Carpenter has "tied my hands." Allen knows he can "answer to someone else." Skinner stormed out of the pressroom, and some enterprising reporters followed him, for the last time, to "the musty club house" in the stadium. "They've ruined Allen," the ex-manager concluded, "so nobody can handle him."

Back at the press conference, journalists ignored the announcement about a new manager and questioned Carpenter about Allen. Had he treated Allen like other players? "In many phases he was treated much more severely," said Carpenter, "in other phases more leniently." Reporters then trailed Carpenter to a kitchen behind the first base grandstand. He uncorked a Scotch bottle and poured a drink that, said one writer, he obviously needed. "I've never seen Skinner mad before," Carpenter said in a low voice. "I really like him." "I told Skinner I didn't know how to handle Allen. The guy just doesn't want responsibility. . . . I don't understand him."

In October the Phillies traded Allen to the Cardinals. Although Allen went to St. Louis, Curt Flood, the other half of the trade, refused to report to the Phillies. In part because Flood regarded the city as a hotbed of racism, he chose to fight the baseball reserve clause that bound him to Philadelphia. His landmark case went to the Supreme Court. Although Flood lost, he never played in Philadelphia, and his stand was critical to the revolution of labor relations in 1970s baseball.

The prolonged disputes, first with Allen and then with Flood, brought all the strains in the Phillies organization into the open—bad management, disaffected players, poor performance, low attendance. The team limped along for the next few years until Carpenter handed over the reins to his son Ruly in 1972. Sandy Grady, a dean of the Philadelphia sports press, wrote that Connie Mack Stadium had "more arguments per square foot than Belfast." Grady perceptively noted that the problems of the franchise went far beyond Allen, but "in the heart of it all flames the electric talent of Rich Allen, burning millionaire [Carpenter] and manager alike." Allen, wrote Grady, did not cause but focused much discontent.

Allen surely focused racial discontent in the franchise. He was a moody and impulsive athlete with a club that did not know how to respond appropriately even with the best of intentions, if indeed there was an appropriate response. Carpenter admitted that he had not treated Allen as he had treated other players. But at the same time, Carpenter changed his views about black athletes. He appreciated Allen's virtues as a player and wanted them displayed in Philadelphia. In a few years Allen taught Carpenter much about the irrelevance of race to ability.

Allen symbolized discontent in the franchise but also in the city. More Philadelphians discussed Allen's life-style and attitudes, said one writer, than worried about the quality of city government or the striking social concerns of the era. If Nixon loses in 1972, said Carpenter reflectively, "they'll blame it on Allen." In addition to racial antagonism, however, fans understood the demands of justice. One observer said, "You'd sit in the stands with these guys, and feel their anger. They'd scream every time he struck out or made an error." Still, this fan went on, "If you knew anything about baseball, you knew that Allen was such a pure talent . . . when he'd hit one of those home runs, they'd love him, worship that ability." White rooters seemed to come to the stadium to witness in Allen's behavior the attraction and revulsion of this time of shifting racial relations. The park was the place where many white people expressed puzzlement, rage, and a modicum of grudging respect. At Connie Mack Stadium Allen represented the confusion of the 1960s.

Grady had concluded his essay on Carpenter and Allen by mentioning the healing aspect of the new park into which the Phillies were to move in 1971. Then under construction, Veterans Stadium was an enormous, antiseptic piece of architecture, located miles from the racial conflicts of the old stadium neighborhood. Fans and team looked on it as Nirvana.

In late 1967 Bob Uecker, then catching for the Phillies, said that Connie Mack Stadium brought out the worst fans and the worst in them. "They work in sewers for eight hours, then they come out to this sewer and all their emotions are expressed." Uecker added that the fans in the old park would "boo unwed mothers on Mother's Day." Allen called the field a "house of gloom." After the *Bulletin* wrote about him in the editorial "The Right to Boo," letters to the paper also connected the hooters and the locale. The "sadistic, atavistic, uncivilized, and ugly" Philadelphia fans, wrote one out-of-town rooter, disgraced even "the dilapidated environs" of Connie Mack Stadium. The fans were not fit for "a modern sophisticated showplace." Philadelphia, wrote one young man, did not "deserve" another park. After the Phillies sold Allen to St. Louis and the team prepared to move to the Vet, Sandy Grady had the last word. They should name the new stadium, he said, after Cardinal general manager Bing Devine, "who emancipated Rich Allen from Philadelphia—and vice versa."

10

Urban Renewal?

In the nineteenth century blacks lived in North Philadelphia around Tenth and Columbia. They moved west along Columbia and then obliquely northwest along Ridge Road, which intersected Columbia. The residential angle formed two arms that embraced, in time, a large segment of this part of the city. Nevertheless, for a long time black people were only one of many lower-income groups occupying what was later called "the inner city." Eventually, however, north Broad became more commercial and black. By the Depression blacks, along with the poor and aged who could not escape, made the southern part of North Philadelphia a distinct enclave. More prosperous white Philadelphians wanted to contain the inhabitants in that enclave.

At the same time, while Philadelphia's total population changed little from 1920 to 1970, the black numbers grew from 134,000 to 650,000, from 7 percent to 34 percent. Despite containment, large ghetto districts flowered. Blacks expanded through Lower North Philadelphia to Upper North Philadelphia, north of Lehigh. The social result said much about the plight of all the old U.S. urban areas.

The changing national and international economy produced a rejuvenated center-city residential region. Affluent whites lived there and worked in nearby downtown corporate headquarters and white-collar service centers. An ever more diseased part of Philadelphia surrounded this section. In various slums lived those people who did not have the wherewithal after World War II to get to the suburbs, new housing, and better jobs. Most were blacks who had marginal employment and substandard dwellings. Their communities could not escape crime, vice, and squalor.

North Penn and its sister neighborhoods to the north were newer areas than those below Lehigh. Urban experts called the latter "streetcar suburbs." In the nineteenth century their residents depended on rapid transit to their jobs. When they changed jobs, or employers themselves moved, the neighborhoods altered. These older communities south of

Lehigh deteriorated rapidly with changes in the city's economic order. Blacks quickly increased their presence there as middle-class whites vacated these early suburbs in the first part of the twentieth century.

Upper North Philadelphia above Lehigh differed. Newer by twenty or thirty years, its communities were originally more homogeneous and more exclusively oriented to the industries a walk or a bus ride away. Experts would call them "streetcar industrial" or "walking industrial." These white working-class sections in Upper North Philadelphia were stable for longer periods than the more mixed, comparatively more middle-class area that initially existed in Lower North Philadelphia.

The blocks immediately around Shibe Park were a peculiar walking industrial zone. The park solidified economic stability through various kinds of employment and often directly contributed to the quality of the housing stock. Baseball made for ancillary employment that gave neighbors an overriding interest in their land. The stadium generated parking lots, residential rooming, the rooftop seats, eating establishments, and bars, all stimulating residents to look after their property.

The Athletics' departure in 1954 struck the first blow at this economy. Some small businessmen did not care. A petshop owner on Twenty-second was pleased that customers could park in front of his shop. A realtor was relieved that he could park near his own office. But the departure hurt other businesses. It pressed taprooms and small eating places most. During the first inconclusive negotiations over the Athletics, one bartender related that people were "jumping with joy" when word came that the franchise was staying. When the sale went through, the owner of Athletics Lunch said that his business would lose "the gravy" and that he would cut down on staff. Charley Quinn at the Deep Right Field Café adopted a wait-and-see attitude, putting the best face on things. One proprietor projected that a five-thousand-dollar loss of business might force him to sell. A drop in customers would hit the neighbors who ran small, independent parking operations equally hard. Moreover, although the Phillies picked up some of the Athletics' employees, the franchise fired fifty-three full-time workers. They sat around Connie Mack Stadium "with the air of mourners at a funeral." Three hundred and fifteen part-timers had their income carved in half. Most of these workers lived in the community.

The Phillies, however, were there in the fifties and sixties. Even though Connie Mack Stadium deteriorated, the franchise functioned as an aging and inefficient enterprise. Unable to move, it remained in business and was a positive element in the community. In the 1960s, however, Philadelphia's economic troubles made the environs of Connie Mack Stadium a beleaguered precinct.

The problems of the franchise and the neighborhood were not unique. In a 1972 federal study, the director of Housing and Urban Affairs mentioned seven cities with similar miseries in the 1960s. Six of the seven were homes to professional baseball; they represented eleven of the original sixteen major league teams and five abandoned parks.

In the 1950s, when Upper North Philadelphia went black, Lehigh Avenue set off "the Jungle" from the more habitable regions to the north. But as the 1960s marked a turning point in national urban affairs, so in Philadelphia the 1964 riot symbolized a grim new era when race relations were the gravest of the city's concerns. The troubles above Lehigh Avenue increased. Undiscriminating about blacks, the white business leadership raced to leave all of North Philadelphia, just as the Phillies did.

From 1965 to 1972 the great number of small but vital Acme supermarkets throughout North Philadelphia closed down. As workers boarded up stores, old black residents shuffled in to say good-bye; some cried. The store at Twenty-fifth and Lehigh went first. The A&P's and the Penn Fruit at Twenty-second and Lehigh imitated the Acmes. Factories, offices, theaters, bakeries, physicians, and pharmacies left in addition to the chain stores. "Thousands of people and entire city blocks have vanished," wrote one commentator. As one black politician put it, local shopping districts changed into "ghost towns" in the late 1960s.

Most symptomatically, banking in North Philadelphia collapsed. Or, rather, machines replaced banks. At Twenty-second and Lehigh, First Pennsylvania Bank appeased the neighborhood and opened a "center," which real people, at least, staffed. But the branch did not offer savings or checking accounts, safe deposit boxes, or loan facilities. Instead the center handled money orders, mass transit passes, and food stamps; distributed welfare checks; and accepted utility payments.

The tragedy was not just a black one. Although far better equipped economically than the city's blacks to endure travail, the Roman Catholic church suffered in many of its urban parishes. In fifteen to twenty years, the once proud Saint Columba's went from 3,500 familes to 350, reflecting the comparatively tiny number of black Catholics. The church fell into disrepair as vandals and muggers haunted it. Irish priests uncomfortably ministered to black female communicants. The population of the adjacent Saint Columba's school dropped from 1,800 to about 460, 90 percent black. The school itself had broken windows. A German shepherd patrolled the yard.

At Saint Mary of the Eternal at Twenty-second and Clearfield the Italians did just as badly. The church closed after 8:00 A.M. mass and did away with evening services. "People are afraid to go out," said the priest in charge. As one observer wrote about all the North Philadelphia parishes, "Bewildered by what seemed to them a cruel blow, the clergymen left behind by their white parishioners did nothing but watch, saddened and angry, as it all began to deteriorate. Income from collections dropped to almost nothing. Mass attendance dwindled . . . church property was not maintained."

After the riot, to a greater extent south of Lehigh but also north of Lehigh, a new phenomenom occurred. One writer argued that "the Jungle" was dying. Philadelphia's population, constant in mid-century, declined 13 percent from 1970 to 1980, from over 1.9 million to under 1.7 million. In North Philadelphia, however, the decline was twice that, 29 percent or 86,000 people. Habitable housing ceased to exist as people and politicians abandoned or demolished residences, business establishments, and industries.

Many factors caused the disappearance of housing. Residents found mortgage money impossible to obtain in North Philadelphia. The banks that had closed their local branches adopted policies in their main offices that assisted decline. They frustrated the desire for ownership and the stake in property values that ownership meant. Bankers were afraid to invest mortgage money in North Philadelphia. Moreover, people with small incomes and low rents could not pay increases. Unable to cover costs, landlords cut maintenance and often gave up entirely on rental units. The city itself drove out real estate speculators by buying up many properties and then letting them deteriorate. Washington paradoxically aided depopulation with its program of "Home Ownership for the Poor." When low-income citizens could not meet mortgage payments on housing purchased under this program, the federal government foreclosed on thousands of buildings and then abandoned them. People thrown out of housing went elsewhere. Others who were able to meet mortgage or rent payments struggled to leave dwellings near unsightly, boarded-up firetraps that tempted drunks or drug dealers.

The delay in finishing Veterans Stadium that forced the Phillies to stay in North Philadelphia pleased many residents. The owners of local parking lots smiled. "It's a blessing," said the proprietors of Peg and Dave's Luncheonette at Twenty-second and Somerset, opposite the bleacher entrance. The taprooms, as one owner put it, could avoid "disastrous times" till the Phillies went.

When the franchise did leave, along with the Acmes and the banks, North Penn reached its nadir. A real estate analyst wrote that in the five-year period from 1966 to 1971 one multistory warehouse declined in value from $1.3 million to $400,000, a real estate "catastrophe." Experts blamed the catastrophe on the neighborhood's "going bad" and cited the purse snatching, robbery, assault, and burglary making their way north of Lehigh and upsetting "good, honest, hard working blacks in neat porch-front row homes."

Gang warfare did spread to Upper North Philadelphia in the early 1970s as various bands—Tenderloin, Twentieth and Cambria, and Mad Dog—contested for turf in the neighborhood. At Twenty-third and Somerset someone shot and stabbed "Geronimo," the leader of the Kool World Valley. According to reports, five murders, forty-four robberies, thirty-two assaults, and four rapes took place in the community in 1969. Gangs killed some small businessmen. Others closed their shops. Some black merchants but also some Jewish ones who had not been able to leave bought guns to protect themselves. They toted thirty-eight-caliber revolvers on their hips in their stores, or kept shotguns—"equalizers"—under their counters.

Thieves regularly burglarized Saint Columba's now. A growing number of violent crimes culminated in the knifing of a priest. The uneasy give-and-take between blacks and whites above Lehigh before the 1964 riot gave way to what one observer called "a wordless, seething anger." Racial disorders closed Dobbins High School at Twenty-second and Lehigh. Packs of black and white students moved up and down Lehigh demonstrating. But crime, assault, and protest were never just racial. As one black neighbor said, "Everyone always used to write about how the white folks was afraid to come up here. Well it ain't any better now." Gangs "don't worry about discrimination. Don't matter whether your skin's black or white." The *Chat*, which now spoke out for black interests in all of North Philadelphia, held on into the mid-seventies and then ceased publishing.

Things may have just "gone bad," but withdrawing services and capital abetted the process. When mortgage lenders assessed the area as risky, they contributed to its riskiness. When insurance carriers placed the neighborhood "off limits," they killled businesses. Without insurance for property damage, fire, or burglary, employers moved if they could. Vandals easily entered vacant establishments. Such a series of events ended in the empty warehouse whose value had depreciated so strikingly by the early 1970s. This happened repeatedly around Connie Mack Stadium. Entrepreneurs and other members of the "development community," like the food chains and banks, participated in the process they found catastrophic. Federal and municipal governments, eager to demolish buildings without plans for future use, assisted developers.

Connie Mack—or rather his image and name—epitomized how the black neighborhood and the urban power structure accommodated each other. By 1965, in the Park and Recreation Center named after Mack, his statue presided over a rubble of litter and broken bottles. Both the bronze and the little park looked "rundown" and "unkempt," said the newspaper. Charley Quinn started a movement to get the statue transferred to the site of the new stadium. Officials, however, had anticipated Quinn. Before erecting the statue in 1957, its proponents decided to move it if the city financed a new facility. After the Phillies left, workers uprooted the statue. Politicians rededicated it in August 1971 at the corner of Broad Street and Pattison Avenue. Quinn himself hung on till he died in 1974. Shortly thereafter his wife sold out.

Inside the Connie Mack Recreation Center officials channeled the energies of young people away from gang warfare by arranging athletic contests for competing groups of "disaffected youth." If Kool World, the Villagers, and Twenty-first and Norris could fight it out on the playing field, social workers reasoned, they would not kill each other or other North Philadelphians. But the center did not repeat the contests after a trial year. In the early seventies the city cut back on the center's funds and deferred repairs. Local government disinvested in North Philadelphia the same way that private enterprise had.

The community's black leadership complained that cuts came *because* the neighborhood went from white to black. As if to emphasize the fact and to offer a palliative, after the untimely death of the NAACP leader, the city council later renamed the Connie Mack Center the

"Cecil Moore Recreation Center." One could not help wonder how permanent this tribute to Moore would be, especially when Reyburn or Connie Mack had never caught on and when some residents still talked about the Square. At the same time the city proposed to name a middle school at Nineteenth and Somerset after Connie Mack. The community protested that Mack had banned black ballplayers from his park and wanted no part of his name. Instead of changing the name, the city dropped plans for the school.

When Jerry Wolman bought the stadium and the Eagles in 1964, his interest was in making money through speculation in real estate and sports franchises. Nonetheless, at least until 1970, Connie Mack Stadium was directly connected to sport, whatever the state of Wolman's enterprises. After the Phillies moved their baggage out in early February 1971, the field, as one writer suggested, "formally became just another piece of Wolman's real estate holdings."

By that time Wolman was bankrupt, although he still lived in an expensive Maryland suburb. The nature of his concern and that of other developers for Twenty-first and Lehigh revealed the problems North Philadelphia faced if it was again to become a viable community. Assisted by the inability or unwillingness of the city to push him, Wolman did nothing with his property. As taxes and mortgages went unpaid, the parcel nourished the evils that made North Philadelphia a no-man's-land. Even if Wolman had interests other than money, he or other capitalists alone could do little to make the area livable. Rehabilitation costs were so great that public financing was necessary.

In 1971, before it stopped publishing, the *Chat* best analyzed the plight of the area. The Phillies, said the newspaper, were through with the community in which they had lived for over thirty years. Now government and the real estate and development communities must act. The fate of the stadium would resemble the fate of this part of the city. If the elite allowed the park to "rot slowly," like a "stiff . . . infect[ing] the neighborhood," then the community had to infer that the power structure believed this was "about par for North Philadelphia." The local civic association, too, linked the neighborhood's "spiritual and physical decline" with "the rise and fall" of the ball park.

Wolman purchased the stadium as part of a larger strategy of making money from municipal development projects. Even when he was in financial straits in the late sixties, he used the property as leverage. He attempted to form a holding company in which Connie Mack Stadium and his other assets would operate as a unit to pay off his debts and yet enable him to maintain ownership. Then Wolman planned to sell everything except the Eagles to meet the demands of creditors. In 1970, as the Phillies departed, Wolman deeded the grounds to a new "straw" owner, the Connie Mack Stadium Ltd. Partnership. Wolman held most of its stock and negotiated a new mortgage. The partnership might take advantage of the situation the Phillies' move created. Someone would raze the property, and perhaps a real estate bonanza might occur, funded by Washington.

Six months after this reorganization Louis M. Grayboyes and Sollis Tollin took over the mortgage. Partners in a real estate corporation, Grayboyes and Tollin erected inner-city housing units for the Philadelphia Housing Authority. At a time when the city was denouncing slumlords in the Connie Mack Stadium area who extracted windfall profits from urban renewal, Grayboyes and Tollin narrowly escaped indictment for the shoddy construction of their housing. The two partners sat on the property. With Wolman in Maryland and the city unable to collect taxes or force demolition, the developers had only to wait till the city destroyed the building or sold the land. Maybe they could still make money. Nothing motivated them to plan. This was the predicament of North Philadelphia. When a reporter asked Grayboyes what he aimed to do with Twenty-first and Lehigh, his humor manifested the atmosphere of indifference. "We may try to bring back the Athletics," he joked.

The potential for a deal was always present. Although the desolation of "the Jungle" was undeniable, in the 1960s Washington's generosity enriched real estate magnates and contractors involved in slum clearance. Urban planners forever conjured up dreams of a garden city in the ghetto. Stories that rehabilitation would take place recurred. Plans for renewal were always a backdrop to the Phillies' departure in the sixties and continued after they left.

In 1966 North City Corporation, a nonprofit civic agency, proposed a $100 million housing and industrial complex over fifty acres in size, part of which would be on the cleared site of the stadium. Built both above and below ground, the complex would have bridges and rooftop amenities. Planners envisioned space for schools, shopping, parks, recreation, and facilities for the elderly. The officials wanted federal funds used "wherever possible." Four years later, with the Phillies ready to go, designs for such a combined commercial and residential center were still extant. Although no one ever acted on the plans, bigwigs added to them a future bicentennial exhibit for 1976.

After Grayboyes and Tollin entered the picture, they tried to sell the property to Philadelphia for municipal buildings. They also supported the local civic association, which urged the city to rehabilitate the park for a children's recreation center or a vocational complex. Plans that required money from its own coffers did not interest Philadelphia, however. City officials did announce that they would seek national funding for an industrial park. Five or six light industries would relocate there and create two to three hundred jobs. Politicians dumped these plans when the community argued instead for housing for the elderly or a vocational skills center. Mainly, though, Philadelphia got no dollars from Washington. Nonetheless, the city regularly expressed its good intentions. A multimillion dollar job training center for unemployed minority youth could go there, said the city's managing director. Politicians floated another proposal for a neighborhood shopping center. Still nothing happened.

In 1968 Tasty Baking Company, with the help of the real estate firm of Jackson-Cross, surveyed the area around the company at Twenty-eighth and Hunting Park. An old firm located near Connie Mack Stadium, Tasty Baking had many advertising ties to baseball. When its Hunting Park neighborhood went black, the company did not leave, primarily because of the cost of rebuilding elsewhere. Company executives worried, however, that the environs might become a slum. They asked Jackson-Cross to define a "conservable" district and formed the Allegheny West Community Development Organization. An agency supported by Tasty and other area businesses, as well as by charitable foundations and urban renewal funds, the organization worked with residents to restore the community at the grass-roots level.

The notion of Allegheny West was extraordinary. It initially defined as a neighborhood a piece of North Philadelphia from Hunting Park to Somerset and from Twenty-second to Twenty-ninth streets. This slice of real estate was never a community; it represented what urban planners believed was salvageable economic territory around Tasty Baking—a "marketing area." The name did not refer to any existing neighborhood. While the boundaries of Allegheny West changed over the years, the Twenty-second Street eastern boundary, the main shopping avenue, usually excluded the immediate area of the old stadium, an essential part of the old neighborhood.

People knew the company that sponsored Allegheny West for its paternalism. Tasty Baking had a long history of being "anti" everything. No union had been able to crack it, and it was antiwomen, anti-Jew, and antiblack. Its president recalled that in the 1950s half of the workers lived around the plant. In the mid-seventies, when the neighborhood was black, the company still had a black work force of only 10 percent, mainly in low-paying jobs. The *Philadelphia Business Journal* gave a revealing description of what Tasty thought of these people, who could not get jobs at the company that professed interest in their well-being. They were folk "anxious to make a good life for themselves, but who had never owned homes and had no experience in organizing a neighborhood."

The same sorts of reformers who demolished North Philadelphia twenty years before praised the 1970s efforts of Allegheny West and similar housing and urban rehabilitation agencies. But in truth these organizations operated on a shoestring and had little power for good or ill. Their resources were tiny compared to what most experts on the city said was necessary to rejuvenate North Philadelphia. At the same time notable triumphs occurred. By the early 1980s Allegheny West had partially revived the north Twenty-second Street business district, and at Twenty-first and Somerset, reformers built a ninety-six-unit town house cooperative. Moreover, the failures of Catholics in the community had to be weighed against the rise of Protestants. Founded in 1899, Saint Bartolomew's Episcopal Church on the south side of Lehigh long served a small group of middle-class whites. By the 1970s it was black and thriving, housing a Get Set School and a day-care service for working mothers. Twelve other Protestant churches held services on Lehigh between Twenty-fourth and Twenty-ninth. Some were Baptist. Others were independent sects. Most moved into old landmarks. Schillings ice cream parlor and bakery at Twenty-fifth and Lehigh was the Kingdom Hall of the Jehovah's Witnesses. Pleasant Grove Baptist Church took over Lindner's candy store at Twenty-eighth Street. The old Lehigh Theater became the Friendship Baptist Church.

In 1969, too, Fidelity Bank bucked a trend and opened a full-service bank at Twenty-third and Lehigh. The staff was black and its customers 70 percent black, city employees, schoolteachers, and working people. In addition, the Colum Federal Credit Union was in business a block away. Although customers were not plentiful, the old Credit Union, a community outfit originally designed to keep Irish money out of the hands of loan sharks, had a growing list of black members. "We're looking forward to helping them as we helped the old Irish families," said its treasurer.

Judging the impact of these victories on the future of the community was difficult. When Allegheny West defined its eastern boundary at Twenty-second Street, the organization wrote out the northeastern edge of old North Penn, including Shibe Park and North Twentieth Street, from whatever funding might come to the agency. Experts called it "triaging" the city. In 1979 the *Inquirer* considered the neglect in an editorial titled "Eleven Forgotten Blocks." One in ten houses was vacant in the area around Twenty-first and Lehigh. The neighborhood, one civic leader said, was "a glaring example of the neglect of the North Central area as a whole." The minute improvements, some critics held, took place in the context of deepening decline.

The Philadelphia "standard metropolitan statistical area" lost a hundred thousand jobs in the 1970s. In the same period the city fell from three to seven in the United States as a corporate headquarters. These figures measured Philadelphia's disadvantages in competing with cites in the South and West and even the weakening of the U.S. economy as it confronted countries such as Japan and West Germany. Tasty Baking stayed, but many others left. A West German steel company acquired Budd Co., the great automobile supplier, and moved the headquarters to Rome, Georgia, at the cost of twelve hundred jobs in Hunting Park.

On the other hand, some analysts argued that blacks would someday get to the worst of the old suburbs, which were now less than desirable: the industry, commerce, and housing built there after World War II were almost fifty years old and increasingly unattractive. In turn, vacant North Philadelphia, close to central city employment, where government was giving away housing ripe for improvement, would attract middle- and upper-middle-class whites. Powerful governmental funding agencies were not eager for more low-income housing in North Philadelphia and were insisting that municipalities place such housing in outlying districts. Laws mandating such changes, it was argued, could in time promote "gentrification" in the inner city and new ghettos in the oldest post–World War II suburbs. The forces necessary to "push" poor blacks out of Philadelphia and "pull" affluent white groups into it might be coming into existence. Perhaps the future of the area lay

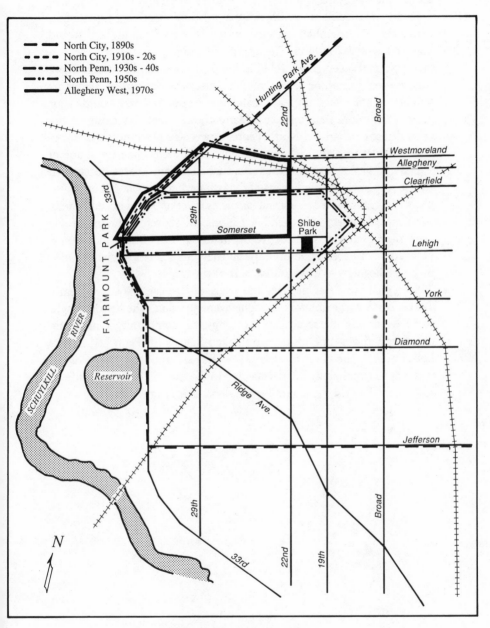

North City, 1890s
North City, 1910s - 20s
North Penn, 1930s - 40s
North Penn, 1950s
Allegheny West, 1970s

Hunting Park Ave.

Broad

22nd

Westmoreland
Allegheny
Clearfield

33rd

29th

Somerset

Shibe
Park

Lehigh

York

Diamond

FAIRMOUNT PARK

SCHUYLKILL RIVER

Reservoir

Ridge Ave.

Jefferson

29th

33rd

22nd

19th

Broad

N

Map 6. Changing boundaries

in town houses for the fortunate. At the same time, at the end of the century, it was still a neglected and run-down section of the city.

Decay or rehabilitation were not the only options. Other experts predicted that Philadelphia's population would stop declining and would hold steady at 1.7 million. The city would come to rest, as it were, at a lower but still acceptable level of industry, services, and housing. There was so much cheap or vacant property near the downtown neighborhoods that one could not realistically assume that renewal would occur in anything more than enclaves. Many choicer spots lay closer to the central district than old North Penn. It was also presumptuous to believe that urban planning commitments could determine the shape of the city. It was unclear, for example, that Allegheny West's decision to "triage" the immediate environs of the ball park in the late 1970s would mean anything. Other renewal agencies overlapped with Allegheny West and, in effect, competed for funds. Moreover, ordinary people went their own way, irrespective of "urbanologists." This is not to say, however, that experts had no impact. They might assist in giving a new name—Allegheny West—to that part of the city.

Seen in longer perspective, the trials of the late 1960s and early 1970s, some commentators thought, were aberrant. The district might still have a long life as a black working-class community. One astute observer and old-time resident remarked that North Penn had always been "more or less poor but stable. . . . The basic problem," he went on, was that the trees along the streets died in the early 1970s. "If the streets had trees," he said, "it would be the same as it always was."

11

Last Days, 1969–1976

Professional baseball came of age in the early twentieth century as an urban phenomenon. The geography of the cities shaped the parks. Sports entrepreneurs built their stadiums in the towns and argued that the game reduced the tensions of industrial work. In the late twentieth century, however, the heirs of these entrepreneurs vacated their facilities because they could not cope with the crime, traffic, and racial problems of the workplace. They moved to suburban facilities. Restrictive street patterns might not constrain the new grounds, but these stadiums were not "natural." They were often not parts of neighborhoods. Their covering was astroturf, and fans were not permitted on it. Some were "all-weather." Their shape had to be conducive to at least two sports—the new Veterans Stadium was an "Octorad palace," whatever that meant.

Although these complaints might be excessive, a transformation had occurred in the move to the new sports complexes. In Philadelphia in the late 1960s and early 1970s, the transformation generated a torrent of public expression.

Bob Carpenter scheduled the Phillies to play in Veterans Stadium sometime early in 1970 and even prepared the team to leave Connie Mack Stadium at the end of 1969. But troubles at the new site prevented the franchise from moving out of its old quarters until early 1971, after the 1970 season. A fire damaged the abandoned building soon after the Phillies departed, paving the way for its 1976 demolition. From 1969 to 1976, and afterward, effusive public statements about the virtues of the new stadium contradicted the sadness about moving. Relief at getting out of North Philadelphia joined with emotional outpourings about Shibe Park that grew as the deserted field became a more distant memory. The positive recollections increased in proportion to the actual decline at the site.

The papers described opening night in 1969 as "dreary." The park was "old," "tired," and "rusting"; the seats unpainted. Next year, reported

the *Inquirer*, suburbanites would enjoy baseball without "slums or worries." Observers thought that the last home game of that season would
be the last game played in Connie Mack Stadium, certainly the last end-
of-season game, and "quite a few" gray and bald heads stood out among
the 6,875 hardy fans at the 1969 finale. Many men brought their families "to whom they could unburden memories and point out particles
of the past." Two seventy-year-olds who had seen the 1909 opener
when they were nine discussed how they had sat "right behind first
base" that April 9, sixty years before. One of them had also been at the
1929 World Series game in which the A's scored ten runs in one inning.
John Murphy had lit a cigar and made up his mind that he "wouldn't
take it out of my mouth until they stopped scoring." When the tenth
run scored, Murphy went on, the cigar was "a wisp and then dropped
on the floor." How many more runs, Murphy mused, would the A's
have gotten had he been able to hold the cigar longer? Another man had
gone to the second game of the 1911 series and witnessed Frank Baker's
home run. Two others reminisced about Connie Mack's selling off his
teams. "He didn't have any money himself," they agreed. Someone else
talked about the spite fence. "They had seats over here on top of the
houses," he pointed out. It was, for a last game, a quiet and understated
afternoon.

Early the next year, however, contractors had not finished the Vet,
and the Phillies were to begin the season at their old grounds. They had
also hired Bill Giles as vice president for business operations. Giles,
who stepped up to the presidency of the Phillies in 1981, concerned
himself with publicity. Appointing an executive who emphasized baseball entertainment was the final concession Bob Carpenter made to the
franchise.

The "modernization" begun in the 1940s and 1950s when Carpenter
took over continued in the 1960s. On the sporting side, his son, who
started working for the franchise in the early sixties, sponsored contract
research at the University of Delaware. Scholars designed studies to se-
lect prospects more efficiently and by "more objective means." The club
invested in personality appraisals and hitting and eye evaluations. On
the business side, the team surveyed the "marketing area" of its customers, prepared a "public relations primer" for its players, and employed
consultants on how to sell "the product." Giles fit into this aspect of the
business. His showmanship contrasted with the conservative Carpenter's intense, if unsuccessful, focus on sport.

Phillies officials hoped Giles would increase attendance, especially with the impending move. In 1970 it became clear that the team would play its first home contest at Connie Mack Stadium. Because Giles believed that the team would leave in midsummer, he celebrated the starting game as a major event. He tried to resurrect an older plan to have a parachutist in a Phillies suit deliver the first ball from three thousand feet in the air. This would generate "excitement galore—flares on the field. . . . Rescue ambulances awaiting any emergency, Firemen and Police in attendance." When the parachutist was vetoed, Giles settled for the first daytime opener in fifteen years.

The new Phillies manager, Frank Luchesi, came to the park early and looked around the empty stands. "Then I stood in the dugout and thought what an honor it was to be in the same place where Mr. Connie Mack managed those great Athletics teams." Sandy Grady reported that it was "an odd, nostalgic crowd" of "beefy red-faced men" and that there was "a soft and sentimental air" about the occasion. "This was a day," he said, "when Connie Mack [Stadium] should have been trapped in amber, a festival out of the past, and nuts to that futuristic mudhole in South Philly." But, Grady added, "How many picnics can you have in a haunted house?" Another writer concluded that the stadium was "a better legend than a ball park."

Despite Giles's efforts, the opener drew only sixteen thousand, the smallest crowd in the National League by ten thousand, a distinction attributable not just to Connie Mack Stadium but also to years of bad baseball. A new home was the fastest way to lift patronage, and the franchise kept hoping to move to the Vet. But as the days passed, it became certain that the Phillies would end 1970 at their old grounds. The team scheduled more day games to entice fans. Most people were "afraid to spend an evening in the neighborhood." The franchise estimated its loss for the extra year in North Philadelphia at $2 million.

Sportswriters were ambivalent. One said, "That's where they steal hubcaps while the car is running." The *Bulletin* reported that coming back to a "gaunt, flaking, cracking, senile stadium" upset fans. At the same time, in his column "My Philadelphia," *Inquirer* writer Al Haas said, "Like most of the males born in this city Connie Mack Stadium was part of my childhood." Watching baseball there, he had grown up assuming "life was as uncomplicated as strikes and balls, as . . . honest as a line drive to left." Haas would go out to Shibe Park "one more time before it is too late."

Fans like Haas got their wish in Giles's special promotion of the last game, on October 1, 1970: "Farewell to Connie Mack Stadium." He oversaw a series of festivities that his staff organized. Employees wore old-fashioned clothes; concessions sold peanuts for a nickel; and an old-time bicycle group performed. The Phillies handed out memorabilia, including slats from the stadium seats and other parts of the park—bases, locker room chairs, uniforms. A publicity man wrote a two-minute eulogy to be read by Connie Mack, Jr., who would be introduced with other dignitaries at the start of the game. At the end of the contest a helicopter would take the old home plate to Veterans Stadium.

Giles's promotion got wide attention. Learning of the evening, Jerry Wolman thought that perhaps after the closing he could hold a giant public auction with the proceeds split fifty-fifty between local charities and his creditors. This proposal went nowhere, but the closing ceremonies themselves came off without a hitch. Connie Mack, Jr., read his lines well: "I feel sadness about this old ball park that has been so important a part of my life . . . and I will always have my memories." The Phillies did well too, defeating the Montreal Expos 2–1 in ten innings and escaping the National League cellar. The franchise made money with Giles's hype. The 31,822 fans—contrasted with under 7,000 the year before at the preliminary closing—consumed 16,000 hot dogs, 40,000 slices of pizza, 20,000 bottles of beer, and 25,000 sodas.

All this was incidental to the main event of the evening, a destructive rampage on the part of those who attended and a substitute for Wolman's proposed auction. Some people brought in their own tools. From early in the game there were sounds of hammering and the splintering of wood. Folks with no hammers and saws sat in the long rows of wood-and-metal chairs anchored in concrete and rocked on them in unison until they could pry out seats. Distinguished-looking men and women joined youngsters in chopping out anything they could move. As the game ended, the masses ran onto the grounds. As Giles screamed, "Keep off the field. Keep off the field," the crowd ripped up whatever it could, including souvenir sod. Although patrons were not able to dislodge home plate, the helicopter also left without this prize, after hovering for an hour. The customers did cart off urinals, pieces of the bullpen, and turnstiles. In the melee thirty-five people had their heads bashed with the souvenir slats of wood.

The next day Giles affected astonishment at what occurred. The insurance company, he said, had dropped its policy for the last few games. "I guess they knew this would happen," he said. The Phillies "encouraged" the finale, said the *Chat*. Over at the Deep Right Field Café a genuine baseball enthusiast charged that Giles's large crowd was not made up of baseball fans; "they are all vandals."

Yet what happened was more complicated than vandalism or a silly and irresponsible attempt to cash in on nostalgia. Outside the park before the game, thugs stabbed a man buying a ticket. Across the street a blind peanut vendor, soon to be out of work after thirty-six years, said that what he would miss most was "the roar of the crowd." Inside the park before the festivities started, former light heavyweight champ Bob Montgomery "walked reverently around the bases, pausing at each one as if at the grave of a loved one." Montgomery had had some successful fights at the park. "I just wanted to say so long," he said. "I made a lot of money in this place." No one could decide how to behave, whether the proper response was tearfulness or holiday high-spiritedness. A lot of people took refuge in a clichéd American conflict of emotions. "This is sad," said one fan, "but I guess you have to move to make way for progress."

The result was that the franchise paved the way for a peculiar kind of riot. In Giles's view the idea was to publicize the team and to make some money from the last game. He had little sense that this might be offensive to those who thought of baseball as more than a mere spectacle; nor did he realize his culpability for the behavior of the fans. At the same time the loss of control was a significant community ritual, like the festive celebration at a wake. The shenanigans at the last game did not display anger but rather joy for the past mingled with sorrow at its loss.

The next day outraged newspapers took the high road of condemning hooliganism, a "destructive assault" on property. "Instead of dying like the graceful, grand place it was, Connie Mack Stadium ended its life literally shrieking in pain from the torments of being torn apart." The *Daily News* said that the fans "raped" the old park; it was a "homicide." The riot, said the *Bulletin*, was "an extended moment of madness that was in fact the epitaph of a shoddy old ballpark that no one really wanted to play in."

The *Bulletin* distinguished the activity of the enflamed crowd from what the activity brought to mind. Above the din of rampaging fans, the newspaper editorialized, "floated memories of other times when giants of the earth stalked these acres, Jimmie Foxx and Lefty Grove and the Whiz Kids and many more. And those, in turn, evoked even more golden recollections of days of municipal glory when Philadelphia was a two-league baseball town and champions of the world played here."

The next spring the Phillies had left what their new yearbook called the "confining antiquity" of their "penitentiary of a ball park." At the Vet an "awesome panorama" and "massive splendor" greeted patrons. One columnist wrote:

> Six months ago, we had a coal yard for parking, a stadium that resembled a warehouse, warm beer, cold hot dogs, seats that made you want to stand, ushers with five o'clock shadows, a scoreboard with a hole in the middle, a near coronary walking to the upper deck, and "50 cents to watch your car, Mister?" Today there's the Palace on Pattison Ave., well lighted, attended parking with plenty of room, escalators to take you up, pretty Fillies to show you to your seats, escalators to take you down, comfortable seats, a scoreboard with the color and excitement of Disneyland.

Roger Angell, baseball's most articulate and sensitive observer, was less full of gush but in some ways even less discerning. In 1972 Angell published many of the essays he had written in the 1960s in a celebrated book, *The Summer Game*. He was eloquent about the destruction of his New York Polo Grounds in 1964. He wrote that he had no wish to watch the end of this old park, "the first fierce blows of ball and hammer." Angell spoke of "the irrevocable deprivation of habit" and "the death of still another neighborhood" that helped us remember who we were, what we had been, and what we loved. Yet the boroughs of New York circumscribed his feeling of loss. He could muster only one sentence about Connie Mack Stadium. The game's "most nagging current affliction," said Angell in *The Summer Game*, were "tired franchises" like that of Philadelphia where "shabby, badly situated ball parks" meant low attendance. The year 1971, wrote Angell, brought an "artificial boost" to the Phillies draw when the team moved.

Richie Ashburn, the Phillies star, started to announce games after his career ended. He began his new job at Connie Mack Stadium. In 1971 he broadcast from the Vet. The difference was like that "between chicken salad and chicken shit," said Ashburn. His fellow announcer, By Saam, later said the old park was "a shit-house."

In the months after it closed, the stadium suffered minor vandalism but was not deserted. The Phillies dismantled more seats and sent them to the ball park of their minor league club in Spartanburg, South Carolina. In the spring the franchise removed more turf and sold it to respectable souvenir hunters. Neighborhood kids opened the new season playing there.

In August revivalists planned a week-long meeting in the park under a big tent erected on the field. Two stepbrothers, aged nine and twelve, who lived near Twenty-third and Lehigh, snuck into the building to see the tent go up. They lit a small fire for the hell of it and ran from the park when it did not go out. The five-alarm blaze that followed destroyed many more seats. The intense heat twisted some of the steel girders that held up the stands. The fire burned the roof and stands from first base around home plate out to left field. The decks along third base collapsed.

Community onlookers were matter-of-fact. One said he would rather "see it burn down then go all rotten and fall down." Another commented, "I wish I had all the dollars I spent in that place." The papers were sadder. The *Bulletin* remarked that the fire was "a final indignity mocking the joyous days, the color and enchantment of another time in Philadelphia." A writer for the *Inquirer* noted that this attack on "the gaunt old stadium" was the "fiery prelude to the bulldozer's blade."

As the remains of the park and the neighborhood deteriorated further, people's relief at not having to deal with baseball in North Philadelphia made tender emotions easy to express. In a "super piece of irony," the fire occurred simultaneously with the rededication of Connie Mack's statue outside the new facility. Inside the Vet the Phillies were sponsoring an old-timers' night. Dick Allen was on hand too, now playing for the Dodgers. One journalist suggested that Philadelphians would blame the fire on him. Allen himself was indifferent. "That place," he said "has been dead for a long time." Among the retired players Satchel Paige was refreshingly cynical. When asked about his memories of Connie Mack Stadium, he furrowed his brow and commented, "Well . . . they wouldn't let me and my boys play there." Stan Musial, Bob Feller, and Joe DiMaggio were more sentimental, as were Del Ennis and Jimmie Dykes. After his initial succinct comparison, Ashburn continued to ruminate. Sure it was "a crummy place," he exclaimed, but it had "an atmosphere all its own . . . and memories." Later Ashburn visited the gutted building, reporting on its sad condition and telling people that the park was "an old friend . . . with whom I shared many years of happiness. . . . It had . . . a heart beat, a personality."

After the fire the state of the building was precarious. The outfield wall, the scoreboard, and the bleachers were intact. But debris from the fire, rainwater, and petty destruction marred the offices, the clubhouses, and the dugouts. The grandstand looked toothless from successive raids on the seats by fans, junk dealers, and Phillies officials. Broken bottles, piles of scorecards, damaged lockers, and miscellaneous baseball rubbish were everywhere. Weeds on the field were "hip deep." Odd trees had taken root; one was eighteen feet high by 1975.

The city's Licenses and Inspections Department said that the large cost of demolition made it unfair to raze the stadium "at the expense of many smaller community demolition projects. . . . As long as the structure was kept sealed," it did not endanger the public. But intruders bent on doing damage were constant and had easy access, especially through the old right field gate. Every few weeks workers boarded up obvious entrances. The city's rat-control crew doused the place with poison. Police looking for missing persons found two dogs strung up by the neck in the Phillies bullpen.

At the same time the frenzied hunt for souvenirs gave way to pilgrimages and individual quests for relics. People came and walked around the park "like old friends at a funeral." They recollected: home plate was there, where that little tree was growing. They saw Jimmie Foxx or Del Ennis in the batter's box. The pitcher's mound, now a hole filled with junk, was there, and Eddie Plank or Lefty Grove or Robin Roberts would be "standing on the high ground dominating the hitters." They remembered Connie Mack "over there" in the dugout and recalled how he waved his scorecard. One man whose father had refused to let him run the bases after games a quarter century before fulfilled a boyhood promise to himself and came to circle the infield, jogging through knee-high grass and uncertain of the base path.

These fans also took more seats, signs, and turnstiles, but it seemed more loving. Tony Taylor, the popular Phillies infielder of the 1960s and 1970s, visited to "reminisce." He brought a bat with him and took some cuts at home plate. An old grounds keeper almost cried when he saw the field. "It makes me sick," he said. The city judge who was, at last, empowered to order the park torn down received mail from all over the country asking for memorabilia.

Nostalgia also gripped the neighborhood, both old and new. The Irish who fled in the 1960s began in the 1970s to hold yearly banquets at catering establishments far from their old haunts. These former North Penn residents called the events "Old Swampoodle" nights. They traded stories about the 1920s, 1930s, and 1940s; about Saint Columba's during its salad days; about the cops, Freihofer's Bakery, or the old icehouse; and of course about Shibe Park—their summer employment, where the ballplayers lived, the home runs on Twentieth Street.

Back near Twentieth Street itself the nostalgia took a different form. To fight the decline of the business district around the remains of the park, the North Twenty-second Street Merchants Association began a yearly street fair. The business people were determined that purse snatching, mugging, and other urban crimes should not drive customers away. The fair featured discounts on goods, a rock band, and a drum and bugle corps. The occasions were called "Swampoodle Days." The woman who owned the florist shop at 2937 North Twenty-second Street said, "Years ago this area was called Swampoodle, and they used to have these days all the time. . . . There was shopping and parades in the streets. . . . We're returning to the Swampoodle Day tradition."

The merchants were fighting an uphill battle as the wretchedness of Lower North Philadelphia, for a time more or less halted at Lehigh Avenue, crept farther north in the late 1960s. The loss of major employers in Nicetown and Hunting Park accompanied the loss of smaller businesses. The Phillies were an atypical employer, but baseball gave people work in the community for over sixty years. Without jobs, area residents could not keep up their properties. Vacant, unmaintained structures were common around the park. In the early seventies they were much like the park itself.

Jerry Wolman still could not pay his mortgage or taxes on the site. In 1971 the neighborhood petitioned him to tear the park down after the fire had left it "a home for rats and drunks." The *Bulletin* reported, too, that the "derelict" stadium was "a heavy burden in an already blighted area of the city." But Wolman had no interest in doing anything. Prompted by community pressure in 1975, the Licenses and Inspections Department suddenly noted violations such as "overgrowth in the old playing field, broken windows, pipes, seats, exposed wires, and a major rat problem." Toward the end of 1975 a city order cited Connie Mack Stadium as "a major fire hazard and public nuisance." The judge overseeing the case instructed Wolman to "demolish and level all structures" within thirty days. Without money, Wolman said, he could not comply. He was not able to pay off the first mortgage, which would give him clear title to the property and permit demolition. "I suggest that the City of Philadelphia go ahead and take whatever action is necessary to demolish the stadium."

The city had no easy means to compel Wolman to act and did not act itself for several months. Then for over a hundred thousand dollars officials hired Geppert Brothers, a suburban wrecking company, to raze the park over a period of two months.

The city still stalled. Apparently "plans" for future use had to precede razing, and no such adequate plans existed. Whereas officials had few qualms about destroying small single-family dwellings in North Philadelphia, they delayed for as long as they could with the huge old building. In the late spring of 1976 the neighbors demonstrated about the danger of the park as a fire hazard and a haven for winos and junkies. In mid-June the local civic association blocked Lehigh Avenue in protest. Finally, irritated over the indecision, Mayor Rizzo gave the order: "Tear the fucking thing down!"

On June 22, 1976, the Geppert Brothers crew began its job. A three-ton solid concrete ball stood on third base. The scoreboard clock was dead at 12:02. "With a flick of his wrists," wrote the *Inquirer*, "Bill Claffey smashed down the right field wall." Jimmie Foxx and Dick Allen stepped aside. "The heavy hitters are in town." The man who operated the wrecking crane was as contemplative as the *Inquirer*. "Lean back and close your eyes," he said. "You can almost hear the crowd roaring." Three weeks later, with the heavy work all but complete, one fan wrote in the *Inquirer*, "Connie Mack Stadium is dying today."

In the years after the Phillies vacated the park, fans, employees, neighbors, workers, and onetime ballplayers considered the site a place where extraordinary, even sacred, events had occurred. People wrote of the park as a person. Echoing the thoughts of many, the *Bulletin* editorialized: "Any structure that has borne the hopes, the despair, and the triumph of a city for 61 years is more than a ballpark, more even than an institution or a tradition. It is, in some part, a fragment of the city's collective soul, just as a house that one family lives in for 61 years becomes part of its life force."

If, according to reflective writers, Connie Mack Stadium began to die when patrons went at her with hammer and saw during the last game, the death agonies continued after demolition. As one writer put it, "Burial was deferred." Over a year later the *Daily News* wrote that clearing the site was only "the beginning of the end." At that time Twenty-first and Lehigh was a junk-strewn urban disaster. Large piles of concrete and twisted steel, once part of the structure, transformed the block into a war zone. Refuse in dank pools of water and weeds "taller than the men who used to catch fly balls in center field" filled the landscape. One resident of Twentieth Street said that when the demolition crew left, "the litter bugs arrived." They first started dumping, noted another neighbor, "near old third base," but the debris was soon everywhere. "Sometimes it's somebody with a plastic bag, other times it's a truck filled with junk." "Ain't it a damn shame," said one customer of the old Deep Right Field Café. "Life is hard enough in North Philadelphia, let alone having a dump for your neighbor."

After the *Daily News* reported on the trash, the city cleaned it up, but significant amounts of garbage regularly accumulated over the next decade. During the Philadelphia Sanitation Department's strike of July 1986, the empty parcel was an informal place for rubbish disposal. Although another cleanup occurred after the city settled the strike, the area remained popular for getting rid of unwanted material. Along with the trash went filthy puddles, a persistent stench, and rats "as big as cats."

Disputes over legal ownership and nasty conditions did not put off occasional visitors who were not from the neighborhood. Usually they were middle-aged men, though occasionally they were even older or much younger. As if at a shrine, they wandered over the site, oblivious of the junk, their heads in a different time and place. One could see them estimating where the third base line was, where the right field wall stood. They were imagining, one knew, days long gone. As one of them put it, the seekers "heard the distant sounds of balls striking bats and gloves." They were nine years old, sitting with their father along first base. Or they were patrolling the outfield with Elmer Valo, or in the Musial crouch trying to hit Curt Simmons. Or they dreamed of mighty deeds they had not witnessed in person. Memory played funny tricks. They would conjure up images of Rube Waddell on the mound, yet Mack had released him before Shibe built the park; or of Grover Cleveland Alexander, yet he had pitched in Baker Bowl; or of Howard Ehmke's great 1929 World Series victory, yet it had been at Wrigley Field; or about Jim Bunning's perfect game, yet it was pitched, as it turns out, in Shea Stadium in New York. Or they talked about Eddie Waitkus being shot after a game, yet the incident took place in Chicago. They recalled a catch, a home run, or a fielding play that had never happened. Frequently the pilgrims would poke about in the trash. One found a broken fungo bat and took it home as a treasure. It could have dated from 1950 or might have been dumped there two weeks before.

Descriptions of the last years of Connie Mack Stadium repeatedly associated conflicting images. These descriptions also exemplified the brevity of memories and the often limited scope of people's feelings. The newspapers were worst, exhibiting a cavalier attitude toward the past. By the late seventies essays on the "old ball park" were as likely to get the name of the stadium right as wrong. Did Ben or Tom Shibe build it? Was it located at Twentieth or Twenty-first, Lehigh or Allegheny? Four—or was it eight?—World Series were played there. Recollection sometimes went back no further than the Whiz Kids. One writer could only dredge up names from the sixties, Chico Fernandez, Johnny Callison, Bob Bowman, "memories racing through the mind."

When the Phillies finally came up with one fine team in the late 1970s and early 1980s, that present imposed itself on the past. Sports commentators wrote nostalgia pieces that denigrated Connie Mack's Athletics in comparison to the powerful National League team. A franchise that at least had a few great moments now suffered in memory in comparison to the actually hapless Phillies.

As the years went by, concerned citizens tried to get Wolman to behave responsibly about "his" property. But he claimed financial invalidism. Hardly anyone bothered about the land because the title had so many liens against it, the latest being the city's bill to the Geppert Brothers.

Not quite no one. Reverend Sarah Potter Smith, a North Philadelphia minister in her seventies, was praying in her kitchen in 1974. A voice whispered to her: "Shibe Park." Smith later explained that the voice wanted her to build a "Temple of Faith" on the site, consisting of a day-care and youth activities center, a facility for senior citizens, a counseling service for unwed mothers, and an information bureau. Above the temple a symbol of Jesus, a 250-foot-high "Tower of Light," would project hope over the city.

Although Smith's style differed from that of the city planners and urban developers who wanted to rehabilitate North Philly, she was no fool. In a year she headed the Sarah Potter Smith Community Development Corporation and in 1977 submitted a prospectus to officials to secure part of a $92 million grant earmarked for Philadelphia neighborhoods. The newspapers said that Jerry Wolman, always agreeable, was "very interested" in the $15 million temple. Philadelphia politicians and philanthropic agencies "studied the proposal" before letting it die. Nonetheless, Reverend Smith's idea was less farfetched than those of the officials and developers, the "honky politicians" or their "flannel-mouth bagmen," as the whites were called.

In 1981 Deliverance Evangelistic Church at 4700 North Broad, some twenty blocks from the site, bought the parcel and the one across the street between Twentieth and Twenty-first and Lehigh and Somerset. The church had "the same vision" as had Sarah Potter Smith. Its plans for Twenty-first and Lehigh called for a colony of stores as well as a complex for the elderly, church groups, recreation, and education. By the mid-1980s the church realized half of the plan. At Twentieth and Lehigh, where parking lots had for so long dominated the terrain, the church erected a small shopping center. The new buildings contrasted happily with Bobo's Lounge, which now occupied the old quarters of Kilroy's Bar and Quinn's Deep Right Field Café. Then, five years later, ignoring the mindset and economic priorities of the Allegheny West Corporation, the church began to bring its dream to fulfillment. In 1990 it broke ground for its Temple of Faith.

Common Ground

In the twentieth century the ecological niche of Philadelphia baseball altered in substantial ways. The move into Shibe Park signified a change in the sport's business stability. As the stadium aged, various kinds of public transportation gave way to the private automobile. White ethnic neighborhoods became black and then disintegrated. The property itself was involved in the struggles of real estate entrepreneurs and urban planners. The revenue basis of professional baseball came to depend less on the cash fans spent at the stadium and more on the sale of rights to broadcast the contests as entertainment.

This interplay between capitalism and baseball, the private ownership of the means of community pleasure, compels attention and speculation. Connie Mack sold stars because he made a narrow calculation of profit and loss that meant more to him than the 1929–1931 A's. What social ethic gave him the right to do that to his fans? If Mack had kept his teams winning, the growth of the North Philly ghetto would have prompted him to move anyway. The degradation of human life there exemplified the grotesque failures of the business system in which baseball has thrived. Part of the story of Shibe Park is one of proprietorial rapacity, cynicism, and the limitations of even admirable people in an industrial society.

At the same time baseball had something about it that not even U.S. corporate avarice could destroy. The sport continued to attract fans to Shibe Park. They needed to witness the achievement, and to participate in the fantasy and shared memory, that the game provided. The unique aspect of Shibe Park baseball was not the failures or successes of management or the feats or defeats on the field. The unique element was that the sport magically taught people about excellence and joined them communally to something not available in day-to-day experience. Shibe Park was a place where uncommon deeds gave people a sense of commonality. In this, its special beauty, the game at Shibe Park rose above the flaws of its businessmen, its players, and its fans.

Some commentators made this point by saying that the precious places of baseball were really in people's hearts and minds. One fan stated it more concretely. In defending her role in the ruckus at Connie Mack Stadium's last game, she said, "The people took the park home with them. . . . That way we'd have it forever." Another old resident of the neighborhood wondered what happened to all the emotions expressed in the park. He speculated that they continued "to cheer the spirits of baseball players past." Another fan, who claimed to be a "philosopher," went even further. He asserted that past time was never gone. What happened at the ball park was somehow around forever, like Amos Strunk's anger, still smoldering on the page. Baseball exploits were "essences." They could always be called to mind and could never vanish. An A's fan in the late 1940s and early 1950s, the philosopher argued that "Eddie Joost, number one, still leads off. Elmer Valo still crashes into the wall. Bobby Shantz still beats the Yankees. Connie Mack still waves his program. Shibe Park still stands. The Philadelphia Athletics still live."

Although baseball was fundamental to the stadium, it was not the only thing that drew people to Twenty-first and Lehigh. Shibe Park had a wide role in urban life and was instrumental in creating a sense of the past that was central to the existence of many Philadelphians. The temporal span actually critical to most persons is brief and extends backward to parents and perhaps grandparents and forward only to children and perhaps grandchildren. This short span of "real" time becomes prized, meaningful, when someone finds in it events that are of abiding worth, that are memorable. For much of the twentieh century Shibe Park was a structure that provided historical coherence to people's lives: it was the spot where a father saw the hundred-thousand-dollar infield and the Loughran-Delaney fight and took his son to see Al Simmons; where FDR came and spoke and the Eagles played; where the son took his children to see the Whiz Kids and the rodeo; and where the grown-up children would go with their friends to a jazz concert. The park enabled individuals to associate themselves with cherished people who came before and after them; and it enabled men and women to give their lives a deeper significance by joining them to matters of consequence. The integrity of the souls of urban Philadelphians depended on a semisacred collection of beliefs, handed-down stories, and recollections about sports, politics, and mass entertainment. Shibe Park was home to these activities.

Individuals attach meaning to places. At Shibe Park, small things remembered—a man selling water ice, the hum of voices on Lehigh, the green grass inside, a glimpse of Connie Mack—turned an ordinary locale into a fanciful landscape. Nonetheless, baseball fans did not merely store up in memory what they saw on the field. The play-by-play was only momentarily absorbing. Imagination and interpretation produced what was crucial. These constructive forces joined with memories of other times that the game in progress evoked. "A hit? . . . They didn't give Allen an error? Ferris Fain would have gotten to that one in his sleep. I remember one game with the Browns, late innings. And this guy . . . I forget his name but he played with the White Sox later, left-handed. Anyway, he bunts down the first-base line, and Fain . . ."

Group remembrance made the location part of the silent infrastructure of a shared life. The joint use of space, a relatively weak form of cohesion after all, underlined the lasting import of the deeds that people witnessed. During much of the period that Shibe Park stood the city was the principal entity through which multitudes of people escaped solitude, and Philadelphia was the unifying force at the stadium. The link to the city's accomplishment and status enlarged the compass of people's lives. Glory became imperishable because it was civic. This enlarged meaning was usually exaggerated, idealized—it certainly is in sports—because individuals needed to put so much weight on the collective expression of conquest.

Shibe Park hosted events distinctive to Philadelphia's sense of itself as an urban center: a big fight, a political rally, high school football championships, the circus. Legendary happenings also took place there—Ty Cobb's visits in 1909 and 1910, the fourth and fifth games of the 1929 series, the "snow game" of 1948, Bobby Shantz's twentieth victory in 1952, the Phillies games at the end of September 1964. For many individuals these occurrences were their only experience of physical contest and victory, of valor and endurance, of grace under pressure and dignity in defeat. These were things to admire and aspire to, and they struck a deep chord in many people. The competition between cities—with Detroit, Chicago, but especially with New York—nurtured a taste for combat but also an array of community emotions, the feelings of pride, triumph, and perhaps most of all in Philadelphia, resignation.

Caring about what happened at Shibe Park—really caring—is a capacity nearly gone from our lives. It almost no longer matters *what* we care about, how frail or foolish the object of concern, if we can resuscitate the feeling. Baseball's sense of history—the passing down of achievements from generation to generation—made the sport more than an arbitrary exercise. Dick Allen was not just hitting a long ball. At Shibe Park he was continuing the line of Frank Baker, Jimmie Foxx, and Del Ennis. Even so, the perhaps insignificant physical effort involved in the game and the selfishness of those who controlled it were not enough to make us skeptics. Believing in what might be trivial was the price we paid to escape private interests for those of a more overarching enterprise.

Meaning and the items that bear it are fragile. The meanings accrue over time in their visible embodiments, artifacts like Shibe Park. Memories do not exist in the mind's isolation but are connected to objects and stored in them. The destruction of artifacts can thus sever the present from the past and the accumulated significance the past embodies. We do not create the legacy of the city but find it in our memories, because in cooperation with others we locate this legacy in the world around us and make it salient in our lives.

Social critics have argued that a generation can be condemned for squandering its heritage and demolishing places where the public past is manifest. In return, these critics say, we receive a terrifying world in which attainment vanishes and beliefs are soon forgotten. The easy destruction of architecture weakens our ability to act humanely in the present or to trust in the future. The value of an event in our lives accrues from its relation to other events in the same temporal order. The present has its origin in earlier events and its destiny in later ones. Without the things that are the carriers of this time, we impoverish the individual and the city. Expectation, for example, means not accepting the finality of the present. We see each moment full of possibilities. We know from experience that at some time a dismal past has turned into a better present. And we know that a terrible here-and-now may not truly indicate a final condition for us or for our community. Knowledge that nothing is forever tempers immediate disappointment. Without places for the past to dwell and to remind us of beginnings, personal lives become shriveled and public life impossible. When the Athletics' fans and later those of the Phillies cried, "Wait 'til next year" at Shibe Park, they were not only expressing anticipation; they were also defining a tradition. They were members of a community of memory and hope. The traditions that inhere in the city's built environment, say the social critics, demand respect and preservation.

At Shibe Park, certainly, abandonment, neglect, and demolition testified to the transience of this respect. But manufactured sentimentality also displayed the fleeting nature of regard. In the late 1980s one oldster wrote for *Phillies Report* his reminiscences of the ball park and the great A's-Yankees rivalry of the late twenties and early thirties. The editors asked the author to "revise" his recollections so they would be about the Whiz Kids. By the 1980s the Depression was too distant to awaken a response in readers. The author changed his story and memorialized the Phillies. But "it was harder to get excited about them," he sighed.

The penchant for renaming, less damaging but more insidious, also indicated infidelity to the past. Shibe Park became Connie Mack Stadium. The Philadelphia Athletics became the Kansas City Athletics, who became the Oakland Athletics. A part of North Penn was designated Allegheny West. Donegal Square became the Square, which became Reyburn Park, which became Connie Mack Park, which became Cecil Moore Park.

At many of the new dedication ceremonies and when the stadium itself was torn down, people professed—they had to profess—enduring concern. But who could blame them for the comparative superficiality of their feelings, their lack of an eternal perspective? In 1990 one woman proudly carried the scar she had received over forty years before when jostling autograph seekers scraped her arm against the Shibe Park wall. Yet even with tender and devoted care, no scar can last. All of us die. The crowd and the players at the park were always the same age, but the individual in the crowd grew older every season. Who would always remember? The very passage of time, which is necessary for the past and thus for respect for it, must bring oblivion, freedom from the bondage of the past. All buildings eventually come down. We are, after all, like the grass.

The social critic demands too much from people. They do care. But their caring is limited in the nature of things, and in time they have to care less.

We cannot keep faith with the past. Life forces us to forget most of it. By the time Connie Mack Stadium closed, many patrons did not know that it was first named after someone else. Soon after it was leveled, people could not remember where it had been located. By then few knew that Oakland was the inheritor of the old Philadelphia A's, if they had heard about these early A's at all.

We cannot keep faith, too, because in the end what we do remember we transform and often love simply because it is past, no matter what its character at the time. People nostalgically called to mind events that never happened at the ball park. They rehearsed sentiments they never had and recalled passions that never existed. In later years fans fondly recollected the car watchers they detested; they talked about enjoying the bad teams Connie Mack fielded; they recounted their admiration for "Dick" Allen.

This lore, an endless stream of the make-believe and the remembered, frequently links parents and children. Baseball, said the fans, must be in the blood. Baseball and life are the same, said one old player. A longtime rooter exclaimed how strange it was that "baseball and my life got so entangled." A father takes a daughter to a game, a grandmother takes a grandson. The grown-ups remember their own parents, and the concerns of their youth: Would Al Simmons win the batting title? Would Robin Roberts deliver up a home-run pitch? Could you look your New York relatives in the eye after the twenty-three-game losing streak? Baseball carries people back to a never-never land of childhood. There is in people, morally, this home base, just as there is, literally, one in the sport. Always, *always*, the past is a simpler, easier era. Ball park memories are not about the game but about a romantic vision of past family life, about a good old time whose potential the present has not fulfilled. Why, asked one commentator, did baseball lend itself to elegy? Why did its memories so often leave us close to tears?

The children cannot be bothered about whether Eddie Joost was a better infielder than Tony Taylor. What they like is to be let into the adult sphere of times gone by. It is as if change existed only so that we could reshape it and comfort ourselves by passing on the result to children or grandchildren.

Social critics correctly wrote about the breakable quality of the past as places contained it. But they too little appreciated the entirely breakable character of human life and too little valued our obviously compromised attempts at effecting permanency; they were too hard on citizens who finally discarded their heritage. There used to be a ball field at Twenty-first and Lehigh, but Shibe Park had its time, and then its time was over. In some more time it will be forgotten. It is good to remember it as long as we can; but we cannot expect to remember forever.

• ESSAY ON SOURCES AND NOTES •

The notes below are keyed to the appropriate pages of the text and should reveal what is documented and what is my own interpretation, but the documentation also needs explanation. Much of the anecdotal material is open to doubt; newspapers frequently offer conflicting stories; many recollections are shaky, and generalizations are impressionistic; often the sources I have used to ascertain matters of fact are less reliable than I would wish. I have tried to suggest these limitations in the notes. Although I have made every effort at accuracy, I have learned that in writing this peculiar kind of cultural history, one must accept these deficiencies. Indeed, I have tried to make a virtue of these defects by arguing that the best history of Shibe Park emphasizes what went on in people's heads. At the same time I hope that readers who find inaccuracies will inform me of them.

Various collections of material have proved useful. There are documents in the Phillies files at Veterans Stadium (hereafter V); the Urban Archives in Paley Library, Temple University (UA); the Free Library of Philadelphia (FLP); and various departments of records of the city of Philadelphia (P).

Another important source is a connected series of federal court cases: *Roy, Earle, and Cornelius McGillicuddy vs. Edward A. McGinnes* (Director of Internal Revenue), Civil Action Cases, File Numbers 29086, 29087, and 29088, Federal Records Center, 5000 Wissahickon Avenue, Philadelphia; and the newspaper report on the settlement, "Connie Mack's Heirs," *Philadelphia Inquirer*, 17 September 1964 (CAC).

A rich collection of business records of the Philadelphia Phillies is located at the Eleutherican-Mills, Hagley Foundation in Wilmington, Delaware (PP).

Some of my reasoning is based on examination of a series of maps of the city found mainly in either FLP or UA. The following collection is abbreviated as MAPS: G. W. Bromley and Co., *Atlas of the City of Philadelphia* (Philadelphia, 1888) (UA); Bromley, *Atlas* (1901) (FLP); C. W.

Baist, *Detail Property Atlas of the City of Philadelphia* (Philadelphia, 1901); Elvino V. Smith, *Atlas of the City of Philadelphia* (Philadelphia, 1908) (UA); Bromley, *Atlas* (1910) (FLP); *Hexamer Property Atlas of the City of Philadelphia* (Philadelphia, 1895-1915) (UA); Bromley, *Atlas* (1922, 1925) (UA); 1930 and 1940 Maps of Foreign Born Population and Negro Population (UA); 1934 Ethnicity Map (FLP); 1939 WPA Map (UA); 1942 WPA Land Use Map (FLP); Sanborn Map Co., *Insurance Maps of Philadelphia* (Philadelphia, 1931–1956) (FLP); 1970 and 1982 Land Use Maps, City of Philadelphia (UA); 1986 Land Use Map, City of Philadelphia, City Planning Commission Office (P).

I have abbreviated as SSDL statistical material on the census tracts around Shibe Park from 1890 to 1970, which was generated from more comprehensive studies done by William Yancey and his colleagues at Temple University's Social Science Data Lab.

Newspapers have been important, chief among them the *Philadelphia Bulletin, Daily News, Inquirer, Record,* and *New York Times*—hereafter abbreviated, respectively, as *B, DN, I, R,* and *NYT.* Particularly useful were the morgues of three of these papers, in which material is arranged topically in packets of clippings (hereafter clips). The *I* morgue is located at the newspaper's headquarters at 400 North Broad Street; *B* at UA; and *R* at the Historical Society of Pennsylvania. When citing this material, I have, where it has been feasible, given not just the date of the newspaper but also some further identification. Other significant newspapers, the *Chat* of North Penn (*C*), the *Philadelphia Independent* (*PI*), and the *Philadelphia Tribune* (*T*), are on microfilm at the FLP.

Interviews were another part of the research. I began by selecting certain obvious people to talk to, but soon responded to various "offers" as people learned of my research. In the course of my writing many less formal resources came my way through unprompted letters, telephone calls, and conversations. I took notes on the calls and conversations, and many of these sources later proved useful. On three occasions my research called to mind words of my father, and I have cited my memories of him. In all I used the words of thirty-seven individuals, and they are cited in the notes. In the listing immediately below, I have identified fans as F and residents as R, with approximate time of residence. Below, also, the letter I designates interview; T, interview by telephone; L, letter; C, conversation: Frank Barrett, R, 1920s–1950s, T, 27 July 1989. Joseph Barrett, R, 1920s–1950s, I, 15 April 1988; T, 5 May and 20 September 1989. Josephine Barrett, R, 1920–1950s, I, 15 April 1988.

Wayne Bodle, F, C, 30 November 1989; L, 14 January 1989. Samuel J. Boyd, nephew of Amos Aaron Strunk, T, 11 January 1988. James Brown, F, T, 21 December 1988. Frank K. Carner, F, C, 11 January 1989. Robert Carpenter, owner Phillies, I, 1 April 1988. Harry Cerino, R, 1940s–1950s, I, 1 November 1988. Andy Clarke, park manager, I, 5 February 1988. Rita Clarke, R, 1930s–1940s, I, 5 February 1988. Mary Maples Dunn, F, C, 17 February 1990. John Feffer, R, 1950s–1960s, I, 21 December 1988 and 27 April 1989. Bernard Freeman, F, C, 6 May 1988. Pat Gorman, R, 1930s, C, 6 May 1987. Ira Harkavy, F, C, 20 November 1989. Charles Hoffman, F, L, 12 and 31 July 1989. Robert Jones, C, 18 August 1987. William Kelley, F, I, 30 December 1988. Frank Kerrigan, R, 1910s, I, 8 February 1988. Rudolph Klinger, F, L, 17 January 1990. Harry McFadden, R, 1920s, I, 29 October 1988. Mary Marscher, F, L, 17 November 1988. Robert Nauss, F, T, 4 December 1987. John Raeburn, F, L, 27 July 1987. John Rooney, R, 1920s–1930s, L, 18 February 1988. Joseph Rooney, R, 1920s–1930s, L, 28 January 1988. Gerald Rosen, F, L, 17 September 1987. Charles Rosenberg, C, 9 December 1989. Reverend Joseph Ross of Deliverance Evangelistic Church, T, 17 May 1989. Joseph Rossi, F, C, 17 October 1989. Mike Ruane, F, C, 4 May 1989. Larry Shenk, Phillies executive, I, 15 November 1987. Alan Trachtenberg, R, 1940s, C, 15 March 1988. Russell Weigley, F, C, 17 October 1988. Oliver Williams, F, C, 24 March 1989. Hattie Woodington, F, L, 6 March 1988.

Information on players and statistics comes from Joseph R. Reichler, *The Baseball Encyclopedia* (New York, 1988), and David S. Neff and Richard M. Cohen, *The Sports Encyclopedia—Baseball* (New York, 1987). For the Phillies, Frank Bilovsky and Rich Westcott, *The Phillies Encyclopedia* (New York, 1984). Details about individual games come from newspaper accounts and, in appropriate instances, Neff and Cohen, *The World Series* (New York, 1986).

Two final abbreviations: SABR for Society for American Baseball Research; and *BRJ* for *Baseball Research Journal.* For the convenience of the reader, all the abbreviations that are used in the notes are listed below.

ABBREVIATIONS

B	*Philadelphia Bulletin*
BRJ	*Baseball Research Journal*
C	*Chat* of North Penn

CAC   Civil Action Cases
DN   *Philadelphia Daily News*
FLP   Free Library of Philadelphia
I   *Philadelphia Inquirer*
MAPS Collection of city maps
NYT   *New York Times*
P   Philadelphia city records
PI   *Philadelphia Independent*
PP   Philadelphia Phillies records
R   *Philadelphia Record*
SABR Society for American Baseball Research
SSDL Social Science Data Lab
T   *Philadelphia Tribune*
UA   Urban Archives, Temple University
V   Veterans Stadium, Phillies files

INTRODUCTION

3 Last night: V, Connie Mack Stadium files, from which the Strunk letter also comes; on Strunk see also *I*, 1 October 1970.

5 Carpenter: hole in the head, *B*, 9 November 1954; progress, *B*, 2 October 1970.

5 The grounds: Deeds and Records, P, Deed to 2000 W. Lehigh (reference number ELT 284 396).

6 Common affection: my approach in writing about baseball differs from that of SABR's baseball historians and of those interested in "sport and society." Although I am interested in the "internal" history of the sport and in baseball's connection to urban culture—mainly to industrial capitalism, a central concern of social historians—they are not what is crucial to me. My primary interest is the way sport is instrumental in ordinary people's construction of a meaningful past for themselves. For an elaboration of my concern, which recurs throughout this book, see my unpublished "Writing the History of Practice: Baseball," heavily indebted to Alasdair MacIntyre's *After Virtue* (South Bend, Ind., 1981). An up-to-date review of the field is given in Elliott J. Gorn, "Doing Sports History," *Reviews in American History* (1990), pp. 27–32.

1. BEN SHIBE AND SHIBE PARK

11 Opening: *I*, 13 April 1909; interview with Harry McFadden, 29 October 1988.

12 Baseball in the late nineteenth and early twentieth century: Harold Seymour, *Baseball*, vol. 1 (New York, 1960), pp. 31–32, 76; David Quentin Voigt, *American Baseball*, vol. 1 (Norman, Okla., 1966); Charles C. Alexander, *Ty Cobb* (New York, 1984), pp. 24–30; John Rickards Betts, "The Technological Revolution and the Rise of Sport, 1850–1900," *Mississippi Valley Historical Review* (1952–53), pp. 231–56; Steven A. Riess, *Touching Base: Professional Baseball and American Culture*

in the Progressive Era (Westport, Conn., 1980), pp. 13–15, 35–36; Peter Levine, *A. G. Spalding and the Rise of Baseball* (New York, 1985), pp. 51–52, 61; Stephen Hardy, "The City and the Rise of American Sport," *Exercise and Sports Sciences Reviews* (1981), pp. 183–219. Steven A. Reiss, *City Games: The Evolution of American Urban Society and the Rise of Sports* (Urbana, Ill., 1989), can also be authoritatively consulted on all the topics of urban history I have considered. For the beginnings of the sport, see *Playing for Keeps: A History of Early Baseball* (Ithaca, N.Y., 1989) by Warren Goldstein. Explanations of baseball's popularity: Thomas L. Altherr, "'The Most Summery, Bold, Free & Spacious Game': Charles King Newcombe and Philadelphia Baseball, 1866–1871," *Pennsylvania History* (1985), pp. 82–83. Social class of fans: Seymour, *Baseball*, vol. 1, pp. 90–91, 326–27, 329.

13   Treatments of commercialism, which also consider the ball park itself as a focus of profit, are: Melvin L. Adelman, *A Sporting Time: New York City and the Rise of Modern Athletics, 1820–1870* (Urbana, Ill., 1986), pp. 9–10, 149–68; George B. Kirsch, *The Creation of American Team Sports: Baseball and Cricket, 1838–72* (Urbana, Ill., 1989), pp. 230–56.

14   The aesthetic dimension essential to this book is shaped by George Santayana's "Philosophy on the Bleachers," *Harvard Monthly* (July 1894), reprinted in *George Santayana's America*, ed. James Ballowe (Urbana, Ill., 1967), pp. 121–30.

14   Johnson and Somers: Eugene Murdock, *Ban Johnson: Czar of Baseball* (Westport, Conn., 1982), pp. 21–49, 74–76; David Quentin Voigt, *American Baseball*, vol. 2 (Norman, Okla., 1970), pp. 7–9. Syndicate baseball: *NYT* editorial, 23 September 1900.

15   Mack: Mack, *My 66 Years in the Big Leagues* (New York, 1950), p. 28; Frederick G. Lieb, *Connie Mack: Grand Old Man of Baseball* (New York, 1945), pp. 61–67.

15   Shibe family: B clips; obituaries, all papers, Ben, d. 14 January 1922 (in *Sporting News*, also 19 January 1922); Tom, d. 16 February 1936; Jack, d. 13 July 1937; R, 26 May 1940 (article on Wilson Shibe); Edward Mott Woolley, "The Business of Baseball," *McClure's Magazine* (July 1912), p. 255; Seymour, *Baseball*, vol. 1, p. 353; Lieb, *Mack*, pp. 61–67. Joanne Fulcoly has deposited genealogical material on the family at the Historical Society of Pennsylvania.

15   Dour and crusty: Bob Considine, "Mr. Mack: Did He Invent Baseball?" *Life* (29 July 1948), reprinted in *The Baseball Reader*, ed. Charles Einstein (New York, 1983), p. 68. Early history of Shibe's baseball manufacturing: William R. Vogel, "The History and Manufacture of the Baseball," Philadelphia Central High School Senior Thesis, 1912, in the possession of Lisa Elliott (Elliott is the great-granddaughter of Vogel, whose mother was a Shibe).

16   Reach and Shibe: Frank Bilovsky and Rich Westcott, *The Phillies Encyclopedia* (New York, 1981), pp. 322–24; Stan Baumgartner, "The Philadelphia Phillies," in *The Book of Major League Baseball Clubs: The National League*, ed. Ed Fitzgerald (New York, 1952). Ownership and value of stock: CAC.

17   Athletics and publicity: Mack, *66 Years*, pp. 147–50, 183, 186; Harry Robert, "The Philadelphia Athletics," in *The Book of Major League Baseball Clubs: The American League*, ed. Ed Fitzgerald (New York, 1952), p. 133.

17   Jack Shibe: *B*, 25 February 1936; *I*, 7 August 1936; all papers, obituaries; *B*, 14 August 1951; *B*, 21 September 1969 (Brookhauser article).
18   *Sporting News*: 16 February 1907. Finances: CAC.
18   Waddell: Lieb, *Mack*, p. 120.
18   Old and new ball parks: Reiss, *Touching*, pp. 85–120.
19   Transportation patterns: MAPS.
21   North Philadelphia streets: Robert I. Alotta, *Street Names of Philadelphia* (Philadelphia, 1955), pp. 45–47.
21   North Philadelphia parks: *B*, 6 August 1969; Bill Conlin, "Up from the Cellar," in *The Phillies: 100 Years*, supplement to the *DN*, April 1983, p. 4; Philip J. Lowry, *Green Cathedrals* (Cooperstown, 1986), pp. 68–69; Martin Leventon, "The Brief History of Baseball Parks, Their Teams, and Owners in Philadelphia and Its Relationship to the Development of Transit Lines, Politics, Class and Neighborhoods from 1870–1910" (paper for Urban Studies 611, 1976, Temple University), UA. I also consulted the unpublished work of Jerrold Casway of Howard Community College for material on the nineteenth-century parks.
21   Rejected sites: *Souvenir Program* (Opening of Shibe Park, 12 April 1909), pp. 8–9, and *B*, March 1950 (Pollock article).
22   North City communities and street patterns: MAPS; *B* clips for each community; and on the one around the ball park, Joseph P. Barrett, "The Life and Death of an Irish Neighborhood," *Philadelphia Magazine* (March 1970), pp. 85, 130; interview with Barrett, 20 September 1989. I have not been able to pinpoint Smokey Hollow on a map. See also the unpublished papers for the Centennial Conference on North Philadelphia, April 1985, Temple University (organized by Noel Cazenave, Department of Sociology, Temple University); and for the structure of the city, Theodore Hershberg et al., "A Tale of Three Cities: Blacks and Immigrants in Philadelphia: 1850–1880, 1930 and 1970," *Annals, American Academy of Political and Social Sciences* (January 1979), pp. 55–81.
24   Twenty-first and Lehigh parcel: MAPS and deeds to 2000 W. Lehigh, Deeds and Records, P (reference numbers WSV 1071; WSV 1058; 195765; 186110; 186111). Anecdotes about hospital: interview with Frank Kerrigan, once a patient there, 8 February 1987.
24   Steele and Co.: *B* clips; William Steele and Sons, *The Steele Idea* (Philadelphia, ca. 1919); *Souvenir Program*, p. 9, which also has material on grading the field.
25   Undervaluation and hospital: *Bureau of Health, Annual Report, Philadelphia*, 1907, pp. 19, 219; 1908, p. 22; 1909, pp. 21–22 (quote), 348; CAC.
25   Ferro-concrete: *Souvenir Program*, pp. 5, 9; John Burchard and Albert Bush-Brown, *The Architecture of America* (Boston, 1961), pp. 136–37; Carl W. Condit, *American Building: Materials and Techniques from the First Colonial Settlements to the Present* (Chicago, 1968), pp. 241, 290–91; David P. Billington, "The Rational and the Beautiful: Maillart and the Origins of Reinforced Concrete" (1988 ms in possession of author, Department of Civil Engineering, Princeton University).
25   Lasting monument: *Souvenir Program*, p. 3.
26   Design of parks: United States Baseball Federation, Inc., *A Baseball Facility: Its Construction and Care* (Trenton, N.J., 1980, 1984, 1987), pp. 2–3; Thomas C. Atwood, "The Ampitheater, Theater and Stadium, Ancient and Modern," *Ameri-*

can City 16 (January 1917), p. 9; "Orientation of Baseball Fields," *American City* 30 (April 1924), p. 439.

26   Description of park: *The Brickbuilder* (June 1909), p. 127, plates 75, 80; Connie Mack, "Philadephia's Giant Ballstand," *Baseball Magazine* (13 October 1908); *B*, 3 December 1908; Philip H. Bess, "Preface," to Lowry, *Cathedrals*, p. 10. Quotes: *Souvenir Program*, pp. 3, 4, 28. Alterations of 1913: CAC; *B*, 9 January 1913; *B*, 8 August 1957. See also Paul Goldberger, "Wrigley Field: A Baseball Park That Radiates Joy," *NYT*, 18 September 1988 (section H, p. 36).

26   Sun and geography: MAPS and material cited above for design of parks.

28   Boats: *B*, 14 August 1951.

28   Architectural description: *Souvenir Program*, pp. 9–10. Later recollection of elegance: *Spitball: The Literary Baseball Magazine* (Spring 1987), p. 2. Scoreboard: Seymour, *Baseball* vol. 2 (New York, 1971), p. 58.

29   Cost: CAC. Intimacy: Robert Bluthardt, "Fenway Park and the Golden Age of the Baseball Park, 1909–1915," *Journal of Popular Culture* (1987), pp. 43–52; *Souvenir Program*, p. 44.

29   Business motives: Seymour, *Baseball* vol. 2, pp. 20–21; Reiss, *Touching Base*, pp. 49, 76–77; David Quentin Voigt, *American Baseball*, vol. 3 (University Park, Pa., 1983), pp. 304–5, whose similar interpretations differ from mine; and the source, *Souvenir Program*, p. 3.

30   Game description and Reyburn quote: *I*, 13 April 1909.

2. THE ATHLETICS AND NORTH CITY, 1909–1923

31   Cobb: Charles C. Alexander, *Ty Cobb* (New York, 1984), pp. 81–82, 115. The 1912 Detroit-A's game: Furman Bisher, *Strange but True Baseball Stories* (New York, 1966), pp. 91–97. *Sporting News* from Richard C. Crepeau, *Baseball: America's Diamond Mind* (Orlando, Fla., 1980), p. 162.

32   Hundred-thousand-dollar infield: Ed Winkler, "Historical Survey of Best Fielder by Position," *BRJ* (1980), p. 45.

33   VanZelst: *B* clips.

33   McGraw: Charles C. Alexander, *John McGraw* (New York, 1988).

33   The 1911 series: Harold Seymour, *Baseball*, vol. 2. (New York, 1971), pp. 90, 280; Eugene C. Murdock, *Ban Johnson: Czar of Baseball* (Westport, Conn., 1982), p. 87. Baker's greatest moment: obituary, *B*, 28 June 1963. Home Run Alley: *B*, 13 July 1952. Rain: Frederick G. Lieb, *Connie Mack: Grand Old Man of Baseball* (New York, 1945), pp. 155–56. Food: *R*, 6 June 1943 (Basenfelder article). "Horseshoes": in *Best Short Stories of Ring Lardner* (New York, 1957), pp. 205–6. *The Celebrant* (New York, 1983), pp. 173–75.

34   Mack sources: Bob Considine, "Mr. Mack: Did He Invent Baseball?" *Life* (29 July 1948), reprinted in *The Baseball Reader*, ed. Charles Einstein (New York, 1983), pp. 64–79; Lieb, *Mack* (whose "1945 fifth impression" has material through 1947); Harry Robert, "The Philadelphia Athletics," in *The Book of Major League Baseball Clubs: The American League*, ed. Ed Fitzgerald (New York, 1952),

pp. 122–56; Wilfrid Sheed, "Mr. Mack and the Main Chance," in *The Ultimate Baseball Book*, ed. Daniel Okrent and Harris Lewine (Boston, 1979), pp. 105–20; John R. Tunis, "Cornelius McGillicuddy," *Atlantic Monthly* (August 1940), pp. 212–16.

34 Mack's acquisition of 50 percent of franchise: David Quentin Voigt, *American Baseball*, vol. 2 (Norman, Okla., 1970), pp. 17–20, 112; Robert, "Athletics," p. 140. Especially important are the deed of sale in Deeds and Records, P (reference number ELT 284 396); CAC; B, 1 August 1950 (Pollock article).

35 Irish advancement: Alexander, *McGraw*, p. 14. Roosevelt: John Morton Blum, *The Republican Roosevelt* (New York, 1954, 1962), pp. 24–36. Mollycoddle: Connie Mack, *My 66 Years in the Big Leagues* (Philadelphia, 1950), p. 99. And see Allen Guttman, "Who's on First? or Books on the History of American Sports," *Journal of American History* (1979–80), p. 350.

35 Deacon: Jimmie Dykes and Charles O. Dexter, *You Can't Steal First Base* (Philadelphia, 1967), p. 17. McInnes anecdote: Lieb, *Mack*, p. 15. Mack key to city: Lieb, *Mack*, p. 144. Unrecognized: "The Methods of Baseball Managers," *Literary Digest* (8 June 1912).

36 Analysis of Mack: Robert, "Athletics," p. 126. Quotes on your club, you win, tail end: Tunis, "McGillicuddy," pp. 214–15. Expect too much: B clips—Mack (Lynn C. Doyle "Close-ups on Sports," some Philadelphia newspaper, 21 December 1947). Nothing more: Considine, "Mr. Mack," pp. 72–73.

36 Final lesson: CAC. In addition to the 1913 transaction and the sale of the franchise in 1950 and 1954 (discussed in Chapter 7), the value of the stock was adjusted on at least three occasions: in 1920, when the A's settled an excess-profits tax matter with the Internal Revenue Service; in the late 1930s, when Mack gained majority control of the franchise and sold stock to his sons; and in the early 1960s, when the Mack heirs sought a reduction in the capital-gains tax they paid when the A's stock was sold.

37 Mack and McGraw: Alexander, *McGraw*, pp. 117, 156, 177.

37 Collegians: B, 14 March 1950 (Kelly article), and Francis Wallace, "College Men in the Big Leagues," *Scribners* (October 1927), pp. 490–95. Thomas: Mack, *66 Years*, p. 181. Jackson: Donald Gropman, *Say It Ain't So, Joe* (New York, 1979), pp. 42–76. Johnson: in Voigt, *American Baseball*, vol. 2, pp. 17–18.

38 Collins and Strunk: B clips.

39 Strunk finances: B, 27 January 1917. Will not sell him: B, 4 September 1919, and B, 26 December 1919. Back at Shibe Park: B, 2 May 1924. My understanding of Strunk's view of Mack comes from an interview with Strunk's nephew, Samuel J. Boyd, 11 January 1988.

40 Red Smith: U.S. House of Representatives, *Organized Baseball*, Report no. 2002 to accompany H.R. 95, 82d Cong., 2d sess., 1952, pp. 73, 103; and see Mack, *66 Years*, pp. 179, 181.

40 Players' addresses: B clips, and for Bender, Robert Tholkes, "Chief Bender—the Early Years," *BRJ* (1983), p. 8.

41 Mack: Lieb, *Mack*, p. 74, and B, 11 March 1916. Auto: Lieb, *Mack*, p. 133. Elephant: Seymour, *Baseball*, vol. 2, p. 78. Trolley rides: B, 26 March 1919.

41   Physical aspects of neighborhood: MAPS. Reyburn: *I*, 13 April 1909. Day old-
ers: interview with John Feffer, 21 December 1988. Donegal Square: Joseph Bar-
rett, "The Life and Death of an Irish Neighborhood," *Philadelphia Magazine*
(March 1970), pp. 85, 130, 131. Lubin: *B* clips; Joseph P. Eckhardt and Linda
Kowall, *Peddler of Dreams: Siegmund Lubin and the Creation of the Motion Picture
Industry* (Philadelphia, 1984).

43   Kilroy: *B* clips.

43   Neighborhood: 1910 census (on microfilm in FLP); MAPS; SSDL.

44   Multiethnic neighborhoods: Dennis Clark, "A Pattern of Urban Growth: Residential Development and Church Location in Philadelphia," *Records of the American Catholic Historical Society* (September 1971), pp. 164–65, 169–70; Clark,
Irish in Philadelphia (Philadelphia, 1972), pp. 142–46; Caroline Golab, "The Im-
migrant and the City: Poles, Italians, and Jews in Philadelphia, 1870–1920," in
The Peoples of Philadelphia, ed. Allen F. Davis and Mark Haller (Philadelphia,
1973), pp. 203–30. Also Theodore Hershberg et al., "A Tale of Three Cities:
Blacks and Immigrants in Philadelphia: 1850–1880, 1930 and 1970," *Annals,
American Academy of Political and Social Sciences* (January 1970), pp. 55–81.
Chase scenes: Eckhardt and Kowall, *Peddler of Dreams*, p. 9.

44   Irish culture: Barrett, "Life and Death"; Barrett interview, 20 September 1989;
Barrett, "The Devil in the Bottle" and "A Triology of the Church in the Modern
World" (mss); interview with Harry McFadden, 29 October 1989; with Frank
Kerrigan, 8 February 1988; with Harry Cerino, 1 November 1988; with Rita
Clarke, 5 February 1988.

45   Street paving: Clay McShane, "Transforming the Use of Urban Space," *Journal
of Urban History* (May 1979), pp. 279–307. Street cleaning: Martin Melosi, *Garbage in the Cities: Refuse, Reform, and the Environment, 1880–1980* (Chicago,
1981), pp. 134–51.

46   Playgrounds and streets: Dominick Cavallo, *Muscles and Morals: Organized
Playgrounds and Urban Reform, 1880–1920* (Philadelphia, 1981); Jane Allen
Shikoh, "The 'Higher Life' in the American City of the 1890's: A Study of Its
Leaders and Their Activities in New York, Philadelphia, St. Louis, Boston, and
Chicago" (Ph.D. diss., New York University, 1972).

46   Baseball and class: Francis G. Couvaris, *The Remaking of Pittsburgh: Class and
Culture in an Industrializing City, 1877–1919* (Albany, 1984), pp. 124–31; Roy
Rosenzweig, *Eight Hours for What We Will: Workers and Leisure in an Industrial
City, 1870–1920* (Cambridge, 1983), pp. 172–79, 182–85, 226–28.

46   Quote: Kerrigan interview. This is the only specific piece of information I have
on the Philadelphia working class and baseball in the 1910s. Kerrigan, who died
on 11 May 1988, was an amateur boxer.

47   America's game: Dennis Clark, "Sports Cults among the Latter Day Celts" (ms,
1989). Italians: conversation with Pat Gorman, 6 May 1987. Italian sense of importance: Cerino interview.

47   Theories of fandom: conversation with Joseph Rossi and Russell Weigley, 17
October 1989.

48   Honey Fitz: *B*, 9 October 1914.

48 Poll: *B*, 23 January 1950 (Yeutter column). Voigt, *American Baseball*, vol. 2, p. 125. See also *B* for October and November 1914; *B*, 3 October 1948 (Yeutter column).

48 Laying down: Mack, *66 Years*, 36–38; Sheed, "Mr. Mack," pp. 108, 113.

49 Cohan: Eliot Asinof, *Eight Men Out: The Black Sox and the 1919 World Series* (New York, 1963), p. 211; Lieb, *Mack*, p. 4; Victor Luhrs, *The Great Baseball Mystery: The 1919 World Series* (South Brunswick, N.J., 1966), pp. 98–99, where the only sophisticated discussion of what might occur in a "fix" is presented (pp. 243–54).

50 Ruth: Robert W. Creamer, *Babe: The Legend Comes to Life* (New York, 1972), pp. 81–82.

50 *Harpers*: 11 April 1914, N. B. Beasley, "Baseball—a Business, a Sport, a Gamble," p. 27. The debt (not liquidated until 1922): CAC.

50 Rosters: *B* clips (Athletics-Rosters). Mohicans: Lieb, *Mack*, p. 191. Rice: from Adrian O'Connor, "Baseball Coverage of the Charlotte Observer," *BRJ* (1980), p. 176.

50 Parallels: Robert, "Athletics," p. 142. Civic pride: *B*, 1 February 1918. Cobb: Alexander, *Cobb*, p. 124. Three teams: Frank Yeutter, *Jim Konstanty* (New York, 1951), p. 84. World War I: *Sporting News*, 4 July and 18 August 1918.

51 The most interesting collection of episodes of *You Know Me Al* is in Ring Lardner's *You Know Me Al* (New York, 1979). Farrell: *Father and Sons* (New York, 1940), in *The Baseball Reader*, ed. Charles Einstein (New York, 1983), pp. 52–55; Dykes, *You Can't Steal*, pp. 12–13.

3. DAYS OF GLORY, 1924–1932

52 Mack: Frederick G. Lieb, *Connie Mack: Grand Old Man of Baseball* (New York, 1945), pp. 199–206.

53 Remodeling: *B*, 25 May 1925; Lieb, *Mack*, pp. 199, 225–26; Noel Hynd, "The Wall Went up and the A's Came Tumbling Down," *Sports Illustrated* (17 August 1987, regional article), p. 10.

54 North Penn: MAPS; SSDL; Joseph Barrett, "The Life and Death of an Irish Neighborhood," *Philadelphia Magazine* (March 1970), pp. 87, 132–33; *C*, 1932–34. Strawberry Mansion: Meredith Savey, "Instability and Uniformity: Residential Patterns in Two Philadelphia Neighborhoods, 1880–1970," in *The Divided Metropolis: Social and Spatial Dimensions of Philadelphia, 1800–1975*, ed. William Cutler and Howard Gilette (Westport, Conn., 1980), pp. 193–226; Maxwell Whiteman, "Philadelphia's Jewish Neighborhoods," in *The Peoples of Philadelphia*, ed. Allen Davis and Mark Haller (Philadelphia, 1973), pp. 231–54. Black community: references in Chapters 9 and 11. White and decent: interview with Josephine Barrett, 15 April 1988.

54 Athletics B&L: *C*, 4 April 1935. Lehigh National: Barrett, "Life and Death," p. 87. Greenfield: *C*, 1930, passim. Churches: *C*, 29 September 1932.

55 Industrial employment: material in Chapter 4 on emergent ethnicity.

55   Grove: interview with Harry MacFadden, 29 October 1988. Bishop and rookies: Joseph Barrett, "The Sweeper" (ms). Mack: interview with Frank Kerrigan, 8 February 1987. Dykes and Boley: *C*, 2 July 1930. Simmons: John J. Rooney, "Bleachers in the Bedroom," *Philadelphia Magazine* (August 1984), pp. 84–85.

55   A's-Yankees: George T. Wiley, "Yankees vs. Athletics, 1927–1932," *BRJ* (1979), pp. 113–20; Larry Swindell, "Really the Greatest Ever," *I Magazine* (15 August 1976), pp. 22–29. See also Charles C. Alexander, *Ty Cobb* (New York, 1984), p. 207.

55   A's at home: Barrett, "Sweeper." Savage: Nathaniel Burt, *The Perennial Philadelphian* (Boston, 1963), p. 315. Huckster: Rooney, "Bleachers," p. 85; letter from Rooney, 18 February 1988. Kesslers: William G. Nicholson, "Bleacher Bums of Yesteryear," *Baseball Historical Review* (1981), p. 27. Game sounds: Barrett, "Sweeper."

57   Home runs and glazier: *B*, 4 August 1949. Ruth story, which I have not been able to confirm, occurs in *B*, 16 August 1926; 15 July 1956; *I*, 2 April 1961 (Red Smith: "Babe Ruth's Home Run into Opal St."). Gehrig: *B*, 3 June 1932. Foxx: *B*, 22 July 1928; and on Foxx, Francis X. Sculley, "The Maryland Drummer Boy" (ms available from SABR). Kids' question: Rooney, "Bleachers," p. 86.

58   Saloon and Prohibition: Perry Duis, *The Saloon: Public Drinking in Chicago and Boston, 1880–1920* (Urbana, Ill., 1983) and its excellent bibliography. Irish and Prohibition: Dennis Clark, *The Irish in Philadelphia* (Philadelphia, 1972), pp. 154–55. Kids drawn into system: interview with Joseph Barrett, 20 September 1989.

59   McLoon: *B*, 12 July 1916; *B* clips; all papers from 9 August 1928. Two later surveys: *B*, 18 March 1951; 6 December 1953. Phanatic: Mark H. Haller, "Philadelphia Bootlegging and the Report of the Special August Grand Jury" (ms, 1984).

60   Enthusiasm for the 1929 A's: *B*, 7 August 1929.

60   Ehmke: Lieb, *Mack*, pp. 222–25; Rooney, "Bleachers," p. 89. Scoreboard: *B*, 8 and 9 October 1929.

60   Cubs ride Mack: Kessler interview in *B*, 30 March 1961. Tears: Taylor Grant, "1929: An Inning to Remember," *Welcomat* (21 October 1986). Hoover, Mackey, Mack, fans, and beer: *B*, 11 and 12 October 1929; "President Hoover's Trials at the World Series," *Literary Digest* (2 November 1929), pp. 63–67; Lieb, *Mack*, pp. 228–29.

61   Philadelphia Award: all papers, 13 and 14 February 1930. New York papers and *Sporting News* quote: Richard C. Crepeau, *Baseball: America's Diamond Mind* (Orlando, Fla., 1980), pp. 63, 130–31.

62   Breakup of team: for background, see Marc Newman, "The Determinants of Baseball Attendance" (ms available from SABR); David Quentin Voigt, *American Baseball*, vol. 2 (Norman, Okla., 1970), pp. 249–50. Specifically: Mack, *My 66 Years in the Big Leagues* (New York, 1950), pp. 38–42.

63   Spur of moment: *B*, 29 September 1932. Pale and trembling: *B*, 13 December 1933. Forced to sell: *B*, 18 December 1933. See also Jimmie Dykes and Charles O. Dexter, *You Can't Steal First Base* (Philadelphia, 1967), pp. 61–63;

Crepeau, *Diamond Mind*, p. 176; Bob Considine, "Mr. Mack: Did He Invent Base-ball?" *Life* (29 July 1948), in *The Baseball Reader*, ed. Charles Einstein (New York, 1983), pp. 71–72.

63   Salary: *R*, 21 August 1932. Tower: *B*, 7 November 1930. Corporate executive: "The House That Mack Built on Seven Cellars," *American Magazine* (June 1930), p. 86.

63   Policy: *B*, 23 April 1936. Press conference: *B*, 18 December 1933.

64   Opening day: Considine, "Mr. Mack," p. 72.

4. SHIBE PARK AND DEPRESSION ERA CONFLICT

67   Irish: MAPS and SSDL. Italians: interviews with Harry Cerino, 1 November 1988, and John Feffer, 27 April 1989; Richard A. Varhero, "Philadelphia's South Italians in the 1920s," in *The Peoples of Philadelphia*, ed. Allen F. Davis and Mark Haller (Philadelphia, 1973), pp. 255–75. Irish imagination: interview with Jo-seph Barrett, 4 May 1989. Church structure: Varhero, "South Italians"; Feffer interview. Strawberry Mansion Jew: conversation with Alan Trachtenberg, 15 March 1988. Multiethnic communities: William Yancey et al., "The Structure of Pluralism: 'We're All Italian Around Here, Aren't We, Mrs. O'Brien,' " *Ethnic and Racial Studies* (1985), pp. 94–116. Kiss-me-ass Irish: Barrett interview.

68   Small businesses: *C*, 1930–1932. Industrial employment: Theodore Hersh-berg et al., "A Tale of Three Cities: Blacks and Immigrants in Philadelphia: 1850–1880, 1930, and 1970," *Annals, American Academy of Political and Social Science* (January 1979), pp. 55–81. Memory: Cerino interview.

68   Emergent ethnicity: William Yancey et al., "Emergent Ethnicity: A Review and Reformulation," *American Sociological Review* (1976), pp. 391–403; Stephanie W. Greenberg, "Industrial Location and Ethnic Residential Patterns in the Industrial-izing City: Philadelphia, 1880," in *Philadelphia: Work, Space, Family, and Group Experience in the 19th Century*, ed. Theodore Hershberg, (New York, 1981), pp. 204–32, and the works cited therein; the qualifications by Dale Light, Jr., "Class, Ethnicity and the Urban Ecology in a Nineteenth Century City: Philadelphia's Irish, 1840–1890" (Ph.D. diss., University of Pennsylvania, 1979).

69   The analyses involved in Yancey's emergent ethnicity give primacy to econom-ics over culture, but my use of these ideas gives cultural factors a more equal weight. This revision has allowed me to bring into my discussion the notion of ethno-cultural politics, a viewpoint that gives primacy to culture over economics. For this approach: John L. Shover, "Ethnicity and Religion in Philadelphia Poli-tics, 1924–40," *American Quarterly* (1973), pp. 499–515; "The Emergence of a Two-Party System in Republican Philadelphia, 1924–36," *Journal of American History* (1973–74), pp. 985–1002. Sad Republicans: interview with Josephine Barrett, 15 April 1988.

70   Blue laws: Phyllis Laverne Ayers, "The History of the Pennsylvania Sunday Blue Laws" (master's thesis, University of Pittsburgh, 1952); J. Thomas Jable, "Sports, Amusements, and Pennsylvania Blue Laws, 1682–1973" (Ph.D. diss.,

Pennsylvania State University, 1974); John A. Lucas, "The Unholy Experiment—Professional Baseball's Struggles against Pennsylvania Sunday Blue Laws, 1926–1934," *Pennsylvania History* (1971), pp. 163–75. See also Harold Seymour, *Baseball*, vol. 2 (New York, 1971), pp. 365–66.

70 Discrimination: *B*, 26 April 1933 (quoting Gifford Pinchot). Slicker and rube: Lucas, p. 171.

71 Test game: *B*, 22 August 1926; *NYT*, 23 August 1926.

71 Mack endorsement: *B*, 30 October and 18 November 1930.

71 Camden: *B*, 2 and 4 August 1930; 28 March 1931; 27 March 1933. Religion and morale: *B*, 4 November 1933.

72 Frugality: *B*, 9 January 1933; 18 July 1954 (letter from R. W. Demko). Forney: *B*, 9 April 1934.

72 Beer in thirties: *R* clips (Shibe Park—Beer). Late forties through early sixties: *B*, 13 June 1948; 23 August 1949; *B* clips (Connie Mack Stadium—Beer).

73 Spite fence: *B*, 13 July 1952. Relief pitchers: Bill Fleishman, "Home Sweet Home," in "The Philadelphia Phillies: 100 Years," supplement to the *DN*, April 1983, p. 44. Rooftop stands 1910–1914: *B*, 7 October 1914; *Sporting News*, 15 October 1914. In the late twenties: Noel Hynd, "The Wall Went up and the A's Came Tumbling Down," *Sports Illustrated* (17 August 1987, regional article), p. 11.

74 Bleachers: *R*, 7 October 1929. Conflicts with city: *R* clips (Shibe Park—Rooftop Stands). Simmons: *B*, 21 September 1929. Shibe: *B*, 16 May 1933. Harvey: *B*, 4 June 1931.

75 Building of fence: *I*, 10 December 1934; *R*, 9 December 1934; *B*, 10 December 1934; *R*, 8 April 1935.

75 Durkin: *P*, Zoning and Variances (for 2731 North Twentieth); *C*, 21 March 1935. Dilworth: John P. Rossi, "Our Mayoral Quagmire," *Welcomat* (4 November 1987), pp. 30–32. Rooney: John J. Rooney, "Bleachers in the Bedroom," *Philadelphia Magazine* (August 1984), p. 83.

75 1950: *I*, 3 October 1950.

75 Throwing in unison: Chuck Barris, "First Person," *Sports Illustrated*, 1983 (clipping collection, Stadiums, FLP). Tin monster: *B*, 17 May 1966 (quoting Johnny Callison); Hynd, "Wall," p. 10. Mack's cheapness: my father on various occasions.

76 Lights: *R* clips (Shibe Park—Lights); *I*, 20 August 1938; *R*, 17 May 1939 (Red Smith article). FDR: Oscar Eddleton, "Under the Lights," *BRJ* (1980), pp. 37–42. Restaurant: *R*, 31 March 1940.

76 Parkland: *B* clips (Mack Recreation Center).

77 Lehigh Bank: Joseph Barrett, "The Life and Death of an Irish Neighborhood," *Philadelphia Magazine* (March 1970), p. 87. Bankers Trust and Greenfield: "Philadelphia," *Fortune* (June 1936), pp. 186, 188; *B*, 18 October 1938; *I*, 18 April 1940; *C*, 21 November 1946.

77 Mack helps family: conversation with Pat Gorman, 6 May 1987. *C* editorial: 8 April 1935. Suicide: *C*, 29 September 1932.

78 Crime: Steven A. Reiss, *City Games: The Evolution of American Urban Society*

and the Rise of Sports (Urbana, Ill., 1989); Mark Haller, "The Changing Structure of American Gambling in the Twentieth Century," *Journal of Social Issues* (1979), pp. 87–114.

78　Boxing: *B* clips on Max "Boo Boo" Hoff, fight promoter, bootlegger, and sponsor of "knot hole gangs" at Shibe Park (conversation with Bernard Freeman, 6 May 1989).

78　Gambling: *R* clips (Shibe Park—Gambling); *B* clips (Connie Mack Stadium—Gambling). Gamblers Patch, *B*, 22 August 1940. Landis: *B*, 27 June; 4 and 7 September 1944.

78　Italians: Humbert S. Nelli, *The Business of Crime: Italians and Syndicates in the United States* (New York, 1976); Richard Juliani, "Origin and Development of Italians in Philadelphia," in *The Ethnic Experience in Pennsylvania*, ed. John E. Bodnar (Lewisburg, Pa., 1973), pp. 243–44; "The Social Organization of Immigration: The Italians in Philadelphia" (Ph. D. diss., University of Pennsylvania, 1971). See also J. Riggio, "The Over-the-Hill Mob," *Philadelphia Magazine* (November 1972). Toronto Street: Feffer interview.

78　I plotted the residences of some fifteen North Penn Italians who were in trouble with the law from the 1920s to the 1960s and who turned up in my research. Thirteen lived along a diagonal axis where Kennedys Lane ran through the area in the 1880s. From this unscientific study (the 1890 census records have been destroyed), I conclude that the original Italian community of the late nineteenth century produced the criminals.

79　Boxers: interview with Frank Barrett, 27 July 1989; correspondence with Charles Hoffman, 12 and 31 July 1989. Novea and Passamonte: *B* clips.

79　Traitz family: *B*; *I* clips. Jimmy Traitz: Cerino interview; *C*, 7 March 1935; 20 April 1939. Quotes: *U.S. v. Local 30, United Slate, Tile*: 686 F. Supp. 1139 (E.D. Pa. 1988), pp. 1156, 1157, 1162, 1166. An excellent resource is "Roofers: A Selected Bibliography, 1986–1988," compiled by Staff, FLP, Database and Newspaper Center (October 1988). Neither the trial nor the material in the bibliography, however, provides much historical information.

80　Rizzo: *B* clips; Barrett, "Life and Death," p. 129; Joseph R. Daughen and Peter Binzen, *Rizzo: The Cop Who Would Be King* (Boston, 1977), pp. 60–66.

80　Kilroy and Tate: *B* clips; *B*, 13 October 1939; *C*, 29 April 1954. "Small street" anecdote: interview with Joseph Barrett, 20 September 1989.

5. TENANTS AND RENTERS

82　Willkie: *C*, 10 October 1940. FDR: all papers, 27 October 1944. Wallace: see Chapter 9. Anti-Castro: *B*, 26 August 1963. Graham: *I*, 28 February 1971. Witnesses: *B*, 25 June 1959; interview with Andy Clarke, 5 February 1988. Rodeo: *B*, 29 July 1962; *I*, 28 February 1971; Clarke interview. Jazz: *B*, 10 and 16 October 1959. Circus: *B* clips (Circus—Ringling Brothers).

82　Blacks: Gottlieb clips, *B*; Rob Ruck, *Sandlot Seasons* (Urbana, Ill., 1986), p. 118. And see Chapter 9. Black college football: *T*, 20 September 1945.

83　Polidor: *B* clips.

83 Early wrestling: correspondence with Charles Hoffman, 12 and 31 July 1989 (I have not been able to confirm Hoffman's recollection of Londos's wrestling in the park). Later wrestling: *I*, 31 July 1959. Softball: "Baseball News of 1959," video available from *Rare Sportsfilms*, Darien, Ill.

83 Shibe and boxing: Gunnis obituary, *I*, 14 September 1936. Gunnis and Taylor: *B* clips.

83 Shibe Park bouts can be located by examining the newspapers for the stated matches or the *B* clips for each fighter. The most recent survey of boxing and its role in American society is Jeffrey T. Sammons, *Beyond the Ring: The Role of Boxing in American Society* (Urbana, Ill., 1988).

84 Robinson-Angott: *B*, 21 and 22 July 1941.

84 First fights: *B*, 12 July 1917 (Baker fanning); *B*, 25 July 1917 (bleacher rush); *B*, 1 June 1952 (draft dodgers); *B*, 25 July 1917 (advertisement for grand opera); *R*, 6 December 1936 (grand opera).

85 Canopy: *B*, 4 May 1954. Loughran-Delaney: *B*, 7 July 1925.

85 Placement of ring: *B*, 2 July 1926; 3 June 1940. Seating: *B*, 14 September 1959. Searchlights: *B*, 11 September 1928. The 1935 price: *B*, 16 August 1935.

85 Biddle: *B* clips. Dilworth: *R*, 20 October 1944.

85 Bass-Blitman: *B*, 11 September 1928. Turner-Williams: *B*, 10 September 1951. Turner-Fusari: *B*, 9 and 10 July 1951.

86 Yellow Jackets: *B* clips.

86 Eagles: "The Eagles Story," *B*, 18 November 1979.

86 East stands: *B* clips (Connie Mack Stadium—Plans).

87 Van Buren: Myron Cope, *The Game That Was: The Early Days of Pro Football* (New York, 1970), p. 229.

87 Snow game: all papers, 19 and 20 December 1948.

87 Kilroy: *B* clips.

88 Collapse of stands: *B*, 10 December 1945. Football and playing field: Clarke interview; *B*, 21 January 1958.

88 Offers to Eagles: *B*, 9 and 15 November 1956.

88 Franklin Field: *B*, 20 January 1958. *Bulletin* quote: *B*, 21 January 1958. Attendance: *B*, 15 April 1965.

89 Humpty-dumpty: Harold Seymour, *Baseball*, vol. 1 (New York, 1960), p. 207. Futile, laughingstock, proletariat: David Quentin Voigt, *American Baseball*, vol. 2 (Norman, Okla., 1970), pp. 218–19, 272. Owner: interview with Bob Carpenter, 1 April 1988. *Yearbook*: 1949. Tailenders: Frank Yeutter, *New York Post*, 28 July 1943.

89 Voigt: *American Baseball*, vol. 3 (University Park, Pa., 1983), pp. 29, 31. Cellar: conversation with Mike Ruane, 4 May 1989. Graveyard: *B*, 12 November 1969 (Grady article). Boswell: *How Life Imitates the World Series* (New York, 1982), p. 226.

90 The 1927 collapse: *R*, 15 May 1927. The 1933 clubhouse: *I*, 10 December 1933. The 1938 move: *B*, 25 and 30 June 1938; 5 July 1938.

90 Baker and Nugent: J. Roy Stockton, "Them Phillies, or How to Make Failure Pay," *Saturday Evening Post* (4 October 1941), pp. 27, 42–44, 48, 50; Red Smith, *R*, 11 December 1941. *Kid from Tomkinsville* (New York, 1940), p. 217. Few

patrons: "Them Phillies," p. 44, where "ghosts of A's" also appears. Yeutter: *Jim Konstanty* (New York, 1951), p. 2.

91 Joke: Bob Considine, "Mr. Mack: Did He Invent Baseball?" *Life* (29 July 1948), reprinted in *The Baseball Reader*, ed. Charles Einstein (New York, 1983), pp. 72–73.

91 Unhappiest location: William J. Plott, "Double Good/Double Bad" (ms available from SABR). A's-J's: Richard Goldstein, *Spartan Seasons: How Baseball Survived the Second World War* (New York, 1980), p. 170. *Stars and Stripes*: Goldstein, *Spartan*, p. 46. 1930–1950 statistics: U.S. House of Representatives, *Organized Baseball*, Report no. 2002 to accompany H.R. 95, 82d Cong., 2d sess., 1952, pp. 75, 85, 94–96.

92 Nugent and Cox in 1942–1943: *B* clips; clips for Phillies—1942 and 1943.

92 Lardner: *B*, 19 November 1942.

92 Carpenter: *B* clips.

92 Press conference: *B*, 23 November 1943. Signing Roberts: interview with Larry Shenk, 15 November 1987. Carpenter himself: Carpenter interview. Inherited wealth: *I Magazine* (19 March 1950). Grady: *B*, 12 November 1969.

93 Accounting: material in unmarked folder, box 5, PP. Modernization: "Sales Reports," box 3, and Treasurer's Reports, box 4, both in PP. Baumgartner: "The Philadelphia Phillies," in *The Book of Major League Baseball Clubs: The National League*, ed. Ed Fitzgerald, (New York, 1952).

93 Whiz Kids: Harry T. Paxton, *The Whiz Kids* (New York, 1950).

94 Attendance comparisons: Gerald R. Curtis, "Factors that Affect the Attendance of a Major League Baseball Club" (master's thesis, Wharton School, University of Pennsylvania, 1951), pp. 70–76. Carpenter recollection: interview. Bitter pill: Lieb, *Mack*, p. 280.

94 Carpenter on being rich: interview.

6. BASEBALL AND BUSINESS

95 Kelleher: Kevin Kerrane, *Dollar Sign on the Muscle* (New York, 1986), p. 209. *Bull Durham* (1988, a Mount Company Production, directed by Ron Shelton), had Kevin Kostner in the role of Davis. Parisse (and his brother, who was dismissed from the police force for numbers running): *B* clips; Richard Goldstein, *Spartan Seasons: How Baseball Survived the Second World War* (New York, 1980), p. 146.

95 Brown: Lee Allen, "A Study in Suet," in *Armchair Book of Baseball*, ed. John Thorn (New York, 1985), pp. 1–2. Nelson and Beck: Art Hill, *I Don't Care if I Never Come Back: A Baseball Fan and His Game* (New York, 1980), p. 85.

96 Mack Day: all papers, 17 May 1941. Dobbins: *R*, 22 May 1941. Loved and welcome: *C*, 18 December 1941.

96 DiMaggio: Michael Seidel, *Streak: Joe DiMaggio and the Summer of 1941* (New York, 1988), pp. 152–54; Maury Allen, *Where Have You Gone, Joe DiMaggio?* (New York, 1975), pp. 106–7. Williams: Ted Williams with John Underwood,

My Turn at Bat: The Story of My Life (New York, 1969, 1988), p. 87. Grove: *B*, 29 September 1941.

97   Night ball: David Quentin Voigt, *American Baseball*, vol. 2 (Norman, Okla., 1970), pp. 226–28. Dimout: Goldstein, *Spartan*, p. 125. Restaurant: *R*, 26 July 1944 (Basenfelder article). Songfests, poppies, autographed balls: Goldstein, *Spartan*, pp. 129, 37, and 78, respectively.

97   Brancato: William B. Mead, *Baseball Goes to War* (Washington, D.C., 1985), pp. 50, 225–26. Mulcahy: Goldstein, *Spartan*, pp. 37, 67. Marchildon: Goldstein, *Spartan*, p. 250; Mead, *War*, p. 201. Savage: Goldstein, *Spartan*, p. 253. Brissie: Mead, *War*, p. 200. Williams-Angott: *B*, 7 June 1944.

99   Shibe and Schroeder: *R*, 31 March 1940 (A's Fans Like their "Dogs"); *B*, 22 January 1950 (Pollock, Playing the Game); *R*, 6 June 1943 (Basenfelder article). Genius tag: interview with Andy Clarke, 5 February 1988. Traveling kitchen: *R*, 31 March 1940.

99   Parker: *DN*, 14 April 1960; 27 July 1964; *B*, 4 October 1967; *DN*, 9 February 1968. See also "1962 Concession Sales," Ledger Book, unmarked, PP.

99   Gumbert: *R*, 6 June 1943. Friedlander: *I*, 30 September 1951.

100   Renovations: *B*, 24 October 1948; 25 November 1948; 27 March 1949. Langdon: *B* clips.

100   Tunnels: *B*, 4 May 1949 (Pollock, Playing the Game); 5 April 1953.

100   Kessler: *B* clips.

100   Clarke: interview and *B* clips; quote from Joseph Barrett interview, 15 April 1988.

101   Crane: *B* clips. See also *B* clips (Connie Mack Stadium—Employees).

101   Bluecaps: letter from Joseph Rooney, 28 January 1988. Vendor: Chuck Barris, "First Person" *Sports Illustrated*, 1983 (clipping file, Stadiums, FLP). "The Sweeper": ms by Joseph Barrett.

102   Broadcasting: Curt Smith, *Voices of the Game* (South Bend, Ind., 1987), pp. 15, 84–90.

102   Saam: David Quentin Voigt, *American Baseball*, vol. 3 (University Park, Pa., 1983), p. 105; Jim Waltzer, "That Lehigh Avenue Moon," *I Magazine* (9 April 1989); *I*, 24 January 1990, reporting Saam's elevation to the Hall of Fame.

103   Re-creation: Smith, *Voices*, pp. 26–28, 39, 40; David Halberstam, *Summer of '49* (New York, 1989), p. 257. My re-creation is from the Phillies-Dodgers game of 28 May 1941.

103   Loudspeaker: *B*, 20 March 1953 (Answers to Queries); Charles C. Alexander, *John McGraw* (New York, 1988), p. 293; O'Rourke *B* clips. O'Brien: *B*, 29 August 1944, 16 August 1948 (both Pollock, Playing the Game); *I*, 26 July 1955; O'Brien obituary, *I*, 11 April 1989.

104   Radio: *I*, 22 August 1955 (Views of Sports).

104   TV in 1937: Richard C. Crepeau, *Baseball: America's Diamond Mind* (Orlando, Fla., 1980), p. 187. TV thereafter: *B*, 17 May 1951 (Answers to Queries); 29 February 1952; 11 February 1953; 8 April 1954; 14 April 1954; 14 August 1955.

104   Merchandising: Wold and Tannenbaum (of Weightman, Inc., Advertising) to Carpenter, 22 July 1949, box 6, PP.

105   Broadcasters: Philadelphia National League Club, Sales Reports, Radio and Television, 1966, 1967, 1969, box 3, all in PP. See also Agreements, N. W. Ayer Marketing Firm and Phillies, box 6, PP.

106   Mack pitchers: Bob Considine, "Mr. Mack: Did He Invent Baseball?" *Life* (29 July 1948), reprinted in *The Baseball Reader*, ed. Charles Einstein (New York, 1983), pp. 76–77.

106   Waitkus: B clips. *The Natural* of 1984, directed by Barry Levinson for Tri–Star Pictures, was adapted from Bernard Malamud, *The Natural* (New York, 1952).

106   Ashburn's Alley: Bob Broeg with Stan Musial, *Stan Musial* (New York, 1964), pp. 143, 309.

107   Konstanty: Frank Yeutter, *Jim Konstanty* (New York, 1951), p. 19.

107   Mardi Gras: B, 18 April 1950 (Yeutter article). To Shibe Park: letter from Mary M. Marschner, 17 November 1988; interview with Jim Brown, 21 December 1988; interview with Robert Nauss, 4 December 1987; conversation with Frank Kenneth Carner, 11 January 1989.

107   Art Hill: *I Don't Care*, p. 15. Morris: *North toward Home* (New York, 1967), p. 102 (which does not mention Shibe Park). Home team: David Shaw, "The Roots of Rooting," *Psychology Today* (February 1978), p. 49. Lodigiani: John Gregory Dunne review of James Stevenson's *Higher on the Door* in *NYT Book Review* (20 September 1987). Train: letter from novelist Dr. Gerald Rosen, 17 September 1987.

108   First memory: Gordon Tindall, "Extra Innings," *Ballparks Bulletin*, May 1986. Rituals: conversation with Mike Ruane, 4 May 1989; Carner conversation; Bruce Kuklick, "Ballpark Memories," *Beachcomber* (19 June 1986). Game breaks: interview with Joseph Barrett, 20 September 1989.

109   Gouraud: B clips. Doctoral diss.: David John Kammer, "Take Me Out to the Ballgame" (Ph.D. diss., University of New Mexico–Albuquerque, 1982), p. 385.

109   Adelis: B clips, esp. 23 September 1948; Tim Braine and John Stravinsky, *The Not-So-Great Moments in Sports* (New York, 1986), p. 244; B Photo Journalism Collection, UA (photo: Mack and Adelis, 29 July 1953). See also Joe Archibald, *The Richie Ashburn Story* (New York, 1960), p. 169.

109   Mize: Yeutter, *Konstanty*, p. 150. Musial: Broeg, *Musial*, p. 143. Williams: John Updike, "Hub Fans Bid Kid Adieu," *New Yorker* (1960), reprinted in *Baseball Reader*, p. 443; Edward F. Doyle, *Forty Years a Fan* (Philadelphia, 1972), p. 42. Five-home-run inning: I, 9 April 1967 (Homers spice History of Phils' Park). Thompson and Gessner: B, 17 October 1980 (Adrian Lee column). Mays: B, 9 October 1977. See also B, illegibly dated article, 1949 (Dick Cresap, Sports Parade, "How Would You Like a Homer in Your Home?"); B, 30 March 1961 (Hugh Brown column); Broeg, *Musial*, p. 308.

110   *The Old Man and the Sea* (New York, 1952), pp. 21–22.

110   Mummers Parade: Yeutter, *Konstanty*, pp. 17–18. Absolutes: William Ecenbarger, "Opening Day," *I Magazine* (3 April 1988).

110   Frank Bilovsky and Rich Westcott: *The Phillies Encyclopedia* (New York, 1984), p. 336.

110 Zernial: Jack Etkin, *Innings Ago: Recollections by Kansas City Ballplayers of Their Days in the Game* (Kansas City, Mo., 1987), pp. 59, 93–94.

111 Rizzo: *B*, 28 September 1977; conversation with Ira Harkavy, 20 November 1989.

7. THE MACK FAMILY AND SHIBE PARK, 1946–1954

112 Shibe family: *B* clips.

112 Mack acquires control: *New York Post*, 20 December 1940. Mack family: *B* clips, and, for Connie, Jr., Robert Schroeder clips.

113 Stock distribution and separation: Harry Robert, "The Philadelphia Athletics," in *The Book of Major League Baseball Clubs: The American League*, ed. Ed Fitzgerald (New York, 1952), pp. 127–28; Frederick G. Lieb, *Connie Mack: Grand Old Man of Baseball* (New York, 1945), pp. 280–81.

113 Roy and Earle fight: Andy Clarke interview, 5 April 1988. Factional fight: *B*, 13 December 1954; Robert, "Athletics," p. 129.

113 David Halberstam's *Summer of '49* (New York, 1989), pp. 19–24, vividly treats the excitement of baseball after the war.

114 Renovation: *R*, 26 July 1944 (Basenfelder); *B*, 14 July 1948; 16 September 1948; 1 October 1948.

114 Birthdays: Lieb, *Mack*, p. 266. Tunis: "Cornelius McGillicuddy," *Atlantic Monthly* (August 1940), p. 212. World War II: Richard Goldstein, *Spartan Seasons: How Baseball Survived the Second World War* (New York, 1980), p. 42. Umpires: Frank Yeutter, *Jim Konstanty* (New York, 1951), p. 87. TV: Jimmie Dykes and Charles O. Dexter, *You Can't Steal First Base* (Philadelphia, 1967), pp. 173–74. Popular figure: Robert, "Athletics," p. 123.

114 Kell: Art Hill, *I Don't Care if I Never Come Back: A Baseball Fan and His Game* (New York, 1980), p. 37. Lapses and death: Considine, "Mr. Mack: Did He Invent Baseball?" *Life* (29 July 1948), reprinted in *The Baseball Reader*, ed. Charles Einstein (New York, 1983), pp. 75, 79; Harold Seymour, *Baseball*, vol. 2 (New York, 1971), p. 138; Goldstein, *Spartan*, p. 157. Potter, emotional, off the beam, and calamitous moves: Robert, "Athletics," pp. 126–27, 153–55. David Quentin Voigt: *American Baseball*, vol. 2 (Norman, Okla., 1970), p. 80. An analysis of Mack in the forties using the recollections of his players is Ben Yagoda, "The Legend of Connie Mack," *PhillySport* (August 1989), pp. 52–62.

115 Mack captivated and Connie, Jr., overridden: Robert, "Athletics," p. 154, 129, respectively. *Elephant Trail*: (January 1950), p. 3. Motorcade: *B*, 21 April 1950.

116 Veeck: *B*, 26 June 1950. Family struggle: Robert, "Athletics," p. 129. Earle removed: *B*, 18 October 1950. The 1950 fight: *B*, 27 May 1950; 28 August 1950; 22 January 1951; *NYT*, 11 February 1960; *B*, 12 February 1960 (Pollock, Playing the Game).

116 Carpenter and Clark: *B*, 31 July 1950 (Pollock article). McShain: *I*, 29 August 1950.

116   Mortgage: *B*, 28 August 1950 (Cresap article). Assessment and Connecticut General: *I*, 9 June 1950; *B*, 9 September 1951; Assignment of lease, Leases, box 7, PP. Jacobs Brothers: Agreement of 1 December 1954, Concessionaire Contract, box 7, PP; *DN* 10 October 1950 (Delaney article); *B*, 11 August 1954 (Pollock article); 26 January 1972.

117   A's budget: 1 August 1950 (Pollock article). *B* quote: 26 August 1950.

117   Phillies comparison: Lieb, *Mack*, p. 279. Phillies World Series: *B*, 20 September 1950.

117   Knowledgeable commentator: Robert, "Athletics," p. 129.

118   *Daily Worker*: 20 October 1950 (On the Scoreboard). For a sampling of other opinions: *Sporting News* (1 November 1950), pp. 11–12; Tim Cohane, "Connie Mack's Last Year," *Look* (14 February 1950).

118   Elephant Room: *B*, 13 April 1951.

118   Shantz: *B* clips, and Bobby Shantz as told to Ralph Bernstein, *The Story of Bobby Shantz* (Philadelphia, 1953), p. 77.

119   Kelly poem: Bernstein, *Bobby Shantz*, p. 148. Boyd: Douglas Wallop, *The Year the Yankees Lost the Pennant* (New York, 1954), pp. 91–93. Shantz crowds: *B*, 26 February 1957. All-Star game: Bernstein, *Bobby Shantz*, p. 146. *I* editorial: 6 August 1952.

119   Roy Mack: *B*, 26 February 1957.

120   Mack brothers: interview with Andy Clarke, 5 February 1988. Fifty-two years: *B*, 19 July 1953. Fairmount Park and Yankee pressure: *B*, 29 September 1953 (Pollock article). And see all papers for June 1954.

120   Macks see Clark, Save the A's, Clark quotes: *B*, 2 July 1954. Clark attitude: *B*, 9 July 1954 (Pollock article); 8 August 1954; 10 September 1954. And see Lenore Berson, "Philadelphia: The Evolution of Economic Urban Planning, 1945–1980," in *Community and Capital in Conflict: Plant Closing and Job Loss*, ed. John C. Raines et al. (Philadelphia, 1982), p. 182.

121   Initial fan quotes: *B*, 6, 7, 8, 11, 13, 15, 18, and 26 July 1954; *I*, 13 June 1954.

122   Public relations director: *B*, 25 July 1954.

122   Fans on Macks: *B*, 10, 13, 14, 17, and 24 July 1954; 1 August 1954; my father (ain't worth a shit).

122   Save the A's collapses and analyzes Macks: *B*, 29 and 30 July 1954; 1 August 1954.

122   Baseball changes: Neil J. Sullivan, *The Dodgers Move West* (New York, 1987). Two counterexamples stand out: the Washington Senators left the District of Columbia, though they were the only team in the city, and Chicago hung on to both the Cubs and the White Sox.

123   Brown article: *B*, 8 July 1954.

123   Johnson: Ernest Mehl, *The Kansas City Athletics* (New York, 1956). Compare his uncritical understanding (pp. 130, 191–93) with mine, adapted from *B*, 13 October 1954; 8 April 1955.

123   Stock value: *B*, 3–5 and 10 August 1954; 9 September 1954; 21 January 1955 (Pollock article).

124   Carpenter: interview with Carpenter, 1 April 1988; *B*, 27 September 1954.
124   Carpenter does not want park: *B*, 18 October 1954. West Philadelphia: *B*, 9 September 1954. Renovation: *B*, 22 September 1954.
124   Johnson lease: *B*, 9 September 1954. Carpenter purchase: *P*, Deeds and Records, 2000 West Lehigh, 10 December 1954 (reference number 827.323).
125   Sylk: *B*, 6 August 1954. Greenfield: *B*, 10 August 1954. Local syndicates: all papers, August–November 1954. Mack attends meeting: Mehl, *Athletics*, p. 98.
125   Race to apartment: *B*, 13–15 November 1954. Excruciating: *B*, 9 November 1954. Macks: *B*, 4 November 1954; 23 December 1954.
125   Daley: *NYT*, 19 October 1954. Kansas City nickname: Joseph L. Reichler, *The Baseball Trade Register* (New York, 1984), p. 349. For a typical expression of the New York attitude: *New York Herald Tribune*, 11 November 1954.
126   Memorabilia and tower office: *B*, 20 January 1955. Crompton: *C*, 30 August 1956. Mack: *B*, 11 May 1958. Loss of franchise: many conversations with Russell Weigley and others.

8. CONNIE MACK STADIUM, 1953–1970

129   The 1941 change: *B*, 10 May 1941. The 1953 change: *B*, 14 February 1953; 5 April 1953.
129   Phillies ball park: *B*, 13 August 1954; 9 November 1954. Council resolution: *B*, 8 July 1956. Memorial committee: *B*, 24 February 1956; 9 July 1956 (Pollock article).
130   Square: *B*, 20 March 1957, in which appears issue of discrediting Reyburn. Tribute to most famous personality: *B*, 17 April 1957. Ceremonies and *I* quote: 17 April 1957.
130   New offices: *B*, 10 December 1954. Thirty-third and Columbia: *B*, 7 August 1946; 9 June 1954. West Philly and real estate quote: *B*, 9 September 1954.
130   Remodeling: *B*, 10 November 1955. Scoreboard: *B*, 16 May 1956 (there is no confirmation to the story that the scoreboard was the old Yankee Stadium one). The 1941 board: *New York Post*, 12 April 1941. Advertising: illegibly dated *B* clip, 1955, Connie Mack Stadium. Sod: interview with Andy Clarke, 5 February 1988. Forbidden grass: *B*, 5 April 1955. The 1969 fence: *Sporting News* (1 March 1969), p. 21.
131   Three problems: Carpenter interview, 1 April 1988.
131   Automobile and mass transit: James J. Flink, *The Automobile Age* (Cambridge, 1988); Mark S. Foster, *From Street Car to Superhighway: American City Planning and Urban Transportation, 1900–1940* (Philadelphia, 1981); Glen E. Holt, "The Changing Perception of Urban Pathology: An Essay on the Development of Mass Transit in the United States," in *Cities in American History*, ed. Kenneth T. Jackson and Stanley K. Schultz (New York, 1972), pp. 324–55; Jon C. Teaford, *The Twentieth Century American City* (Baltimore, 1986); Richard Deglin, "Spatial Aspects of the Street Railway Network" (paper for Geography 273, 1 December 1975), UA, Papers on Philadelphia. Eric H. Monkkonen adds complexity to con-

ventional views in *America Becomes Urban: The Development of U.S. Cities & Towns, 1780–1980* (Berkeley, 1988), pp. 158–81.

132 Parking lots: MAPS. Square: *B*, 24, 25, and 29 June 1939; 18 May 1940; 25 May 1950; 1 June 1950; *I*, 6 June 1952; *B*, 10 February 1953; 29 March 1953; 19 May 1953. Phils buy block: *I*, 2 August 1957. The 1959 expansion: *B*, 7 May 1959. Neighborhood businesses: *B*, 21 July 1954.

133 Railroad parking and hard surfacing: *B*, 9 June 1954. Dell parking: *B*, 15 June 1954; 17 July 1954.

133 Phillies encourage cars and buses: *Yearbook*, 1951, 1952, and 1953; *I*, 13 May 1970. Group sales: e.g., Philadelphia National League Club, Sales Report, 1957, box 3, PP. Private busing: interview with Robert Nauss, 4 December 1987. Special buses: *B*, 11 April 1951; 12 July 1957.

134 The 1930s car watchers: interview with Harry McFadden, 29 October 1988. The 1940s and 1950s: *B* clips (Connie Mack Stadium—Car Watchers).

134 Stadium study: Eshbach, Nathan, and Bass, "Municipal Sports Stadium Study," 2 vols. (25 July 1957). The 1959 article: *B*, 12 April 1959. The 1964 editorial: *B*, 1 July 1964. Covington: *B*, 10 August 1964 (Bilovsky article). *Magazine*: Charles MacNamara, "The Stadium: Who's Getting Railroaded?" (July 1964). Grady: *B*, 18 April 1968. The 1968 editorial: *B*, 1 October 1968.

135 *Sporting News*: in David Quentin Voigt, *American Baseball*, vol. 2 (Norman, Okla., 1970), pp. 201–6, whence comes material on ball parks in the 1920s to 1950s.

136 The 1953 meeting: MacNamara, "The Stadium." Tate: 8 January 1959. Carpenter quotes: interview.

136 Dilworth: *B* clips. *I* articles: *I*, 11 June 1957 (The Mayor Writes). Dilworth's advisers: *B*, 3 August 1957 (Eisler article). Phillies might leave: *B*, 12 September 1957. Creepy: *B*, 20 September 1961. Ashburn: Joe Archibald, *The Richie Ashburn Story* (New York, 1960), p. 178. Dogs: *B*, 10 October 1962. Idea of stadium: *B*, 14 November 1955; 18 August 1964 (Fine and Semonski article). Carpenter on baseball park: e.g., *I*, 27 August 1957 (Schrage article); *B*, 28 May 1961 (Eisler article). Clarke: interview.

137 The 1910s plan: *I*, 10 August 1964 (Corr article). Kelly idea: 4 August 1954 (Pollock article); 9 November 1954. Cheltenham: *B*, 20 May 1958 (Newhall article). New York: *B*, 15 April 1959. Camden: *B*, 7 January 1959; 22 February 1959; 20 March 1959; Notebook, "New Stadium . . . Camden County," box 7, PP. Later recollection: interview with Carpenter.

138 Football and Carpenter: *B*, 22 January 1958 (brief note titled: Lovely Landlord); 11 November 1959; *I*, 10 October 1957.

138 Torresdale: *B*, 28 June 1961; 21 July 1961; 1 August 1961. Carpenter sells park: *B*, 29 March 1961; 3 April 1961. Lease arrangements, 1954–1959: Treasurers Reports, 1955, 1960, box 4, and Notebook, "New Stadium . . . Camden County," box 7, both in PP.

139 Treasurer: *B*, 9 April 1961 (Pollock article). Time bomb: MacNamara, "The Stadium."

139 Chaotic wrangling: *B*, 28 August 1961 (Grady article). Endless bickering: *I*, 17 May 1970. Decay: MacNamara, "The Stadium."

139 Auto damage in 1960s: *B*, 10 June 1963; 27 July 1964; 26 August 1964. Complaint: *B*, 11 June 1964. Whitey: interview with Joseph Barrett, 20 September 1989.

141 Torresdale: *B*, 21 July 1961. Other recommendations: Citizens Committee on City Planning, *Report* (9 May 1961). South Philly: *B*, 19 July 1957. Thirtieth and Arch: *B*, 1 April 1959.

141 Clarkes: interview. Torresdale preference: Carpenter interview.

141 Overviews of 1964 fighting: *I*, 4 April 1965 (Byrod article); *B*, 8 April 1965 (Calpin article). Phillies' perspective: stadium material, box 6, PP.

141 Wolman: *B* clips. Buys stadium: *B*, 5 December 1963. Helps Phillies: *B*, 24 May 1964 (Lee article). Eagles move: *B*, 27 June 1964. Interests against Thirtieth and Arch: *B*, 10 August 1964. Wolman to rebuild park: *I*, 5 June 1964.

142 Tate: *B* clips. Thirtieth and Arch: *B*, 8 April 1965 (Calpin article). No urban renewal: *B*, 27 May 1964. Wolman will sell: *I*, 5 June 1964; *B*, 7 June 1964.

142 Tate conferences: *B*, 1 and 3 June 1964.

142 Wolman will not move and Tate to purchase park: *I*, 27 June 1964. Wolman refusal: *B*, 27–29 June 1964. August withdrawal: *B*, 12–17 August 1964. Agreement on South Philly: *B*, 18 August 1964.

143 Teams reject alternatives: *B*, 11 May 1967. Eagles' rights: *I*, 7 May 1965; *B*, 1 July 1965. Monstrous design: *B*, 14 December 1965. Quotes on Vet: Publicity Releases, September 1966, Pennsylvania Railroad Papers, UA.

143 Carpenter timetable and lease: Treasurers Report, 1966; Digest of Stadium Leases, File on Financial Data—Other Clubs, box 5, PP. Quotes: *I*, 26 January 1967; *B*, 10 May 1967.

144 Aggression: *B*, 15 April 1969; 18 September 1969; 5 and 7 July 1970. In 1970: *I*, 17 May 1970 (Ryan article, which is a good survey of post-1965 problems).

144 Wolman goes bust: e.g., *B*, 14 and 15 November 1967.

9. RACE RELATIONS

145 Mack and Jim Crow: David Quentin Voigt, *American Baseball*, vol. 3 (University Park, Pa., 1983), p. 46. Black performances at Shibe Park: John Holway, *Blackball Stars: Negro League Pioneers* (Westport, Conn., 1988); Donn Rogosin, *Invisible Men: Life in Baseball's Negro Leagues* (New York, 1985), p. 183.

145 Wharton School study: Gerald R. Curtis, "Factors That Affect the Attendance of a Major League Baseball Club" (master's thesis, University of Pennsylvania, 1951). Landis: Rogosin, *Invisible Men*, pp. 183–84, 197–98.

145 Campanella (two conflicting accounts): Kevin Kerrane, *Dollar Sign on the Muscle* (New York, 1986), p. 258; Campanella, *It's Good to Be Alive* (New York, 1959), pp. 94–98.

146 Phillies in early forties: J. Roy Stockton, "Them Phillies, or How to Make Failure Pay," *Saturday Evening Post* (4 October 1941), p. 50. Father Divine: *PI*, 20 September 1942. Gottlieb: *B* clips. His involvement with Phillies: *B*, 20 January 1980 (Red Smith article). Veeck: Bill Veeck with Ed Linn, *Veeck as in Wreck* (New York, 1962, 1986), pp. 173–75.

146   Landis: Rogosin, *Invisible Men*, pp. 183–84, 197–98. Mack's leadership in neighborhood: conversation with Oliver Williams, 24 March 1989. Bitter opposition: *T*, 25 August 1945 (Through the Eyes of Rollo Wilson). My sense of Philadelphia's white rooters is impressionistic but corroborated by everyone I interviewed.

147   Gottlieb and Mack: *T*, 8 September 1945 (Through the Eyes of Rollo Wilson). Stars at park: e.g., *T*, 19 May 1945; 1 September 1945; *PI*, 15 August 1947; 6 September 1947. World Series: *PI*, 20 September 1942; *T*, 15 September 1945; *PI*, 27 September 1947.

147   Exploitation: *B*, 4 January 1951. Johnson quotes: Kerrane, *Dollar Sign*, pp. 16, 63; *B*, 11 September 1978.

147   Robinson: Jules Tygiel, *Baseball's Great Experiment* (New York, 1983), pp. 182–85; Maury Allen, *Jackie Robinson* (New York, 1987), pp. 130–31. Doby: Joseph Thomas Moore, *Pride against Prejudice* (New York, 1988), p. 90. Trice: *B*, 8 September 1953.

148   Phillies: Voigt, *American Baseball*, vol. 3, pp. 26–27, 49, 53. Black press: *T*, 26 June 1956. Carpenter quote: Frank Bilovsky and Rich Westcott, *Phillies Encyclopedia* (New York, 1981), p. 335. Dilworth: to Shorter, 5 October 1956, Urban League papers, UA. *PI*: 30 June 1956. Carpenter: to Shorter, 22 June 1956; Carpenter to Shorter, 17 July 1956; Shorter to Carpenter, 19 July 1956, Urban League Papers, UA.

148   Desegregation of housing: *B*, 18 February 1962.

148   Gray: to Shorter, 5 July 1956, Urban League papers, UA.

149   Demographic changes: Kenneth Jackson, *The Crabgrass Frontier: The Suburbization of the United States* (New York, 1985); John C. Teaford, *The Twentieth Century American City* (Baltimore, 1986); Eric Lampard, "The Nature of Urbanization," in *The Pursuit of Urban History*, ed. Derek Fraser and Anthony Sutcliffe (London, 1983), pp. 3–53. For Philadelphia: Theodore Hershberg et al., "A Tale of Three Cities: Blacks and Immigrants in Philadelphia, 1850–1880, 1930 and 1970," *Annals, American Academy of Political and Social Science* (January 1979), pp. 55–81; John Bauman, *Public Housing, Race, and Renewal: Urban Planning in Philadelphia, 1920–1974* (Philadelphia, 1987). For North Penn: MAPS and Joseph Barrett, "The Life and Death of an Irish Neighborhood," *Philadelphia Magazine* (March 1970).

150   Black housing: Bauman, *Public Housing*, p. 219. Quotes: interview with Frank Kerrigan, 8 February 1988; with Josephine Barrett, 15 April 1988.

150   Strike and Jubilee: Alan M. Winkler, "The Philadelphia Transit Strike of 1944," *Journal of American History* (1971–72), pp. 73–89; G. Gordon Brown, *Law Administration and Negro-White Relations in Philadelphia* (Philadelphia, 1947); Frederick G. Lieb, *Connie Mack: Grand Old Man of Baseball* (New York, 1945), pp. 273–74; *B*, 3, 4, and 5 August 1944; Thomas Roberts, "A History and Analysis of Labor-Management Relations in the Philadelphia Transit Industry" (Ph.D. diss., University of Pennsylvania, 1959).

150   The 1948 election: Bruce Kuklick, *The Good Ruler* (New Brunswick, N.J., 1988), pp. 84–85, 88–90.

151   Williams-Beau Jack, Wallace, and West: *B*, 17 May 1948; 13, 14, 26, and 31 July 1948; 3 and 8 August 1948.

152 Late 1940s and early 1950s: Barrett, "Irish Neighborhood"; interview with Barrett, 20 May 1988. Forbidden zone: interview with Harry Cerino, 1 November 1988.

153 Liberals and North Philadelphia: John Bauman, "Visions of a Post-War City: A Perspective on Urban Planning in Philadelphia and the Nation, 1942–1945," *Urbanism Past and Present* (1980), pp. 1–11; Bauman, *Public Housing*; Nancy Klieniewski's essays: "From Industrial to Corporate City: The Role of Urban Renewal," in *Marxism and the Metropolis*, ed. W. K. Tabb and L. Saweres, 2d ed. (New York, 1984), pp. 206–22; and "Local Business Leaders and Urban Policy: A Case Study," *Insurgent Sociologist* 14 (1987), pp. 33–56.

154 Blacks move: Bauman, *Public Housing*, p. 248; Josephine Barrett and Cerino interviews. Demographic change: SSDL; Barrett, "Irish Neighborhood." White island: interview with John Feffer, 21 December 1988.

155 C: 12 October 1954; 1 July 1965; 9 February 1967; 15 June 1967; 2 November 1967; 11 April 1968.

155 Early sixties: Conrad Weiler, *Philadelphia: Neighborhood, Authority, and the Urban Crisis* (New York, 1974).

156 Riot and Phillies: B, 28 August–2 September 1964; *NYT*, 31 August 1964; 2 September 1964.

156 Allen: Thomas Boswell, *How Life Imitates the World Series* (New York, 1982), pp. 138, 140; Mark Lazarus, "Dick Allen's 1972," in *National Pastime*, ed. John Thorn (New York, 1987), pp. 318–25; B, 26 April 1977.

157 Allen blasts: letter from Wayne Bodle, 14 January 1989. Beating heat: interview with Robert Jones, 18 August 1987. Tate: letter from John Raeburn, 27 July 1987. Home run distance: B, 2 June 1966; I, 9 April 1967; B, 10 July 1967; 15 April 1969; 17 June 1969. Fearsome: Lazarus, "Allen," p. 325. Fans' memories: Dick Allen and Tim Whitaker, *Crash: The Life and Times of Dick Allen* (New York, 1989), pp. xvi, 179.

157 Angell: *The Summer Game* (New York, 1972), p. 102. The 1964 Phillies: *PhillySport* (June 1989) is devoted to the subject; Steve Wulf, "The Year of the Blue Snow, *Sports Illustrated* (25 September 1989), pp. 76–86.

158 Board up the park: B, 2 September 1964. Vulnerability: interview with Larry Shenk, 15 November 1987. Racial troubles in 1960s: Lenora Berson, "Philadelphia: The Evolution of Urban Economic Planning, 1945–1980," in *Community and Capital in Conflict: Plant Closing and Job Loss*, ed. John C. Raines et al. (Philadelphia, 1982), pp. 187–90. White observer: David Ley, *The Black Inner City as Frontier Outpost: Images and Behavior of a Philadelphia Neighborhood* (Washington, D.C., 1974), pp. 58–59.

158 Rizzo: Joseph R. Daughen and Peter Binzen, *Rizzo: The Cop Who Would Be King* (Boston, 1977); Weiler, *Philadelphia*, pp. 192–98. Moore: B clips.

159 Carpenter a big kid: Shenk interview. Circumspect observers: Kerrane, *Dollar Sign*, pp. 62–63, and Voigt, *American Baseball*, vol. 3, p. 53. Conlin: DN, 25 October 1971. Carpenter himself: B, 28 October 1971. Black America's team: Robert Ruck, *Sandlot Seasons* (Urbana, Ill., 1986), p. 184. My sense of black attendance comes independently from interviews with: James Brown, 23 December 1988; William Kelley, 31 December 1988; letter from Joseph Rooney, 28 January 1988.

159   Overview of Allen's career: *I*, 8 May 1975 (nigger lover). See also *B*, 6 July 1965; 26 June 1969; 3 July 1969 (black and militant); 18 August 1969 (nigger); 12 October 1969; 20 August 1979 (racial prejudice). Carpenter quote: interview, 1 April 1988.

160   Abuse: *I*, 12 October 1969. Booed: *B*, 18 January 1969. Editorial: *B*, 19 August 1967. Crash: Allen, *Crash*, p. 69. Crossword: *NYT*, 10 April 1973.

160   Outlaw: Allen, *Crash*, p. 34, whose material is essential for drawing a portrait of Allen.

161   Mauch: *B*, June 1968, especially 11 June (see also *B*, 26 June 1969). Fairness: *B*, 8 August 1969.

161   Decaying: *B*, 5 July 1969. The 1969 fines: *B*, 8 June 1969. Skinner firing: *B*, 8 August 1969.

162   Flood: James Edward Miller, *The Baseball Business: Pursuing Profits and Pennants in Baltimore* (Chapel Hill, N.C., 1990), pp. 181–84.

162   Grady: *B*, 25 August 1969.

162   Allen's importance: *I*, 11 August 1969. Observer: conversation with Wayne Bodle, 30 November 1988.

163   Uecker: *B*, 18 August 1967. Allen: *Crash*, p. 130. And see the peculiar comments about the Rizzo era, pp. 159–60. Fans: *B*, 24 August 1967. Grady: *B*, 9 October 1969.

10. URBAN RENEWAL?

164   Black North Philadelphia: Miriam Ershkowitz and Joseph Zikmund II, eds., *Black Politics in Philadelphia* (New York, 1973); Karl E. Taeuber and Alma Taeuber, *Negroes in Cities* (Chicago, 1965). And see papers delivered at Centennial Conference on North Philadelphia, Temple University, Philadelphia, 1985 (organized by Noel Cazenave, Department of Sociology, Temple University).

164   Philadelphia's economy and guide to the literature on streetcar and industrial suburbs: Theodore Hershberg et al., "A Tale of Three Cities: Blacks and Immigrants in Philadelphia: 1850–1880, 1930 and 1970," *Annals, American Academy of Political and Social Science* (January 1979), pp. 55–81.

165   A's leave: *B*, 18 October 1954; 5 and 9 November 1954.

166   Housing study: Robert Powell Sangster, "Abandonment of Inner City Properties," *Federal Home Loan Board Journal* (February 1972).

166   North Philadephia vacated: Mike Mallowe, "The Barren North," *Philadelphia Magazine* (August 1981), quotes, p. 110.

166   Catholic churches: Joseph Barrett, "The Life and Death of an Irish Neighborhood," *Philadelphia Magazine* (March 1970), pp. 86–87; *B*, 8 November 1970; 28 April 1979. Observer: Kathleen Gavigan, "The Rise and Fall of Parish Cohesiveness in Philadelphia," *Records of the American Catholic Historical Society* (1975), p. 128.

167   Dying Jungle: Mallowe, "Barren North," p. 108. Disappearance of people and housing: Housing Association of the Delaware Valley, "Housing Abandonment: The Future Forgotten" (Philadelphia, 1972); Lynne Kotranski, "The Structure and Determinants of Urban Mortgage Lending Patterns: A Study of Philadelphia, 1968–1974" (Ph.D. diss., Temple University, 1974); Philadelphia City Planning Commission, "Demolition/Vacant House Treatment Study" (1984); George H. Leon and David W. Bartelt, "From Row House to No House: Housing Abandonment and Demolition in North Philadelphia" (ms, ca. 1985).

168 Phillies leaving delayed: *B*, 5 April 1970; *I*, 23 June 1971.

168 Real estate decline: *B*, 14 September 1971 (Seymour article).

168 Gangs: Barrett, "Life and Death," pp. 85–86, 130–31.

168 Anger: Mallowe, "Barren North," p. 108. Dobbins: *B*, 10 and 14 October 1968; see also *B*, 18 December 1970; 15 November 1972. Black neighbor: *I*, 12 April 1971.

169 Analysis of going bad: *B*, 15 August 1969; 15 June 1970; 14 September 1971 (Seymour article), and material on abandonment above. State-financed demolitions and abandonment: Carolyn Teich Adams and Rosemary Conroy-Hughes, "Philadelphia's Population Decline: Economic, Social and Physical Effects" (ms, 1979).

169 Mack statue: *B*, 24 December 1965; *I*, 24 May 1971. Quinn anticipated: *B*, 24 February 1956. August rededication: *B*, 16 August 1971. Quinn dies: Bill Fleischman, "Home Sweet Home," in "The Phillies, 100 Years," supplement to the *DN*, April 1983, p. 44. Mack Center: *B*, 11 December 1975.

169 Black leadership: *B*, 3 December 1975. Middle school: *I*, 25 April 1969; *B*, 31 March 1971; editorial, *I*, 5 September 1979.

170 Real estate quote: *B*, 3 February 1971.

170 *C* analysis: 7 October 1970. Civic association link: *I*, 10 July 1982.

171 Wolman: *B*, 11, 12, and 14 December 1967; 26 August 1968; 26 November 1968; 13 March 1969.

171 Grayboyes and Tollin: *B*, 12 March 1971; *I*, 13 March 1971. Denunciation: illegibly dated *B* clip (Connie Mack Stadium, 1969). Indictment: *B*, 14 October 1969; 14 January 1970. Grayboyes's humor: *B*, 14 October 1973.

171 Plans: *B*, 16 October 1966; *I*, 17 February 1970; *B*, 24 June 1973; *B*, 17 March 1974. Grayboyes and Tollin support: *B*, 24 September 1972 (Brookhauser article); *I*, 4 March 1975 (Dubin article). Industrial park: *B*, 10 February 1976 (Gillespie article). City ideas: *DN*, 10 February 1976; *DN*, 13 April 1976; *B*, 25 December 1977; *I*, 21 January 1978; 20 May 1978.

172 Allegheny West: *B* clips; Allegheny West files, William Penn Foundation; interview with Harry Cerino, 1 November 1988; Lynne Kotranski and Douglas Porpora, "Tasty Baking Company: The Company That Stayed," in *Community and Capital in Conflict: Plant Closings and Job Loss*, ed. John C. Raines et al. (Philadelphia, 1982), pp. 220–33.

173 Recollection of president: "The Triumph of Tastykake," *I Magazine* (25 April 1976). *Journal*: Stuart Mendelson, "Hunting Park Gets a Boost," 15 July 1978.

173 Reformers' limits: Allegheny West files. North Twenty-second Street: *B*, 11 October 1979. Town houses: *B*, 5 October 1979. Protestant and banking triumphs: Barrett, "Life and Death," pp. 132–33.

174 Forgotten blocks: *I*, 30 August 1979 (Tulsky article); 17 September 1979 (editorial); 17 September 1979 (letters).

174 Decline: Adams and Conroy-Hughes, "Population Decline." Budd Co.: Pamela Haines and Gary Klein, "Citizens and Unions Respond," in *Community*, ed. Raines, p. 248.

174 Suburbs and inner-city prediction: Conrad Weiler, *Philadelphia: Neighborhood, Authority, and the Urban Crisis* (New York, 1974), p. 129.

176 Other predictions: Adams and Conroy-Hughes, "Population Decline."

176 Basic problem: Cerino interview. Trees die: *C*, 2 July 1970.

11. LAST DAYS, 1969–1976

177 Ball parks in twentieth century: Joel Spring, "Mass Culture and School Sports," *History of Education Quarterly* 14 (1974), p. 497; Philip H. Bess, "Preface," to Philip J. Lowry, *Green Cathedrals* (Cooperstown, 1986), pp. 9–16; Bess, *City Baseball Magic: Plain Talk and Uncommon Sense about Cities and Baseball Parks* (Minneapolis, 1989). Octorad: Phillies *Yearbook*, 1970.

178 The 1969 opening: *I*, 15 April 1969. The 1969 closing: *B*, 29 September 1969. Giles: *B* clips; interview with Larry Shenk, 15 November 1987; Mike Mallowe, "Bill's Phils," *Philadelphia Magazine* (April 1989).

178 Delaware Studies: "Baseball Research Program," 1962, 1964, 1965, 1966, box 1, PP. Consultants and survey: Philadelphia National League Club, Consulting Proposal, 1969, box 3, PP. Primer: box 3, PP.

179 Parachutist: Powell to Carpenter, 16 March 1966, Promotions, box 3, PP.

179 The 1970 opening and Luchesi: *B*, 8 April 1970 (Kelly and Bilovsky articles). Grady: *B*, 8 April 1970. Legend: Charles NacNamara, "Requiem for a Ball Park," *Philadelphia Magazine* (October 1969), p. 64.

179 Attendance estimate: *B*, 17 May 1970.

179 Hubcaps: *B*, 7 April 1970 (Brookshier). *B* quote: 8 April 1970. Haas: *I*, 17 March 1970.

180 Promotion: Connie Mack Stadium files, V. Wolman auction: *DN*, 21 September 1970. Mack, Jr., sales, riot: *B*, 2 October 1970; conversations with Richard Dunn and many others. Giles on field: *B*, 23 August 1971 (Barniak article). Insurance: *B*, 2 October 1970. Chat: *C*, 7 October 1970. Vandals: *DN*, 2 October 1970 (Fox article).

181 Thugs stab man, Bob Montgomery, and progress quote: *B*, 2 October 1970. Peanut vendor: *New Era* (Lancaster, Pa.), 2 October 1970.

181 Rape: *DN*, 2 October 1970 (Fox article). Other quotes: *B*, 2 October 1970.

182 *Yearbook*: 1971. Laudatory quotes: *Yearbook*, 1972.

182 Angell: *Summer Game* (New York, 1972), pp. 57–58, 205, 253.

182 Ashburn: *B*, 11 April 1971 (Fidati article). Saam: B. G. Kelley, "By Saam," *PhillySport* (May 1989), p. 76.

182 Vandalism and dismantling: interview with Shenk. Turf sold and kids play: *B*, 11 April 1971; *I*, 12 April 1971. Revival, setting of fire, results, and quotes: *B*, 21 and 22 August 1971; *I*, 22 August 1971.

183 Irony and old-timers: *B*, 23 August 1971 (Barniak article, from which all quotes are taken). Ashburn: *DN*, 4 November 1975.

183 After-the-fire descriptions: *Times-Picayune* (New Orleans), 28 October 1975; *B*, 24 September 1972 (Brookhauser article); *B*, 28 October 1975; *DN*, 4 November 1975 (Ashburn).

184 Licenses and Inspections: *B*, 14 October 1973. Access and state: *I*, 4 March 1975 (Dubin article); *DN*, 4 November 1975 (Ashburn).

184 Pilgrimages: many people in conversations; *I*, 13 July 1976 (Bodle article). High ground: 4 November 1975 (Ashburn). Boy running bases: *I*, 9 May 1989 (Ruane article, Metro section). Taylor: Bob Bartosz, "Shibe Park—Remembering Last Visits," *Ballparks Bulletin* (1988), p. 10. Grounds keeper: *DN*, 8 May 1975. Judge: *DN*, 16 December 1975.

184 Swampoodle nights: *B*, 25 November 1977. Swampoodle days: *B*, 27 August 1972.

185 Wolman petitioned: *I*, 24 June 1976. *B* quote: 14 October 1973. Violations and city order: *DN*, 27 October 1975; 16 December 1975; *B*, 10 February 1976.

186 The 1976 demonstration: *DN*, 23 June 1976 (Enoch article). Rizzo story: interview with Joseph Barrett, 20 September 1989.

186 Demolition: *I*, 24 June 1976. Dying today: *I*, 13 July 1976.

186 *B* editorial: 2 October 1970. Deferred: NacNamara, "Requiem," p. 64. *DN* and residents: *DN*, 17 October 1977 (Dougherty article). Cleanup: *DN*, 26 October 1977.

187 Visitors were observed by me on many occasions. Memory lapses started early—see *I*, 3 October 1950, and many fans in conversation. The fungo bat belongs to me. See also B. G. Kelley, "And There Used to Be a Ballpark Right Here," *PhillySport* (April 1989), p. 66, who wrote of the distant sounds.

188 Sixties memories: *I*, 4 March 1975 (Dubin article). Transformation of Phillies: Jay Greenberg, "Mr. Mack's Team," in "The Phillies: 100 Years," supplement to the *DN*, April 1983, pp. 30–31; Ben Yagoda, "The Legend of Connie Mack," *PhillySport* (August 1989), pp. 52–62.

188 Wolman problems: citations in Chapter 10.

188 Smith and Wolman: *B*, 27 November 1977 (Brown article). Deliverance Church: *B*, 22 June 1981 (Herbut article). Same vision: interview with Reverend Joseph Ross of Deliverance Evangelistic Church, 17 May 1989. See also Kelley, "Ballpark," p. 66.

EPILOGUE: COMMON GROUND

190 In *Playing for Keeps: A History of Early Baseball* (Ithaca, 1989), Warren Goldstein writes of two "histories" of baseball, one of the enterprise, the other of its emotional impact. This framework, I think, gets at my sense of the disjunction between the mundane and imperfect social history and the practice's transcendence. For help with expressing my sense of the sport's relation to capitalism, I am much indebted to Jonathan Steinberg.

191 Hearts and memories: brochure for exhibition by Andy Jurinko at Gallery Henoch (1989). Defender of riot: Mary Maples Dunn, conversation, 17 February 1990. Resident: Joseph Barrett in "The Sweeper" (in author's possession). Philos-

opher: Rudolph Klinger, letter of 17 January 1990. For his views Klinger cites Plato's *Republic*, book 7; F. H. Bradley, *Appearance and Reality* (London, 1893), pp. 40–43; George Santayana, *Skepticism and Animal Faith* (New York, 1923); J.M.E. McTaggart, *The Nature of Existence*, 2 vols. (Cambridge, England, 1927), vol. 2, pp. 9–31; and Duke Snider with Bill Gilbert, *The Duke of Flatbush* (New York, 1989), pp. 335–36. (I take this with some skepticism.)

192   Small things remembered: Gerald Danzer, *Public Places: Exploring Their History* (Nashville, 1987), p. xi; also John Brinckerhoff Jackson, *The Necessity for Ruins and Other Topics* (Amherst, Mass., 1980); for the specific memories, conversation with Frank Kenneth Carner, 11 January 1989. Constructive forces in memory: John Hildebidle, "The Intellectual Game: Baseball and the Life of the Mind," *New England Review and Bread Loaf Quarterly* (Winter 1984), pp. 253, 255.

192   Common use of space: William L. Yancey and Eugene P. Ericksen, "The Antecedents of Community: The Economic and Institutional Structure of Urban Neighborhoods," *American Sociological Review* (1979), p. 253.

192   Importance of the city: Nicole Loraux, *The Invention of Athens: The Funeral Oration in the Classical City* (Cambridge, 1986); Morris Cohen, "Baseball," *Dial*, 26 July 1919, p. 57.

192   Sport and valor: David Papineau, "Beyond the Leisure Principle," *Times Literary Supplement*, 2–8 February 1990.

193   Caring: Roger Angell, "1975: Boston Red Sox 7, Cincinnati Reds, 6," in *The Baseball Reader*, ed. Charles Einstein (New York, 1983), pp. 123–24.

193   Social criticism: Philip H. Bess in his "Preface" to Philip J. Lowry, *Green Cathedrals* (Cooperstown, 1986), pp. 9–16; also his *City Baseball Magic: Plain Talk and Uncommon Sense about Cities and Baseball Parks* (Minneapolis, 1989). See also Danzer, *Public Places*, and Jackson, *Necessity for Ruins*. Temporal order: James L. Muyskens, *The Sufficiency of Hope: The Conceptual Foundations of Religion* (Philadelphia, 1979), pp. 24–26. Community of memory and hope: Josiah Royce, *The Problem of Christianity* (Boston, 1913), vol. 2, pp. 49–53.

194   Manufactured sentimentality: Barrett, "The Sweeper" (ms, both versions in possession of author). Quote: interview with Barrett, 15 April 1988. *Phillies Report* has not, as of this writing, published either version. Arm scraping: letter from Mary M. Marschner, 17 November 1988. Forgetting the past: Friedrich Nietzsche, *The Use and Abuse of History* (1874).

195   Keeping faith: Katha Pollitt, "Mandarin Oranges," *New Yorker* (23 February 1987), p. 36.

195   Baseball and blood: many fans to me. Baseball and life: Frank Baker's wife on her husband's views in his obituary, *B*, 28 June 1963. Entanglement of baseball and life: letter from Hattie Woodington, 6 March 1988.

195   Home base: Thomas L. Altherr, "'The Most Summery, Bold, Free & Spacious Game': Charles King Newcombe and Philadelphia Baseball, 1866–1871," *Pennsylvania History* (1985), quoting Newcombe, p. 75. Elegy: Charles Rosenberg, conversation, 9 December 1989.

195   Existence of change: Joe Mantegna, "Let There Be Light! The Better to See Our Memories," *NYT*, 1 August 1988.

·INDEX·